GEORGE BERNARD SHAW (1856–1950) is one
of the world's greatest literary figures. Born
in Dublin, Ireland, he left school at fourteen
and in 1876 went to London, where he
began his literary career with a series of unsuccessful novels. In 1884 he became a founder
of the Fabian Society, the famous British socialist organization. After becoming a reviewer
and drama critic, he published a study of the
Norwegian dramatist Henrik Ibsen in 1891
and became determined to create plays as
he felt Ibsen did: to shake audiences out of
their moral complacency and to attack social
problems. However, Shaw was an irrepress-
ible wit, and his plays are as entertaining as
they are socially provocative. Basically shy,
Shaw created a public persona for himself:
G.B.S., a bearded eccentric, crusading social critic, antivivisectionist, language reformer,
strict vegetarian, and renowned public
speaker. The author of fifty-three plays, hundreds of essays, reviews, and letters, and
several books, Shaw is best known for *Widowers' Houses* (1892), *Arms and the Man* (1894),
Mrs. Warren's Profession (1893), *Caesar and
Cleopatra* (1901), *Man and Superman*
(1903), *Major Barbara* (1905), *Pygmalion* (1913),
Heartbreak House (1919), and *Saint Joan*
(1923). He was awarded the Nobel Prize for
Literature in 1925.

Ask your bookseller for Bantam Classics by these British and Irish writers:

Jane Austen
J. M. Barrie
Charlotte Brontë
Emily Brontë
Frances Hodgson Burnett
Lewis Carroll
Geoffrey Chaucer
Wilkie Collins
Joseph Conrad
Daniel Defoe
Charles Dickens
Sir Arthur Conan Doyle
George Eliot
Henry Fielding
E. M. Forster
Kenneth Grahame
Thomas Hardy
James Joyce
Rudyard Kipling
D. H. Lawrence
W. Somerset Maugham
John Stuart Mill
Sir Walter Scott
William Shakespeare
George Bernard Shaw
Mary Shelley
Robert Louis Stevenson
Bram Stoker
Jonathan Swift
William Makepeace Thackeray
H. G. Wells
Oscar Wilde

Pygmalion
and
Major Barbara
by
George Bernard Shaw

With an Introduction by Michael Holroyd

BANTAM BOOKS
NEW YORK · TORONTO · LONDON · SYDNEY · AUCKLAND

PYGMALION AND MAJOR BARBARA

A Bantam Classic Book / August 1992

PUBLISHING HISTORY

*This Bantam Classic volume has been set directly from the 1907 edition
of* Major Barbara *published in New York by Brentano's and the 1916
edition of* Pygmalion *published in London by Constable and Company.
Spelling and punctuation have not been altered in any way.*

*"L'Ambitieuse," by James Jacques Joseph Pissot.
Courtesy of Albright-Knox Art Gallery, Buffalo, NY.*

ISBN 0-553-21408-X

Published simultaneously in the United States and Canada

Bantam Books are published by Bantam Books, a division of Bantam Doubleday Dell
Publishing Group, Inc. Its trademark, consisting of the words "Bantam Books" and the
portrayal of a rooster, is Registered in U.S. Patent and Trademark Office and in other
countries. Marca Registrada. Bantam Books, 1540 Broadway, New York, New York 10036.

PRINTED IN THE UNITED STATES OF AMERICA

OPM   0 9 8 7 6 5

Contents

Introduction

Early in his career as a dramatist, Bernard Shaw divided his work for the theatre into two categories: *Plays Pleasant and Unpleasant*. His unpleasant plays (*Widowers' Houses, The Philanderer*, and *Mrs. Warren's Profession*) dramatised some of the "unspeakable" social issues of the late nineteenth century—property values versus human values, conjugal rights and wrongs—and treated prostitution as a metaphor for capitalism. In his pleasant plays (*Arms and the Man, Candida, The Man of Destiny*, and *You Never Can Tell*), resolving to "sport with human follies not with crimes," he turned history into comedy and made his audiences laugh rather than feel politically incriminated.

Most of Shaw's subsequent dramas may also be seen as belonging to one or the other of these categories. *Major Barbara* is his most ambitious "unpleasant" play. He wrote it, with much difficulty, between March and September 1905, when he was approaching fifty. He had achieved almost no success in the theatre until his early forties, when *The Devil's Disciple*, his melodrama set in New Hampshire during the American Revolution, had been successfully produced by Richard Mansfield in New York. In Britain he had to wait until the founding of the new repertory experiment at the Court Theatre in London's Sloane Square to get his first taste of success. Between 1904 and 1907 he joined the actor-playwright Harley Granville Barker and the theatre manager J. E. Vedrenne to create a revolution in contemporary English theatre at the Court. This brilliant partnership dispensed with the star system of the famous actor-managers led by Sir Henry

Irving at the Lyceum, and substituted ensemble acting without fame-snobbery. It also gave power to the play-wright (Shaw and Granville Barker usually directed their own plays), encouraged contemporary writers such as John Galsworthy, Laurence Housman, John Masefield, Elizabeth Robins, and W. B. Yeats to write for the theatre, and put on the works of foreign playwrights from Euripides to Ibsen.

Above all, the Court established a theatre of ideas in England. These ideas often turned Victorian values upside down, replacing the woman on a pedestal with woman as huntress, inventing the "new man" (the man of technology), taking the heroic romance out of warfare, and advocating the political blasphemy of socialism and the economic independence of women. It was all wonderfully exciting to young people. They treated the Court Theatre almost as if it were a college extension course, going in as late-nineteenth-century aesthetes and emerging as twentieth-century radicals. In the opinion of Leonard Woolf, "There was no living man to whom the generations which came to maturity between 1900 and 1914 owed so much to as Mr. Shaw. . . . Nothing less than a world war could have prevented [him] from winning the minds of succeeding generations . . . ever since [the war] the barbarians have naturally been on top."

Major Barbara fitted perfectly into the imaginative education being offered at the Court Theatre. "Shaw's play was highly amusing and interesting and very brutal," wrote the young poet Rupert Brooke, who saw a performance there early in January 1906. But the brutality offended some of the older and more staid members of the audience. An anonymous theatre critic of the conservative newspaper *The Morning Post*, for example, attacked G.B.S. (the title Shaw chose for his public persona) for his jeering "insincerity," "deliberate perversity," and unforgivable "offences against good taste and good feeling." He questioned whether it should not be a case for official censorship against blasphemy, demonstrating that simplistic reaction to the challenge of the arts with which we are still familiar today.

Part melodrama and part theatrical debate, *Major Barbara* examines the reliance of twentieth-century capitalism on the modern armaments trade. While not disputing that this was an unholy alliance, Shaw did not pretend that the Church could formulate any easy or adequate dismissal of it. In his own lifetime he was to see perhaps only one world leader open to the catholicity of all religions who extracted the political implications of Christianity and used them in a general strategy. This was Mahatma Gandhi, whom Shaw judged to be "a saint . . . the sort of man who occurs once in several centuries." Shaw looked forward to a future where everyone might be the moral equivalent of Gandhi. But Gandhi's assassination in 1948 strengthened Shaw's belief in the danger of being so far ahead of the age in which one lived.

But at the time, the barbarians were largely in command of the world. In *Major Barbara* Shaw tried to steer a course between short-term pragmatism and visionary optimism that was neither defeatist nor sentimental. In the challenge of Undershaft, the armaments manufacturer, to his Salvation Army daughter Barbara, we may hear a prelude to Stalin's famous dismissal of the Catholic Church with the ironic enquiry: "How many divisions has the Pope?"

According to his friend the political sociologist Beatrice Webb, Shaw was gambling very dangerously with ideas and emotions in this play. He had partly used Beatrice as his model for the robust and sensitive Barbara, and another friend, the classical scholar Gilbert Murray, who was to become an active member of the League of Nations, as the model for Barbara's fiancé, Adolphus Cusins. Undershaft himself owes a good deal to several plutocrats in the armaments trade: to Sir Basil Zaharoff, chief salesman of Vickers, who boasted of selling arms to anyone who would buy them and of creating wars so that he could sell to both sides; to Sir William Armstrong, who insisted that the responsibility for these new engines of war lay with those who used them rather than with those who supplied them; to Alfred Krupp, the Prussian "Cannon King," whose welfare conditions for his workers in Essen resembled those provided by Undershaft at the model town of Perivale St. Andrews; and to Alfred Nobel, who patented dynamite in 1867, claimed that his factories might end war sooner than other people's peace conferences, and used his profits to found the Nobel Peace Prize. "I can forgive Alfred Nobel for having invented dynamite," Shaw was to say after winning the Nobel Prize for Literature in 1925. "But only a fiend in human form could have invented the Nobel Prize."

Zaharoff, Armstrong, Krupp, and Nobel all could have subscribed unashamedly to "the true faith of the Armorer" as expressed by Undershaft:

> To give arms to all men who offer an honest price for them, without respect of persons or principles: to aristocrat and republican, to Nihilist and Tsar, to Capitalist and Socialist, to Protestant and Catholic, to burglar and policeman, to black man, white man and yellow man, to all sorts and conditions, all nationalities, all faiths, all follies, all causes and all crimes.

Major Barbara demonstrates, perhaps more powerfully than any of his other plays, the way in which Shaw's knowledge of contemporary politics was linked to a prophetic understanding of what political themes would still be troubling us at the end of the twentieth century. No military dictator in 1990 would have had difficulty in recognising Undershaft's successors at the Pentagon or the Kremlin. No reader of Anthony Sampson's recent book *The Arms Bazaar* could doubt that Undershaft's army of orphans was still in business. Barbara's opposing forces are still familiar to us also in some of the international relief organisations and the ministrations of remarkable individuals such as Mother Teresa. The Salvation Army, in which Barbara holds the rank of major, had been founded in 1878 by William Booth, who calculated that one Londoner in ten lived "below the standard of the London cab horse." By 1905, when Shaw was writing his play, there were 150,000 paupers in London who spent their nights either in the streets or the workhouse casual wards. Over eighty years later a "cardboard city" had arisen in London for such vagrants, and the casual wards of the workhouses were renamed "government reception centres."

If Barbara represents evangelical Christianity and spiritual passion, then Cusins, the academic, may be said to stand for intellectual passion, while Undershaft embodies material strength and the power of money. The problem Shaw set himself in the final long disquisitory scene was to find a convincing synthesis of those opposing interests. It was a problem that, in various forms, had been obsessing him since the beginning of our century. *Major Barbara* was to be the last of the "big three" dramas of Shaw's middle period. In the dream sequence of *Man and Superman* he had set optimism against pessimism as part of the great Socratic debate between Don Juan and the Devil. In *John Bull's Other Island*, where the defrocked Irish priest, Father Keegan, opposes the philistine English materialist, Tom Broadbent, Shaw had attempted to focus the optimism of his dreams upon waking life. "Live in contact with dreams and you will get something of their charm," he wrote in that play: "live in contact with facts and you will get something of their brutality. I wish I could find a country to live in where the facts were not brutal and the dreams not unreal."

Undershaft's "death and devastation factory" seems an unlikely capital for such an ideal country. For here, surely, is the devil's palace remodelled by the civil engineer Tom Broadbent into a shining garden city. Yet this is where Shaw sets "the real tug-of-war" between the millionaire, the poet, and the saviour of souls. What emerges most potently from this confrontation is Undershaft's religion of money and gunpowder. The audience has already been convinced that "money governs England" and that Undershaft is one of the people who governs the country. He has demonstrated before Barbara that "all religious organizations exist by selling themselves to the rich" and persuaded Cusins that "you must first acquire money enough for a decent life, and power enough to be your own master." In his vocabulary, money means freedom and gunpowder is power. Here, in its purest form, is the philosophy of the marketplace against which Barbara's "larger loves and diviner dreams" seem little more than the sentimentalities of a modern television evangelist. She is indeed "hypnotised" by her father's display of power which also drives Cusins to act against his benevolent temperament and high conscience. "Come and make explosives with me," Undershaft invites them. "Whatever can blow men up can blow society up. The history of the world is the history of those who had courage enough to embrace this truth. Have you the courage to embrace it . . . ?"

Shaw's problem is how to conjure the politics of death into the mystical operations of the Life Force. To solve the problem he uses the philosophy of William Blake. "There is no wicked side: life is all one," Barbara says to Cusins, who asks her: "Then the way of life lies through the factory of death?" To which she answers: "Yes, through the raising of hell to heaven and of man to God, through the unveiling of an eternal light in the Valley of the Shadow." Shaw wanted to see the poet, the intellectual, men and women of vision and unbribable integrity become involved in the muddy business of politics. He would have welcomed in our own time the election of a philosopher, Zhelyu Zhelev, as president of Bulgaria, and a dramatist, Vaclav Havel, as president of Czechoslovakia. Like Plato, he believed that "society cannot be saved until either the Professors of Greek take to making gunpowder, or else the makers of gunpower become Professors of Greek."

In Undershaft's powerful speech against the crime of poverty, he accuses Barbara of failing the "half-starved ruffian" who had come to the Salvation Army shelter. "I will drag his soul back again to salvation for you," he promises her.

Not by words and dreams; but by thirty-eight shillings a week, a sound house in a handsome street, and a permanent job. In three weeks he will have a fancy waistcoat; in three months a tall hat and a chapel sitting; before the end of the year he will shake hands with a duchess at the Primrose League meeting, and join the Conservative Party.

This is a similar transformation to that performed by Professor Henry Higgins on Eliza Doolittle in *Pygmalion*, the most "pleasant" of all Shaw's plays: Shaw was a natural writer of social and romantic comedies. He described *Pygmalion*, which he composed between March and June 1912 at the age of fifty-five, as "A Romance in Five Acts." It was, he liked to say, comparable to Shakespeare's *As You Like It*, which was to say, the public liked it. "There must be something radically wrong with the play if it pleases everybody," he admitted, "but at the moment I cannot find what it is."

He liked to speak of *Pygmalion* as a didactic entertainment in which he demonstrated how the science of phonetics could be used to subvert an antiquated British class system. By teaching the unkempt cockney flower girl a new speech and culture, the dedicated phonetician changes her into a completely different person with new expectations. Shaw had taken his title from Greek mythology: Pygmalion, king of Cyprus, made an ivory statue of a girl which was so beautiful that he fell in love with it and prayed to Aphrodite to give the statue life. His wish was granted and he married her. Shaw had already adapted this metaphor in one of his early novels, *Love Among the Artists*, as had Tobias Smollett in *Peregrine Pickle*, and W. S. Gilbert in *Pygmalion and Galatea*. Shaw may well have also been aware of the similarity of his theme to Swift's poem "Cadenus and Vanessa," which describes the tutorial-erotic relationship between a passionate young woman and a self-protective older pedagogue.

But the real source for Shaw's *Pygmalion* lay in his own adolescence and the revival of adolescent feelings for Mrs. Patrick Campbell, the celebrated actress whom he wanted to play Eliza Doolittle. He intended to use this theatrical romance for the feminist purpose of conceiving a Shavian new woman—an educated woman able to earn her own living in a male-dominated society. But behind the new woman of his invention lay the dominating woman behind his life: his mother.

The good news is that Shaw loved his mother; the bad news is that she did not love him. Lucinda Elizabeth Shaw, nicknamed Bessie, was a ladylike lapsed Protestant who had married a redundant civil servant, George Carr Shaw, who she discovered was a failed if ardent teetotaller. She came to despise her husband and seems to have felt that their son, George, was tainted with the same male ineffectualness. Indeed, she appears to have been contemptuous of all men except one, a musician called George Vandeleur Lee, who later became a model for George du Maurier's Svengali. Lee, who invited the Protestant Shaws to share his much smarter house in Dublin, was a Catholic. So it was a doubly unconventional ménage in which the child grew up. Lee was the centre of their household. Mrs. Shaw sang for him and became the right-hand woman of his prosperous Amateur Musical Society in Dublin. But early in 1873, after running into difficulties, Lee somewhat hurriedly left Ireland to seek his fortune in London. A fortnight later, on her twenty-first wedding anniversary, Lucinda Elizabeth Shaw followed him. Over the next months she took her two daughters to join her, but left her son, the youngest of her children, in Dublin with his father.

Shaw was sixteen, and the effect on him was devastating. He questioned his own legitimacy—had he been named after George Carr Shaw or George Vandeleur Lee? What seemed certain was that Lee was the sort of man his mother admired. Later he dropped the name George, the symbol of unhappy ambiguity, and created a public personality known as G.B.S., largely influenced by Lee. This famous and feted figure was to take the place of the neglected child.

When looking back at his childhood, Shaw wrote that he had the choice of making it into either "a family tragedy or a family joke." *Pygmalion* is the most imaginative of his jokes deriving from this background. He re-creates Vandeleur Lee, the teacher of singing, as Henry Higgins, the teacher of speech, and transforms his pupil from Lucinda Elizabeth Shaw into Eliza Doolittle. But there was a double transposition at work in this creative process. As G.B.S. had fashioned his public image on Lee, so Higgins grew into a self-portrait of the playwright himself. And as he fell in love with Mrs. Patrick Campbell, so an aura of traditional romance enveloped the figure of Eliza.

Shaw had often seen Mrs. Pat on stage when he had been a dramatic critic in the 1890s. He saw that she cast an extraordinary aura of glamour over the late-Victorian theatre, and he wanted her for his own play-world. He had written his *Caesar and Cleopatra* for her, though she never became his Cleopatra. The dazzled Caesar who nevertheless retains his full self-possession is G.B.S., the professional critic who watches her from the safety of the stalls. By autumn 1897 everything else had been driven out of his head by a play he wished to write in which she could act an East End girl "in an apron and three orange and red feathers," playing opposite a West End gentleman. It was not until fifteen years later that he wrote this play and persuaded Mrs. Pat, whom he now called Stella, to act in it.

The late-Victorian and Edwardian theatre had very few good roles for actresses. Shaw, who believed in the equality of women and men in the theatre, was a playwright Stella Campbell needed to write for her. She could see that *Pygmalion* was a most fruitful product of their relationship. His play made her laugh, but she underrated the emotional fires she had lit in him.

Shaw had been born with an instinct to show off, which his mother, feeling no pride in his tricks, had stifled. His hunger for love fed on his imagination. Stella fulfilled an important adolescent need in him. "You are a figure from the dreams of my childhood," he told her in 1912. But Stella was planning to marry George Cornwallis-West after he divorced his then-present wife, the mother of Winston Churchill, and she did not want to imperil this arrangement by an affair with Shaw. So she rejected him and married Cornwallis-West during the rehearsals of *Pygmalion*. This rejection deeply distressed Shaw. Of his fifty-seven years, he wrote to Stella, ''I have suffered twenty and worked thirty-seven. Then I had a moment's happiness: I almost condescended to romance. I risked the breaking of deep roots and sanctified ties . . . what have I shrunk into?''

''I call it a romance,'' Shaw told a journalist who had asked him about *Pygmalion*, ''because it is the story of a poor girl who meets a gentleman at a church door and is transformed by him into a beautiful lady. That is what I call a romance. It is also what everybody else calls a romance, so for once we are all agreed.'' But the public's idea of a romance was not Shaw's. They wanted to change Professor Higgins from a Miltonic bachelor into Eliza's lover. There was much in the stage directions and the subtext of the play to support these wishes. Even Higgins's mother believes that her son ''must be perfectly cracked'' about his flower girl. But Higgins himself resists every innuendo. In the second act Eliza complains to Higgins, ''One would think you was my father.'' He replies, ''If I decide to teach you, I'll be worse than two fathers to you.'' Near the end of the play he suggests to her, ''I'll adopt you as my daughter and settle money on you if you like.'' What seems clear is that Higgins can assume almost any family relationship with Eliza except that of husband. ''I've never been able to feel really grown-up and tremendous, like other chaps,'' he tells Colonel Pickering. He explains the reason for this to his mother. ''My idea of a lovable woman is somebody as like you as possible . . . some habits lie too deep to be changed.'' Eliza has changed, but Higgins admits that ''I can't change my nature.'' ''I only want to be natural,'' Eliza says. But can Higgins be natural? The original ending of the play is carefully ambiguous, reflecting Shaw's uncertainties over his romance with Stella. He could not have married her and she could not have remained his pupil as an actress learning from his theatrical direction. But might they have become lovers? The question is left open to our imagination.

The history of *Pygmalion* was to develop into a battle over its ending. Responding to what was suppressed in Shaw's life and lay in the subtext of his play, the public demanded a love affair. "This is unbearable," Shaw cried out. He had dramatised the relationship between Vandeleur Lee and his mother which, he insisted, had always been professional. His very legitimacy seemed to depend on it. And then there was his own affair with Stella Campbell; he could not bear to speculate on what might have been. "Eliza married Freddy [Eynsford-Hill]" he explained; "and the notion of her marrying Higgins is disgusting." In other words, she married a double-barrelled, well-connected nobody like George Cornwallis-West.

In later versions of *Pygmalion,* Shaw tried to remove "virtually every suggestion of Higgins's possible romantic interest in Eliza" and strengthen the role of Freddy Eynsford-Hill. But actors, directors, and audiences conspired to get around these changes. There was one humiliation, however, Shaw was determined to avoid. Oscar Straus had made a sentimental operetta called *The Chocolate Soldier* from his pleasant play *Arms and the Man.* The same thing would not be allowed to happen to *Pygmalion.* When Franz Lehar, creator of *The Merry Widow,* wanted to make a musical of *Pygmalion,* Shaw was adamant that it should not happen. "I have no intention of allowing the history of the Chocolate Soldier to be repeated," he wrote. For the rest of his life he resisted every pressure to "downgrade" his play into a musical. "I absolutely forbid any such outrage," he said when in his ninety-second year. This was one battle with the public he believed he had won.

Composed half a dozen years after Shaw's death, the musical *My Fair Lady* was based on the film version of *Pygmalion,* for which he had written the original script. At a press show only two days before the film's opening, however, Shaw discovered that other screenwriters had been brought in to provide a more sentimental ending to the story. The premieres in London and New York were hugely successful and, less than a year before the beginning of the Second World War, were seen as a timely gesture towards removing the power for change from fighting men to artists and writers, men and women of vision and imagination. But, as Leonard Woolf had written, the barbarians were on top. After the war started, Shaw chose *Major Barbara* as his second film. It struck many people as dramatically topical in 1941. "The house was packed," H. G. Wells wrote to Shaw, ". . . and you could not have had a more responsive audience. They laughed at all the right places. Most young people in uniform they were."

Shaw made a special prologue to this film for the United States which was regarded by many Americans as an invitation for them to join the fight against Hitler. When he was a little boy, he said, the Dublin newspapers reported how America had abolished black slavery. When he grew up, he continued, "I determined to devote my life as far as I could to the abolition of white slavery," the sort of slavery to economic dictatorship that had erupted in the war. Then he lifted one trembling hand to his forehead and held it in a salute. "When my mere bodily stuff is gone, I should like to imagine that you are still working with me . . . at that particular job . . . farewell!"

—MICHAEL HOLROYD

Major Barbara

(1905)

Preface to Major Barbara

First Aid to Critics

Before dealing with the deeper aspects of Major Barbara, let me, for the credit of English literature, make a protest against an unpatriotic habit into which many of my critics have fallen. Whenever my view strikes them as being at all outside the range of, say, an ordinary suburban church-warden, they conclude that I am echoing Schopenhauer, Nietzsche, Ibsen, Strindberg, Tolstoy, or some other heresiarch in northern or eastern Europe.

I confess there is something flattering in this simple faith in my accomplishment as a linguist and my erudition as a philosopher. But I cannot tolerate the assumption that life and literature is so poor in these islands that we must go abroad for all dramatic material that is not common and all ideas that are not superficial. I therefore venture to put my critics in possession of certain facts concerning my contact with modern ideas.

About half a century ago, an Irish novelist, Charles Lever, wrote a story entitled A Day's Ride: A Life's Romance. It was published by Charles Dickens in Household Words, and proved so strange to the public taste that Dickens pressed Lever to make short work of it. I read scraps of this novel when I was a child; and it made an enduring impression on me. The hero was a very romantic hero, trying to live bravely, chivalrously, and powerfully by dint of mere romance-fed imagination, without courage, without means, without knowledge, without skill, without anything real except his bodily appetites. Even in my childhood I found in this poor devil's unsuccessful encounters with the facts of life, a poignant quality that romantic fiction lacked. The book, in spite of its first failure, is not dead: I saw its title the other day in the catalogue of Tauchnitz.

Now why is it that when I also deal in the tragicomic irony of the conflict between real life and the romantic imagination, no critic ever affiliates me to my countryman and immediate forerunner, Charles Lever, whilst they confidently derive me from a Norwegian author of whose language I do not know three words, and of whom I knew nothing until years after the Shavian *Anschauung* was already unequivocally declared in books full of what came, ten years later, to be perfunctorily labelled Ibsenism. I was not Ibsenist even at second hand; for Lever, though he may have read Henri Beyle, *alias* Stendhal, certainly never read Ibsen. Of the books that made Lever popular, such as Charles O'Malley and Harry Lorrequer, I know nothing but the names and some of the illustrations. But the story of the day's ride and life's romance of Potts (claiming alliance with Pozzo di Borgo) caught me and fascinated me as something strange and significant, though I already knew all about Alnaschar and Don Quixote and Simon Tappertit and many another romantic hero mocked by reality. From the plays of Aristophanes to the tales of Stevenson that mockery has been made familiar to all who are properly saturated with letters.

Where, then, was the novelty in Lever's tale? Partly, I think, in a new seriousness in dealing with Potts's disease. Formerly, the contrast between madness and sanity was deemed comic: Hogarth shews us how fashionable people went in parties to Bedlam to laugh at the lunatics. I myself have had a village idiot exhibited to me as something irresistibly funny. On the stage the madman was once a regular comic figure: that was how Hamlet got his opportunity before Shakespear touched him. The originality of Shakespear's version lay in his taking the lunatic sympathetically and seriously, and thereby making an advance towards the eastern consciousness of the fact that lunacy may be inspiration in disguise, since a man who has more brains than his fellows necessarily appears as mad to them as one who has less. But Shakespear did not do for Pistol and Parolles what he did for Hamlet. The particular sort of madman they represented, the romantic make-believer, lay outside the pale of sympathy in literature: he was pitilessly despised and ridiculed here as he was in the east under the name of Alnaschar, and was doomed to be, centuries later, under the name of Simon Tappertit. When Cervantes relented over Don Quixote, and Dickens relented over Pickwick, they did not become impartial: they simply changed sides, and became friends and apologists where they had formerly been mockers.

In Lever's story there is a real change of attitude. There is no relenting towards Potts: he never gains our affections like Don Quixote and Pickwick: he has not even the infatuate courage of Tappertit. But we dare not laugh at him, because, somehow, we recognize ourselves in Potts. We may, some of us, have enough nerve, enough muscle, enough luck, enough tact or skill or address or knowledge to carry things off better than he did; to impose on the people who saw through him; to fascinate Katinka (who cut Potts so ruthlessly at the end of the story); but for all that, we know that Potts plays an enormous part in ourselves and in the world, and that the social problem is not a problem of storybook heroes of the older pattern, but a problem of Pottses, and of how to make men of them. To fall back on my old phrase, we have the feeling—one that Alnaschar, Pistol, Parolles, and Tappertit never gave us—that Potts is a piece of really scientific natural history as distinguished from comic story telling. His author is not throwing a stone at a creature of another and inferior order, but making a confession, with the effect that the stone hits everybody full in the conscience and causes their self-esteem to smart very sorely. Hence the failure of Lever's book to please the readers of Household Words. That pain in the self-esteem nowadays causes critics to raise a cry of Ibsenism. I therefore assure them that the

sensation first came to me from Lever and may have come
to him from Beyle, or at least out of the Stendhalian atmosphere. I exclude the hypothesis of complete originality
on Lever's part, because a man can no more be completely
original in that sense than a tree can grow out of air.

Another mistake as to my literary ancestry is made
whenever I violate the romantic convention that all women
are angels when they are not devils; that they are better
looking than men; that their part in courtship is entirely
passive; and that the human female form is the most beautiful object in nature. Schopenhauer wrote a splenetic
essay which, as it is neither polite nor profound, was probably intended to knock this nonsense violently on the head.
A sentence denouncing the idolized form as ugly has been
largely quoted. The English critics have read that sentence;
and I must here affirm, with as much gentleness as the
implication will bear, that it has yet to be proved that they
have dipped any deeper. At all events, whenever an English playwright represents a young and marriageable
woman as being anything but a romantic heroine, he is
disposed of without further thought as an echo of Schopenhauer. My own case is a specially hard one, because,
when I implore the critics who are obsessed with the Scho-
penhaurian formula to remember that playwrights, like
sculptors, study their figures from life, and not from philosophic essays, they reply passionately that I am not a
playwright and that my stage figures do not live. But even
so, I may and do ask them why, if they must give the
credit of my plays to a philosopher, they do not give it to
an English philosopher? Long before I ever read a word
by Schopenhauer, or even knew whether he was a philosopher or a chemist, the Socialist revival of the eighteen-
eighties brought me into contact, both literary and personal,
with Mr. Ernest Belfort Bax, an English Socialist and
philosophic essayist, whose handling of modern feminism
would provoke romantic protests from Schopenhauer himself, or even Strindberg. As a matter of fact I hardly noticed Schopenhauer's disparagements of women when they
came under my notice later on, so thoroughly had Mr.

Bax familiarized me with the homoist attitude, and forced me to recognize the extent to which public opinion, and consequently legislation and jurisprudence, is corrupted by feminist sentiment.

But Mr. Bax's essays were not confined to the Feminist question. He was a ruthless critic of current morality. Other writers have gained sympathy for dramatic criminals by eliciting the alleged "soul of goodness in things evil"; but Mr. Bax would propound some quite undramatic and apparently shabby violation of our commercial law and morality, and not merely defend it with the most disconcerting ingenuity, but actually prove it to be a positive duty that nothing but the certainty of police persecution should prevent every right-minded man from at once doing on principle. The Socialists were naturally shocked, being for the most part morbidly moral people; but at all events they were saved later on from the delusion that nobody but Nietzsche had ever challenged our mercanto-Christian morality. I first heard the name of Nietzsche from a German mathematician, Miss Borchardt, who had read my Quintessence of Ibsenism, and told me that she saw what I had been reading: namely, Nietzsche's Jenseits von Gut und Böse. Which I protest I had never seen, and could not have read with any comfort, for want of the necessary German, if I had seen it.

Nietzsche, like Schopenhauer, is the victim in England of a single much quoted sentence containing the phrase "big blonde beast." On the strength of this alliteration it is assumed that Nietzsche gained his European reputation by a senseless glorification of selfish bullying as the rule of life, just as it is assumed, on the strength of the single word Superman (Übermensch) borrowed by me from Nietzsche, that I look for the salvation of society to the despotism of a single Napoleonic Superman, in spite of my careful demonstration of the folly of that outworn infatuation. But even the less recklessly superficial critics seem to believe that the modern objection to Christianity as a pernicious slave-morality was first put forward by Nietzsche. It was familiar to me before I ever heard of

Nietzsche. The late Captain Wilson, author of several queer pamphlets, propagandist of a metaphysical system called Comprehensionism, and inventor of the term "Crosstianity" to distinguish the retrograde element in Christendom, was wont thirty years ago, in the discussions of the Dialectical Society, to protest earnestly against the beatitudes of the Sermon on the Mount as excuses for cowardice and servility, as destructive of our will, and consequently of our honor and manhood. Now it is true that Captain Wilson's moral criticism of Christianity was not a historical theory of it, like Nietzsche's; but this objection cannot be made to Mr. Stuart-Glennie, the successor of Buckle as a philosophic historian, who has devoted his life to the elaboration and propagation of his theory that Christianity is part of an epoch (or rather an aberration, since it began as recently as 6000 B.C. and is already collapsing) produced by the necessity in which the numerically inferior white races found themselves to impose their domination on the colored races by priestcraft, making a virtue and a popular religion of drudgery and submissiveness in this world not only as a means of achieving saintliness of character but of securing a reward in heaven. Here you have the slave-morality view formulated by a Scotch philosopher long before English writers began chattering about Nietzsche.

As Mr. Stuart-Glennie traced the evolution of society to the conflict of races, his theory made some sensation among Socialists—that is, among the only people who were seriously thinking about historical evolution at all—by its collision with the class-conflict theory of Karl Marx. Nietzsche, as I gather, regarded the slave-morality as having been invented and imposed on the world by slaves making a virtue of necessity and a religion of their servitude. Mr. Stuart-Glennie regards the slave-morality as an invention of the superior white race to subjugate the minds of the inferior races whom they wished to exploit, and who would have destroyed them by force of numbers if their minds had not been subjugated. As this process is in operation still, and can be studied at first hand not only in our Church schools and in the struggle between our modern proprietary classes and the proletariat, but in the part played by Christian missionaries in reconciling the black races of Africa to their subjugation by European Capitalism, we can judge for ourselves whether the initiative came from above or below. My object here is not to argue the historical point, but simply to make our theatre critics ashamed of their habit of treating Britain as an intellectual void, and assuming that every philosophical idea, every historic theory, every criticism of our moral, religious and juridical institutions, must necessarily be either imported from abroad, or else a fantastic sally (in rather questionable taste) totally unrelated to the existing body of thought. I urge them to remember that this body of thought is the slowest of growths and the rarest of blossomings, and that if there is such a thing on the philosophic plane as a matter of course, it is that no individual can make more than a minute contribution to it. In fact, their conception of clever persons parthenogenetically bringing forth complete original cosmogonies by dint of sheer "brilliancy" is part of that ignorant credulity which is the despair of the honest philosopher, and the opportunity of the religious imposter.

The Gospel of St. Andrew Undershaft

It is this credulity that drives me to help my critics out with Major Barbara by telling them what to say about it. In the millionaire Undershaft I have represented a man who has become intellectually and spiritually as well as practically conscious of the irresistible natural truth which we all abhor and repudiate: to wit, that the greatest of evils and the worst of crimes is poverty, and that our first duty—a duty to which every other consideration should be sacrificed—is not to be poor. "Poor but honest," "the respectable poor," and such phrases are as intolerable and as immoral as "drunken but amiable," "fraudulent but a good after-dinner speaker," "splendidly criminal," or the like. Security, the chief pretense of civilization, cannot exist where the worst of dangers, the danger of poverty, hangs over everyone's head, and where the alleged protection of our persons from violence is only an accidental result of the existence of a police force whose real business is to force the poor man to see his children starve whilst idle people overfeed pet dogs with the money that might feed and clothe them.

It is exceedingly difficult to make people realize that an evil is an evil. For instance, we seize a man and deliberately do him a malicious injury: say, imprison him for years. One would not suppose that it needed any exceptional clearness of wit to recognize in this an act of diabolical cruelty. But in England such a recognition provokes a stare of surprise, followed by an explanation that the outrage is punishment or justice or something else that is all right, or perhaps by a heated attempt to argue that we should all be robbed and murdered in our beds if such senseless villainies as sentences of imprisonment were not committed daily. It is useless to argue that even if this were true, which it is not, the alternative to adding crimes of our own to the crimes from which we suffer is not helpless submission. Chickenpox is an evil; but if I were to declare that we must either submit to it or else repress it sternly by seizing everyone who suffers from it and punishing them by inoculation with smallpox, I should be laughed at; for though nobody could deny that the result would be to prevent chickenpox to some extent by making people avoid it much more carefully, and to effect a further apparent prevention by making them conceal it very anxiously, yet people would have sense enough to see that the deliberate propagation of smallpox was a creation of evil, and must therefore be ruled out in favor of purely humane and hygienic measures. Yet in the precisely parallel case of a man breaking into my house and stealing my wife's diamonds I am expected as a matter of course to steal ten years of his life, torturing him all the time. If he tries to defeat that monstrous retaliation by shooting me, my survivors hang him. The net result suggested by the police statistics is that we inflict atrocious injuries on the burglars we catch in order to make the rest take effectual precautions against detection; so that instead of saving our wives' diamonds from burglary we only greatly decrease our chances of ever getting them back, and increase our chances of being shot by the robber if we are unlucky enough to disturb him at his work.

But the thoughtless wickedness with which we scatter sentences of imprisonment, torture in the solitary cell and on the plank bed, and flogging, on moral invalids and energetic rebels, is as nothing compared to the stupid levity with which we tolerate poverty as if it were either a wholesome tonic for lazy people or else a virtue to be embraced as St. Francis embraced it. If a man is indolent, let him be poor. If he is drunken, let him be poor. If he is not a gentleman, let him be poor. If he is addicted to the fine arts or to pure science instead of to trade and finance, let him be poor. If he chooses to spend his urban eighteen shillings a week or his agricultural thirteen shillings a week on his beer and his family instead of saving it up for his old age, let him be poor. Let nothing be done for "the undeserving": let him be poor. Serve him right! Also—somewhat inconsistently—blessed are the poor!

Now what does this Let Him Be Poor mean? It means let him be weak. Let him be ignorant. Let him become a nucleus of disease. Let him be a standing exhibition and example of ugliness and dirt. Let him have rickety children. Let him be cheap and let him drag his fellows down to his price by selling himself to do their work. Let his habitations turn our cities into poisonous congeries of slums. Let his daughters infect our young men with the diseases of the streets and his sons revenge him by turning the nation's manhood into scrofula, cowardice, cruelty, hypocrisy, political imbecility, and all the other fruits of oppression and malnutrition. Let the undeserving become still less deserving; and let the deserving lay up for himself, not treasures in heaven, but horrors in hell upon earth. This being so, is it really wise to let him be poor? Would he not do ten times less harm as a prosperous burglar, incendiary, ravisher or murderer, to the utmost

limits of humanity's comparatively negligible impulses in
these directions? Suppose we were to abolish all penalties
for such activities, and decide that poverty is the one thing
we will not tolerate—that every adult with less than, say,
£365 a year, shall be painlessly but inexorably killed, and
every hungry half naked child forcibly fattened and
clothed, would not that be an enormous improvement on
our existing system, which has already destroyed so many
civilizations, and is visibly destroying ours in the same
way?

Is there any radicle of such legislation in our parliamen-
tary system? Well, there are two measures just sprouting
in the political soil, which may conceivably grow to something valuable. One is the institution of a Legal Minimum
Wage. The other, Old Age Pensions. But there is a better
plan than either of these. Some time ago I mentioned the
subject of Universal Old Age Pensions to my fellow Socialist Mr. Cobden-Sanderson, famous as an artist-craftsman in
bookbinding and printing. "Why not Universal Pensions
for Life?" said Cobden-Sanderson. In saying this, he
solved the industrial problem at a stroke. At present we
say callously to each citizen: "If you want money, earn
it," as if his having or not having it were a matter that
concerned himself alone. We do not even secure for him
the opportunity of earning it: on the contrary, we allow
our industry to be organized in open dependence on the
maintenance of "a reserve army of unemployed" for the
sake of "elasticity." The sensible course would be Cobden-Sanderson's: that is, to give every man enough to live
well on, so as to guarantee the community against the
possibility of a case of the malignant disease of poverty,
and then (necessarily) to see that he earned it.

Undershaft, the hero of Major Barbara, is simply a man
who, having grasped the fact that poverty is a crime,
knows that when society offered him the alternative of
poverty or a lucrative trade in death and destruction, it
offered him, not a choice between opulent villainy and
humble virtue, but between energetic enterprise and cow-
ardly infamy. His conduct stands the Kantian test, which

Peter Shirley's does not. Peter Shirley is what we call the honest poor man. Undershaft is what we call the wicked rich one: Shirley is Lazarus, Undershaft Dives. Well, the misery of the world is due to the fact that the great mass of men act and believe as Peter Shirley acts and believes. If they acted and believed as Undershaft acts and believes, the immediate result would be a revolution of incalculable beneficence. To be wealthy, says Undershaft, is with me a point of honor for which I am prepared to kill at the risk of my own life. This preparedness is, as he says, the final test of sincerity. Like Froissart's medieval hero, who saw that "to rob and pill was a good life," he is not the dupe of that public sentiment against killing which is propagated and endowed by people who would otherwise be killed themselves, or of the mouth-honor paid to poverty and obedience by rich and insubordinate do-nothings who want to rob the poor without courage and command them without superiority. Froissart's knight, in placing the achievement of a good life before all the other duties— which indeed are not duties at all when they conflict with it, but plain wickednesses—behaved bravely, admirably, and, in the final analysis, public-spiritedly. Medieval society, on the other hand, behaved very badly indeed in organizing itself so stupidly that a good life could be achieved by robbing and pilling. If the knight's contemporaries had been all as resolute as he, robbing and pilling would have been the shortest way to the gallows, just as, if we were all as resolute and clearsighted as Undershaft, an attempt to live by means of what is called "an independent income" would be the shortest way to the lethal chamber. But as, thanks to our political imbecility and personal cowardice (fruits of poverty, both), the best imitation of a good life now procurable is life on an independent income, all sensible people aim at securing such an income, and are, of course, careful to legalize and moralize both it and all the actions and sentiments which lead to it and support it as an institution. What else can they do? They know, of course, that they are rich because others are poor. But they cannot help that: it is for the

poor to repudiate poverty when they have had enough of
it. The thing can be done easily enough: the demonstra-
tions to the contrary made by the economists, jurists, moralists and sentimentalists hired by the rich to defend them,
or even doing the work gratuitously out of sheer folly and
abjectness, impose only on the hirers.

The reason why the independent income-tax payers are
not solid in defence of their position is that since we are
not medieval rovers through a sparsely populated country,
the poverty of those we rob prevents our having the good
life for which we sacrifice them. Rich men or aristocrats
with a developed sense of life—men like Ruskin and William Morris and Kropotkin—have enormous social appetites and very fastidious personal ones. They are not
content with handsome houses: they want handsome cities.
They are not content with bediamonded wives and blooming daughters: they complain because the charwoman is
badly dressed, because the laundress smells of gin, because the sempstress is anemic, because every man they
meet is not a friend and every woman not a romance.
They turn up their noses at their neighbors' drains, and
are made ill by the architecture of their neighbors' houses.
Trade patterns made to suit vulgar people do not please
them (and they can get nothing else): they cannot sleep
nor sit at ease upon "slaughtered" cabinet makers' furniture. The very air is not good enough for them: there is
too much factory smoke in it. They even demand abstract
conditions: justice, honor, a noble moral atmosphere, a
mystic nexus to replace the cash nexus. Finally they declare that though to rob and pill with your own hand on
horseback and in steel coat may have been a good life, to
rob and pill by the hands of the policeman, the bailiff,
and the soldier, and to underpay them meanly for doing
it, is not a good life, but rather fatal to all possibility of
even a tolerable one. They call on the poor to revolt,
and, finding the poor shocked at their ungentlemanliness,
despairingly revile the proletariat for its "damned want-
lessness" (*verdammte Bedürfnislosigkeit*).

So far, however, their attack on society has lacked simplicity. The poor do not share their tastes nor understand their art-criticisms. They do not want the simple life, nor the esthetic life; on the contrary, they want very much to wallow in all the costly vulgarities from which the elect souls among the rich turn away with loathing. It is by surfeit and not by abstinence that they will be cured of their hankering after unwholesome sweets. What they do dislike and despise and are ashamed of is poverty. To ask them to fight for the difference between the Christmas number of the Illustrated London News and the Kelmscott Chaucer is silly: they prefer the News. The difference between a stockbroker's cheap and dirty starched white shirt and collar and the comparatively costly and carefully dyed blue shirt of William Morris is a difference so disgraceful to Morris in their eyes that if they fought on the subject at all, they would fight in defence of the starch. "Cease to be slaves, in order that you may become cranks" is not a very inspiring call to arms; nor is it really improved by substituting saints for cranks. Both terms denote men of genius; and the common man does not want to live the life of a man of genius: he would much rather live the life of a pet collie if that were the only alternative. But he does want more money. Whatever else he may be vague about, he is clear about that. He may or may not prefer Major Barbara to the Drury Lane pantomime; but he always prefers five hundred pounds to five hundred shillings.

Now to deplore this preference as sordid, and teach children that it is sinful to desire money, is to strain towards the extreme possible limit of impudence in lying, and corruption in hypocrisy. The universal regard for money is the one hopeful fact in our civilization, the one sound spot in our social conscience. Money is the most important thing in the world. It represents health, strength, honor, generosity and beauty as conspicuously and undeniably as the want of it represents illness, weakness, disgrace, meanness and ugliness. Not the least of its virtues is that it destroys base people as certainly as it fortifies and dignifies noble people. It is only when it is cheapened

to worthlessness for some, and made impossibly dear to
others, that it becomes a curse. In short, it is a curse only
in such foolish social conditions that life itself is a curse.
For the two things are inseparable: money is the counter
that enables life to be distributed socially: it *is* life as truly
as sovereigns and bank notes are money. The first duty of
every citizen is to insist on having money on reasonable
terms; and this demand is not complied with by giving
four men three shillings each for ten or twelve hours'
drudgery and one man a thousand pounds for nothing. The
crying need of the nation is not for better morals, cheaper
bread, temperance, liberty, culture, redemption of fallen
sisters and erring brothers, nor the grace, love and fellowship of the Trinity, but simply for enough money. And the
evil to be attacked is not sin, suffering, greed, priestcraft,
kingcraft, demagogy, monopoly, ignorance, drink, war,
pestilence, nor any other of the scapegoats which reformers sacrifice, but simply poverty.

Once take your eyes from the ends of the earth and
fix them on this truth just under your nose; and Andrew
Undershaft's views will not perplex you in the least. Unless indeed his constant sense that he is only the instrument
of a Will or Life Force which uses him for purposes wider
than his own, may puzzle you. If so, that is because you
are walking either in artificial Darwinian darkness, or in
mere stupidity. All genuinely religious people have that
consciousness. To them Undershaft the Mystic will be
quite intelligible, and his perfect comprehension of his
daughter the Salvationist and her lover the Euripidean republican natural and inevitable. That, however, is not
new, even on the stage. What is new, as far as I know,
is that article in Undershaft's religion which recognizes in
Money the first need and in poverty the vilest sin of man
and society.

This dramatic conception has not, of course, been attained *per saltum*. Nor has it been borrowed from
Nietzsche or from any man born beyond the Channel. The
late Samuel Butler, in his own department the greatest
English writer of the latter half of the XIX century, stead-

ily inculcated the necessity and morality of a conscientious
Laodiceanism in religion and of an earnest and constant
sense of the importance of money. It drives one almost to
despair of English literature when one sees so extraordinary a study of English life as Butler's posthumous Way
of All Flesh making so little impression that when, some
years later, I produce plays in which Butler's extraordinarily fresh, free and future-piercing suggestions have an
obvious share, I am met with nothing but vague cacklings
about Ibsen and Nietzsche, and am only too thankful that
they are not about Alfred de Musset and George Sand.
Really, the English do not deserve to have great men.
They allowed Butler to die practically unknown, whilst I,
a comparatively insignificant Irish journalist, was leading
them by the nose into an advertisement of me which has
made my own life a burden. In Sicily there is a Via Samuele Butler. When an English tourist sees it, he either asks
"Who the devil was Samuele Butler?" or wonders why
the Sicilians should perpetuate the memory of the author
of Hudibras.

Well, it cannot be denied that the English are only too
anxious to recognize a man of genius if somebody will
kindly point him out to them. Having pointed myself out
in this manner with some success, I now point out Samuel
Butler, and trust that in consequence I shall hear a little
less in future of the novelty and foreign origin of the ideas
which are now making their way into the English theatre
through plays written by Socialists. There are living men
whose originality and power are as obvious as Butler's;
and when they die that fact will be discovered. Meanwhile
I recommend them to insist on their own merits as an
important part of their own business.

The Salvation Army

When Major Barbara was produced in London, the second act was reported in an important northern newspaper
as a withering attack on the Salvation Army, and the despairing ejaculation of Barbara deplored by a London daily

as a tasteless blasphemy. And they were set right, not by
the professed critics of the theatre, but by religious and
philosophical publicists like Sir Oliver Lodge and Dr.
Stanton Coit, and strenuous Nonconformist journalists like
Mr. William Stead, who not only understand the act as
well as the Salvationists themselves, but also saw it in its
relation to the religious life of the nation, a life which
seems to lie not only outside the sympathy of many of
our theatre critics, but actually outside their knowledge of
society. Indeed nothing could be more ironically curious
than the confrontation Major Barbara effected of the theatre enthusiasts with the religious enthusiasts. On the one
hand was the playgoer, always seeking pleasure, paying
exorbitantly for it, suffering unbearable discomforts for it,
and hardly ever getting it. On the other hand was the
Salvationist, repudiating gaiety and courting effort and
sacrifice, yet always in the wildest spirits, laughing, joking, singing, rejoicing, drumming, and tambourining: his
life flying by in a flash of excitement, and his death arriv-
ing as a climax of triumph. And, if you please, the playgoer despising the Salvationist as a joyless person, shut
out from the heaven of the theatre, self-condemned to a
life of hideous gloom; and the Salvationist mourning over
the playgoer as over a prodigal with vine leaves in his
hair, careering outrageously to hell amid the popping of
champagne corks and the ribald laughter of sirens! Could
misunderstanding be more complete, or sympathy worse
misplaced?

Fortunately, the Salvationists are more accessible to the
religious character of the drama than the playgoers to the
gay energy and artistic fertility of religion. They can see,
when it is pointed out to them, that a theatre, as a place
where two or three are gathered together, takes from that
divine presence an inalienable sanctity of which the gross-
est and profanest farce can no more deprive it than a
hypocritical sermon by a snobbish bishop can desecrate
Westminster Abbey. But in our professional playgoers this
indispensable preliminary conception of sanctity seems
wanting. They talk of actors as mimes and mummers, and,

I fear, think of dramatic authors as liars and pandars, whose main business is the voluptuous soothing of the tired city speculator when what he calls the serious business of the day is over. Passion, the life of drama, means nothing to them but primitive sexual excitement: such phrases as "impassioned poetry" or "passionate love of truth" have fallen quite out of their vocabulary and been replaced by "passional crime" and the like. They assume, as far as I can gather, that people in whom passion has a larger scope are passionless and therefore uninteresting. Consequently they come to think of religious people as people who are not interesting and not amusing. And so, when Barbara cuts the regular Salvation Army jokes, and snatches a kiss from her lover across his drum, the devotees of the theatre think they ought to appear shocked, and conclude that the whole play is an elaborate mockery of the Army. And then either hypocritically rebuke me for mocking, or foolishly take part in the supposed mockery!

Even the handful of mentally competent critics got into difficulties over my demonstration of the economic deadlock in which the Salvation Army finds itself. Some of them thought that the Army would not have taken money from a distiller and a cannon founder: others thought it should not have taken it: all assumed more or less definitely that it reduced itself to absurdity or hypocrisy by taking it. On the first point the reply of the Army itself was prompt and conclusive. As one of its officers said, they would take money from the devil himself and be only too glad to get it out of his hands and into God's. They gratefully acknowledged that publicans not only give them money but allow them to collect it in the bar—sometimes even when there is a Salvation meeting outside preaching teetotalism. In fact, they questioned the verisimilitude of the play, not because Mrs. Baines took the money, but because Barbara refused it.

On the point that the Army ought not to take such money, its justification is obvious. It must take the money because it cannot exist without money, and there is no other money to be had. Practically all the spare money in

the country consists of a mass of rent, interest, and profit,
every penny of which is bound up with crime, drink, prostitution, disease, and all the evil fruits of poverty, as inex-
tricably as with enterprise, wealth, commercial probity,
and national prosperity. The notion that you can earmark
certain coins as tainted is an unpractical individualist superstition. None the less the fact that all our money is
tainted gives a very severe shock to earnest young souls
when some dramatic instance of the taint first makes them
conscious of it. When an enthusiastic young clergyman of
the Established Church first realizes that the Ecclesiastical
Commissioners receive the rents of sporting public houses,
brothels, and sweating dens; or that the most generous
contributor at his last charity sermon was an employer
trading in female labor cheapened by prostitution as un-
scrupulously as a hotel keeper trades in waiters' labor
cheapened by tips, or commissionaire's labor cheapened
by pensions; or that the only patron who can afford to
rebuild his church or his schools or give his boys' brigade
a gymnasium or a library is the son-in-law of a Chicago
meat King, that young clergyman has, like Barbara, a very
bad quarter hour. But he cannot help himself by refusing
to accept money from anybody except sweet old ladies
with independent incomes and gentle and lovely ways of
life. He has only to follow up the income of the sweet
ladies to its industrial source, and there he will find Mrs.
Warren's profession and the poisonous canned meat and
all the rest of it. His own stipend has the same root. He
must either share the world's guilt or go to another planet.
He must save the world's honor if he is to save his own.
This is what all the Churches find just as the Salvation
Army and Barbara find it in the play. Her discovery that
she is her father's accomplice; that the Salvation Army is
the accomplice of the distiller and the dynamite maker;
that they can no more escape one another than they can
escape the air they breathe; that there is no salvation for
them through personal righteousness, but only through the
redemption of the whole nation from its vicious, lazy,
competitive anarchy: this discovery has been made by ev-

eryone except the Pharisees and (apparently) the professional playgoers, who still wear their Tom Hood shirts and underpay their washerwomen without the slightest misgiving as to the elevation of their private characters, the purity of their private atmospheres, and their right to repudiate as foreign to themselves the coarse depravity of the garret and the slum. Not that they mean any harm: they only desire to be, in their little private way, what they call gentlemen. They do not understand Barbara's lesson because they have not, like her, learnt it by taking their part in the larger life of the nation.

Barbara's Return to the Colors

Barbara's return to the colors may yet provide a subject for the dramatic historian of the future. To go back to the Salvation Army with the knowledge that even the Salvationists themselves are not saved yet; that poverty is not blessed, but a most damnable sin; and that when General Booth chose Blood and Fire for the emblem of Salvation instead of the Cross, he was perhaps better inspired than he knew: such knowledge, for the daughter of Andrew Undershaft, will clearly lead to something hopefuller than distributing bread and treacle at the expense of Bodger.

It is a very significant thing, this instinctive choice of the military form of organization, this substitution of the drum for the organ, by the Salvation Army. Does it not suggest that the Salvationists divine that they must actually fight the devil instead of merely praying at him? At present, it is true, they have not quite ascertained his correct address. When they do, they may give a very rude shock to that sense of security which he has gained from his experience of the fact that hard words, even when uttered by eloquent essayists and lecturers, or carried unanimously at enthusiastic public meetings on the motion of eminent reformers, break no bones. It has been said that the French Revolution was the work of Voltaire, Rousseau and the Encyclopedists. It seems to me to have been the work of men who had observed that virtuous indignation, caustic

criticism, conclusive argument and instructive pamphle-
teering, even when done by the most earnest and witty
literary geniuses, were as useless as praying, things going
steadily from bad to worse whilst the Social Contract and
the pamphlets of Voltaire were at the height of their
vogue. Eventually, as we know, perfectly respectable citizens and earnest philanthropists connived at the September
massacres because hard experience had convinced them
that if they contented themselves with appeals to humanity
and patriotism, the aristocracy, though it would read their
appeals with the greatest enjoyment and appreciation, flattering and admiring the writers, would none the less con-
tinue to conspire with foreign monarchists to undo the
revolution and restore the old system with every circum-
stance of savage vengeance and ruthless repression of popular liberties.

The nineteenth century saw the same lesson repeated in
England. It had its Utilitarians, its Christian Socialists, its
Fabians (still extant): it had Bentham, Mill, Dickens, Ruskin, Carlyle, Butler, Henry George, and Morris. And the
end of all their efforts is the Chicago described by Mr.
Upton Sinclair, and the London in which the people who
pay to be amused by my dramatic representation of Peter
Shirley turned out to starve at forty because there are
younger slaves to be had for his wages, do not take, and
have not the slightest intention of taking, any effective
step to organize society in such a way as to make that
everyday infamy impossible. I, who have preached and
pamphleteered like any Encyclopedist, have to confess that
my methods are no use, and would be no use if I were
Voltaire, Rousseau, Bentham, Mill, Dickens, Carlyle,
Ruskin, George, Butler, and Morris all rolled into one,
with Euripides, More, Molière, Shakespear, Beaumar-
chais, Swift, Goethe, Ibsen, Tolstoy, Moses and the
prophets all thrown in (as indeed in some sort I actually
am, standing as I do on all their shoulders). The problem
being to make heroes out of cowards, we paper apostles
and artist-magicians have succeeded only in giving cowards all the sensations of heroes whilst they tolerate every

abomination, accept every plunder, and submit to every oppression. Christianity, in making a merit of such submission, has marked only that depth in the abyss at which the very sense of shame is lost. The Christian has been like Dickens' doctor in the debtor's prison, who tells the newcomer of its ineffable peace and security: no duns; no tyrannical collectors of rates, taxes, and rent; no importunate hopes nor exacting duties; nothing but the rest and safety of having no further to fall.

Yet in the poorest corner of this soul-destroying Christendom vitality suddenly begins to germinate again. Joyousness, a sacred gift long dethroned by the hellish laughter of derision and obscenity, rises like a flood miraculously out of the fetid dust and mud of the slums; rousing marches and impetuous dithyrambs rise to the heavens from people among whom the depressing noise called "sacred music" is a standing joke; a flag with Blood and Fire on it is unfurled, not in murderous rancor, but because fire is beautiful and blood a vital and splendid red; Fear, which we flatter by calling Self, vanishes; and transfigured men and women carry their gospel through a transfigured world, calling their leader General, themselves captains and brigadiers, and their whole body an Army: praying, but praying only for refreshment, for strength to fight, and for needful MONEY (a notable sign, that); preaching, but not preaching submission; daring ill-usage and abuse, but not putting up with more of it than is inevitable, and practising what the world will let them practise, including soap and water, color and music. There is danger in such activity; and where there is danger there is hope. Our present security is nothing, and can be nothing, but evil made irresistible.

Weaknesses of the Salvation Army

For the present, however, it is not my business to flatter the Salvation Army. Rather must I point out to it that it has almost as many weaknesses as the Church of England itself. It is building up a business organization which

will compel it eventually to see that its present staff of
enthusiast-commanders shall be succeeded by a bureau-
cracy of men of business who will be no better than bish-
ops, and perhaps a good deal more unscrupulous. That has
always happened sooner or later to great orders founded
by saints; and the order founded by St. William Booth is
not exempt from the same danger. It is even more dependent than the Church on rich people who would cut off
supplies at once if it began to preach that indispensable
revolt against poverty which must also be a revolt against
riches. It is hampered by a heavy contingent of pious
elders who are not really Salvationists at all, but Evangeli-
cals of the old school. It still, as Commissioner Howard
affirms, "sticks to Moses," which is flat nonsense at this
time of day if the Commissioner means, as I am afraid
he does, that the Book of Genesis contains a trustworthy
scientific account of the origin of species, and that the
god to whom Jephthah sacrificed his daughter is any less
obviously a tribal idol than Dagon or Chemosh.

Further, there is still too much other-worldliness about
the Army. Like Frederick's grenadier, the Salvationist
wants to live for ever (the most monstrous way of crying
for the moon); and though it is evident to anyone who has
ever heard General Booth and his best officers that they
would work as hard for human salvation as they do at
present if they believed that death would be the end of
them individually, they and their followers have a bad
habit of talking as if the Salvationists were heroically enduring a very bad time on earth as an investment which
will bring them in dividends later on in the form, not of
a better life to come for the whole world, but of an eternity
spent by themselves personally in a sort of bliss which
would bore any active person to a second death. Surely
the truth is that the Salvationists are unusually happy people. And is it not the very diagnostic of true salvation that
it shall overcome the fear of death? Now the man who
has come to believe that there is no such thing as death,
the change so called being merely the transition to an
exquisitely happy and utterly careless life, has not over-

come the fear of death at all: on the contrary, it has overcome him so completely that he refuses to die on any
terms whatever. I do not call a Salvationist really saved
until he is ready to lie down cheerfully on the scrap heap,
having paid scot and lot and something over, and let his
eternal life pass on to renew its youth in the battalions of
the future.

Then there is the nasty lying habit called confession,
which the Army encourages because it lends itself to dramatic oratory, with plenty of thrilling incident. For my
part, when I hear a convert relating the violences and oaths
and blasphemies he was guilty of before he was saved,
making out that he was a very terrible fellow then and is
the most contrite and chastened of Christians now, I believe him no more than I believe the millionaire who says
he came up to London or Chicago as a boy with only
three halfpence in his pocket. Salvationists have said to
me that Barbara in my play would never have been taken
in by so transparent a humbug as Snobby Price; and certainly I do not think Snobby could have taken in any
experienced Salvationist on a point on which the Salvationist did not wish to be taken in. But on the point of
conversion all Salvationists wish to be taken in; for the
more obvious the sinner the more obvious the miracle of
his conversion. When you advertize a converted burglar
or reclaimed drunkard as one of the attractions at an experience meeting, your burglar can hardly have been too
burglarious or your drunkard too drunken. As long as such
attractions are relied on, you will have your Snobbies
claiming to have beaten their mothers when they were as
a matter of prosaic fact habitually beaten by them, and
your Rummies of the tamest respectability pretending to a
past of reckless and dazzling vice. Even when confessions
are sincerely autobiographic there is no reason to assume
at once that the impulse to make them is pious or the
interest of the hearers wholesome. It might as well be
assumed that the poor people who insist on shewing appalling ulcers to district visitors are convinced hygienists,
or that the curiosity which sometimes welcomes such exhi-

bitions is a pleasant and creditable one. One is often tempted to suggest that those who pester our police superintendents with confessions of murder might very wisely be taken at their word and executed, except in the few cases in which a real murderer is seeking to be relieved of his guilt by confession and expiation. For though I am not, I hope, an unmerciful person, I do not think that the inexorability of the deed once done should be disguised by any ritual, whether in the confessional or on the scaffold.

And here my disagreement with the Salvation Army, and with all propagandists of the Cross (to which I object as I object to all gibbets) becomes deep indeed. Forgiveness, absolution, atonement, are figments: punishment is only a pretence of cancelling one crime by another; and you can no more have forgiveness without vindictiveness than you can have a cure without a disease. You will never get a high morality from people who conceive that their misdeeds are revocable and pardonable, or in a society where absolution and expiation are officially provided for us all. The demand may be very real; but the supply is spurious. Thus Bill Walker, in my play, having assaulted the Salvation Lass, presently finds himself overwhelmed with an intolerable conviction of sin under the skilled treatment of Barbara. Straightway he begins to try to unassault the lass and deruffianize his deed, first by getting punished for it in kind, and, when that relief is denied him, by fining himself a pound to compensate the girl. He is foiled both ways. He finds the Salvation Army as inexorable as fact itself. It will not punish him: it will not take his money. It will not tolerate a redeemed ruffian: it leaves him no means of salvation except ceasing to be a ruffian. In doing this, the Salvation Army instinctively grasps the central truth of Christianity and discards its central superstition: that central truth being the vanity of revenge and punishment, and that central superstition the salvation of the world by the gibbet.

For, be it noted, Bill has assaulted an old and starving woman also; and for this worse offence he feels no remorse whatever, because she makes it clear that her malice is as great as his own. "Let her have the law of me, as she said she would," says Bill: "what I done to her is no more on what you might call my conscience than sticking a pig." This shews a perfectly natural and wholesome state of mind on his part. The old woman, like the law she threatens him with, is perfectly ready to play the game of retaliation with him: to rob him if he steals, to flog him if he strikes, to murder him if he kills. By example and precept the law and public opinion teach him to impose his will on others by anger, violence, and cruelty, and to wipe off the moral score by punishment. That is sound Crosstianity. But this Crosstianity has got entangled with something which Barbara calls Christianity, and which unexpectedly causes her to refuse to play the hangman's game of Satan casting out Satan. She refuses to prosecute a drunken ruffian; she converses on equal terms with a blackguard whom no lady could be seen speaking to in the public street: in short, she behaves as illegally and unbecomingly as possible under the circumstances. Bill's conscience reacts to this just as naturally as it does to the old woman's threats. He is placed in a position of unbearable moral inferiority, and strives by every means in his power to escape from it, whilst he is still quite ready to meet the abuse of the old woman by attempting to smash a mug on her face. And that is the triumphant justification of Barbara's Christianity as against our system of judicial punishment and the vindictive villain-thrashings and "poetic justice" of the romantic stage.

For the credit of literature it must be pointed out that the situation is only partly novel. Victor Hugo long ago gave us the epic of the convict and the bishop's candlesticks, of the Crosstian policeman annihilated by his encounter with the Christian Valjean. But Bill Walker is not, like Valjean, romantically changed from a demon into an angel. There are millions of Bill Walkers in all classes of society to-day; and the point which I, as a professor of natural psychology, desire to demonstrate, is that Bill, without any change in his character whatsoever, will react one way to one sort of treatment and another way to another.

In proof I might point to the sensational object lesson provided by our commercial millionaires to-day. They begin as brigands: merciless, unscrupulous, dealing out ruin and death and slavery to their competitors and employees, and facing desperately the worst that their competitors can do to them. The history of the English factories, the American trusts, the exploitation of African gold, diamonds, ivory and rubber, outdoes in villainy the worst that has ever been imagined of the buccaneers of the Spanish Main. Captain Kidd would have marooned a modern Trust magnate for conduct unworthy of a gentleman of fortune. The law every day seizes on unsuccessful scoundrels of this type and punishes them with a cruelty worse than their own, with the result that they come out of the torture house more dangerous than they went in, and renew their evil doing (nobody will employ them at anything else) until they are again seized, again tormented, and again let loose, with the same result.

But the successful scoundrel is dealt with very differently, and very Christianly. He is not only forgiven: he is idolized, respected, made much of, all but worshipped. Society returns him good for evil in the most extravagant overmeasure. And with what result? He begins to idolize himself, to respect himself, to live up to the treatment he receives. He preaches sermons; he writes books of the most edifying advice to young men, and actually persuades himself that he got on by taking his own advice; he endows educational institutions; he supports charities; he dies finally in the odor of sanctity, leaving a will which is a monument of public spirit and bounty. And all this without any change in his character. The spots of the leopard and the stripes of the tiger are as brilliant as ever; but the conduct of the world towards him has changed; and his conduct has changed accordingly. You have only to reverse your attitude towards him—to lay hands on his property, revile him, assault him, and he will be a brigand again in a moment, as ready to crush you as you are to crush him, and quite as full of pretentious moral reasons for doing it.

In short, when Major Barbara says that there are no scoundrels, she is right: there are no absolute scoundrels, though there are impracticable people of whom I shall treat presently. Every practicable man (and woman) is a potential scoundrel and a potential good citizen. What a man is depends on his character; but what he does, and what we think of what he does, depends on his circumstances. The characteristics that ruin a man in one class make him eminent in another. The characters that behave differently in different circumstances behave alike in similar circumstances. Take a common English character like that of Bill Walker. We meet Bill everywhere: on the judicial bench, on the episcopal bench, in the Privy Council, at the War Office and Admiralty, as well as in the Old Bailey dock or in the ranks of casual unskilled labor. And the morality of Bill's characteristics varies with these various circumstances. The faults of the burglar are the qualities of the financier: the manners and habits of a duke would cost a city clerk his situation. In short, though character is independent of circumstances, conduct is not; and our moral judgments of character are not: both are circumstantial. Take any condition of life in which the circumstances are for a mass of men practically alike: felony, the House of Lords, the factory, the stables, the gipsy encampment or where you please! In spite of diversity of character and temperament, the conduct and morals of the individuals in each group are as predicable and as alike in the main as if they were a flock of sheep, morals being mostly only social habits and circumstantial necessities. Strong people know this and count upon it. In nothing have the master-minds of the world been distinguished from the ordinary suburban season-ticket holder more than in their straightforward perception of the fact that mankind is practically a single species, and not a menagerie of gentlemen and bounders, villains and heroes, cowards and daredevils, peers and peasants, grocers and aristocrats, artisans and laborers, washerwomen and duchesses, in which all the grades of income and caste represent distinct animals who must not be introduced to one another or intermarry. Napoleon constructing a galaxy of generals and courtiers, and even of monarchs, out of his collection of social nobodies; Julius Cæsar appointing as governor of Egypt the son of a freedman—one who but a short time before would have been legally disqualified for the post even of a private soldier in the Roman army; Louis XI making his barber his privy councillor: all these had in their different ways a firm hold of the scientific fact of human equality, expressed by Barbara in the Christian formula that all men are children of one father. A man who believes that men are naturally divided into upper and lower and middle classes morally is making exactly the same mistake as the man who believes that they are naturally divided in the same way socially. And just as our persistent attempts to found political institutions on a basis of social inequality have always produced long periods of destructive friction relieved from time to time by violent explosions of revolution; so the attempt—will Americans please note—to found moral institutions on a basis of moral inequality can lead to nothing but unnatural Reigns of the Saints relieved by licentious Restorations; to Americans who have made divorce a public institution turning the face of Europe into one huge sardonic smile by refusing to stay in the same hotel with a Russian man of genius who has changed wives without the sanction of South Dakota; to grotesque hypocrisy, cruel persecution, and final utter confusion of conventions and compliances with benevolence and respectability. It is quite useless to declare that all men are born free if you deny that they are born good. Guarantee a man's goodness and his liberty will take care of itself. To guarantee his freedom on condition that you approve of his moral character is formally to abolish all freedom whatsoever, as every man's liberty is at the mercy of a moral indictment, which any fool can trump up against everyone who violates custom, whether as a prophet or as a rascal. This is the lesson Democracy has to learn before it can become anything but the most oppressive of all the priesthoods.

Let us now return to Bill Walker and his case of conscience against the Salvation Army. Major Barbara, not being a modern Tetzel, or the treasurer of a hospital, refuses to sell Bill absolution for a sovereign. Unfortunately, what the Army can afford to refuse in the case of Bill Walker, it cannot refuse in the case of Bodger. Bodger is master of the situation because he holds the purse strings. "Strive as you will," says Bodger, in effect: "me you cannot do without. You cannot save Bill Walker without my money." And the Army answers, quite rightly under the circumstances, "We will take money from the devil himself sooner than abandon the work of Salvation." So Bodger pays his conscience-money and gets the absolution that is refused to Bill. In real life Bill would perhaps never know this. But I, the dramatist, whose business it is to shew the connexion between things that seem apart and unrelated in the haphazard order of events in real life, have contrived to make it known to Bill, with the result that the Salvation Army loses its hold of him at once.

But Bill may not be lost, for all that. He is still in the grip of the facts and of his own conscience, and may find his taste for blackguardism permanently spoiled. Still, I cannot guarantee that happy ending. Let anyone walk through the poorer quarters of our cities when the men are not working, but resting and chewing the cud of their reflections; and he will find that there is one expression on every mature face: the expression of cynicism. The discovery made by Bill Walker about the Salvation Army has been made by everyone of them. They have found that every man has his price; and they have been foolishly or corruptly taught to mistrust and despise him for that necessary and salutary condition of social existence. When they learn that General Booth, too, has his price, they do not admire him because it is a high one, and admit the need of organizing society so that he shall get it in an honorable way: they conclude that his character is unsound and that all religious men are hypocrites and allies of their sweaters and oppressors. They know that the large subscriptions which help to support the Army are endowments, not of religion, but of the wicked doctrine of docility in poverty and humility under oppression; and they are rent by the most agonizing of all the doubts of the soul, the doubt whether their true salvation must not come from their most abhorrent passions, from murder, envy, greed, stubbornness, rage, and terrorism, rather than from public spirit, reasonableness, humanity, generosity, tenderness, delicacy, pity and kindness. The confirmation of that doubt, at which our newspapers have been working so hard for years past, is the morality of militarism; and the justification of militarism is that circumstances may at any time make it the true morality of the moment. It is by producing such moments that we produce violent and sanguinary revolutions, such as the one now in progress in Russia and the one which Capitalism in England and America is daily and diligently provoking.

At such moments it becomes the duty of the Churches to evoke all the powers of destruction against the existing order. But if they do this, the existing order must forcibly suppress them. Churches are suffered to exist only on condition that they preach submission to the State as at present capitalistically organized. The Church of England itself is compelled to add to the thirty-six articles in which it formulates its religious tenets, three more in which it apologetically protests that the moment any of these articles comes in conflict with the State it is to be entirely renounced, abjured, violated, abrogated and abhorred, the policeman being a much more important person than any of the Persons of the Trinity. And this is why no tolerated Church nor Salvation Army can ever win the entire confidence of the poor. It must be on the side of the police and the military, no matter what it believes or disbelieves; and as the police and the military are the instruments by which the rich rob and oppress the poor (on legal and moral principles made for the purpose), it is not possible to be on the side of the poor and of the police at the same time. Indeed the religious bodies, as the almoners of the rich, become a sort of auxiliary police, taking off the insurrectionary

edge of poverty with coals and blankets, bread and treacle, and soothing and cheering the victims with hopes
of immense and inexpensive happiness in another world
when the process of working them to premature death
in the service of the rich is complete in this.

Christianity and Anarchism

Such is the false position from which neither the Salvation Army nor the Church of England nor any other religious organization whatever can escape except through a
reconstitution of society. Nor can they merely endure the
State passively, washing their hands of its sins. The State
is constantly forcing the consciences of men by violence
and cruelty. Not content with exacting money from us for
the maintenance of its soldiers and policemen, its gaolers
and executioners, it forces us to take an active personal
part in its proceedings on pain of becoming ourselves the
victims of its violence. As I write these lines, a sensational
example is given to the world. A royal marriage has been
celebrated, first by sacrament in a cathedral, and then by
a bullfight having for its main amusement the spectacle of
horses gored and disembowelled by the bull, after which,
when the bull is so exhausted as to be no longer dangerous, he is killed by a cautious matador. But the ironic
contrast between the bull fight and the sacrament of marriage does not move anyone. Another contrast—that between the splendor, the happiness, the atmosphere of
kindly admiration surrounding the young couple, and the
price paid for it under our abominable social arrangements
in the misery, squalor and degradation of millions of other
young couples—is drawn at the same moment by a novelist, Mr. Upton Sinclair, who chips a corner of the veneer-
ing from the huge meat packing industries of Chicago,
and shews it to us as a sample of what is going on all
over the world underneath the top layer of prosperous plutocracy. One man is sufficiently moved by that contrast to
pay his own life as the price of one terrible blow at the
responsible parties. Unhappily his poverty leaves him also

ignorant enough to be duped by the pretence that the innocent young bride and bridegroom, put forth and crowned
by plutocracy as the heads of a State in which they have
less personal power than any policeman, and less influence
than any chairman of a trust, are responsible. At them
accordingly he launches his sixpennorth of fulminate,
missing his mark, but scattering the bowels of as many
horses as any bull in the arena, and slaying twenty-three
persons, besides wounding ninetynine. And of all these,
the horses alone are innocent of the guilt he is avenging:
had he blown all Madrid to atoms with every adult person
in it, not one could have escaped the charge of being an
accessory, before, at, and after the fact, to poverty and
prostitution, to such wholesale massacre of infants as
Herod never dreamt of, to plague, pestilence and famine,
battle, murder and lingering death—perhaps not one who
had not helped, through example, precept, connivance,
and even clamor, to teach the dynamiter his well-learnt
gospel of hatred and vengeance, by approving every day
of sentences of years of imprisonment so infernal in its
unnatural stupidity and panic-stricken cruelty, that their
advocates can disavow neither the dagger nor the bomb
without stripping the mask of justice and humanity from
themselves also.

Be it noted that at this very moment there appears the
biography of one of our dukes, who, being Scotch, could
argue about politics, and therefore stood out as a great
brain among our aristocrats. And what, if you please, was
his grace's favorite historical episode, which he declared
he never read without intense satisfaction? Why, the young
General Bonapart's pounding of the Paris mob to pieces
in 1795, called in playful approval by our respectable
classes "the whiff of grapeshot," though Napoleon, to do
him justice, took a deeper view of it, and would fain have
had it forgotten. And since the Duke of Argyll was not a
demon, but a man of like passions with ourselves, by no
means rancorous or cruel as men go, who can doubt that
all over the world proletarians of the ducal kidney are now
revelling in "the whiff of dynamite" (the flavor of the

joke seems to evaporate a little, does it not?) because it was aimed at the class they hate even as our argute duke hated what he called the mob.

In such an atmosphere there can be only one sequel to the Madrid explosion. All Europe burns to emulate it. Vengeance! More blood! Tear "the Anarchist beast" to shreds. Drag him to the scaffold. Imprison him for life. Let all civilized States band together to drive his like off the face of the earth; and if any State refuses to join, make war on it. This time the leading London newspaper, anti-Liberal and therefore anti-Russian in politics, does not say "Serve you right" to the victims, as it did, in effect, when Bobrikoff, and De Plehve, and Grand Duke Sergius, were in the same manner unofficially fulminated into fragments. No: fulminate our rivals in Asia by all means, ye brave Russian revolutionaries; but to aim at an English princess—monstrous! hideous! hound down the wretch to his doom; and observe, please, that we are a civilized and merciful people, and, however much we may regret it, must not treat him as Ravaillac and Damiens were treated. And meanwhile, since we have not yet caught him, let us soothe our quivering nerves with the bullfight, and comment in a courtly way on the unfailing tact and good taste of the ladies of our royal houses, who, though presumably of full normal natural tenderness, have been so effectually broken in to fashionable routine that they can be taken to see the horses slaughtered as helplessly as they could no doubt be taken to a gladiator show, if that happened to be the mode just now.

Strangely enough, in the midst of this raging fire of malice, the one man who still has faith in the kindness and intelligence of human nature is the fulminator, now a hunted wretch, with nothing, apparently, to secure his triumph over all the prisons and scaffolds of infuriate Europe except the revolver in his pocket and his readiness to discharge it at a moment's notice into his own or any other head. Think of him setting out to find a gentleman and a Christian in the multitude of human wolves howling for his blood. Think also of this: that at the very first essay he finds what he seeks, a veritable grandee of Spain, a noble, high-thinking, unterrified, malice-void soul, in the guise—of all masquerades in the world!—of a modern editor. The Anarchist wolf, flying from the wolves of plutocracy, throws himself on the honor of the man. The man, not being a wolf (nor a London editor), and therefore not having enough sympathy with his exploit to be made bloodthirsty by it, does not throw him back to the pursuing wolves—gives him, instead, what help he can to escape, and sends him off acquainted at last with a force that goes deeper than dynamite, though you cannot make so much of it for sixpence. That righteous and honorable high human deed is not wasted on Europe, let us hope, though it benefits the fugitive wolf only for a moment. The plutocratic wolves presently smell him out. The fugitive shoots the unlucky wolf whose nose is nearest; shoots himself; and then convinces the world, by his photograph, that he was no monstrous freak of reversion to the tiger, but a good looking young man with nothing abnormal about him except his appalling courage and resolution (that is why the terrified shriek Coward at him): one to whom murdering a happy young couple on their wedding morning would have been an unthinkably unnatural abomination under rational and kindly human circumstances.

Then comes the climax of irony and blind stupidity. The wolves, balked of their meal of fellow-wolf, turn on the man, and proceed to torture him, after their manner, by imprisonment, for refusing to fasten his teeth in the throat of the dynamiter and hold him down until they came to finish him.

Thus, you see, a man may not be a gentleman nowadays even if he wishes to. As to being a Christian, he is allowed some latitude in that matter, because, I repeat, Christianity has two faces. Popular Christianity has for its emblem a gibbet, for its chief sensation a sanguinary execution after torture, for its central mystery an insane vengeance bought off by a trumpery expiation. But there is a nobler and profounder Christianity which affirms the sacred mystery of Equality, and forbids the glaring futility and folly of vengeance, often politely called punishment or justice. The gibbet part of Christianity is tolerated. The other is criminal felony. Connoisseurs in irony are well aware of the fact that the only editor in England who denounces punishment as radically wrong, also repudiates Christianity; calls his paper The Freethinker; and has been imprisoned for two years for blasphemy.

Sane Conclusions

And now I must ask the excited reader not to lose his head on one side or the other, but to draw a sane moral from these grim absurdities. It is not good sense to propose that laws against crime should apply to principals only and not to accessories whose consent, counsel, or silence may secure impunity to the principal. If you institute punishment as part of the law, you must punish people for refusing to punish. If you have a police, part of its duty must be to compel everybody to assist the police. No doubt if your laws are unjust, and your policemen agents of oppression, the result will be an unbearable violation of the private consciences of citizens. But that cannot be helped: the remedy is, not to license everybody to thwart the law if they please, but to make laws that will command the public assent, and not to deal cruelly and stupidly with lawbreakers. Everybody disapproves of burglars; but the modern burglar, when caught and overpowered by a householder, usually appeals, and often, let us hope, with success, to his captor not to deliver him over to the useless horrors of penal servitude. In other cases the lawbreaker escapes because those who could give him up do not consider his breach of the law a guilty action. Sometimes, even, private tribunals are formed in opposition to the official tribunals; and these private tribunals employ assassins as executioners, as was done, for example, by Mahomet before he had established his power officially, and by the Ribbon lodges of Ireland in their long struggle with the landlords. Under such circumstances, the assassin goes free although everybody in the district knows who he is

and what he has done. They do not betray him, partly
because they justify him exactly as the regular Government
justifies its official executioner, and partly because they
would themselves be assassinated if they betrayed him:
another method learnt from the official government. Given
a tribunal, employing a slayer who has no personal quarrel
with the slain; and there is clearly no moral difference
between official and unofficial killing.

In short, all men are anarchists with regard to laws
which are against their consciences, either in the preamble
or in the penalty. In London our worst anarchists are the
magistrates, because many of them are so old and ignorant
that when they are called upon to administer any law that
is based on ideas or knowledge less than half a century
old, they disagree with it, and being mere ordinary home-
bred private Englishmen without any respect for law in
the abstract, naïvely set the example of violating it. In this
instance the man lags behind the law; but when the law
lags behind the man, he becomes equally an anarchist.
When some huge change in social conditions, such as
the industrial revolution of the eighteenth and nineteenth
centuries, throws our legal and industrial institutions out
of date, Anarchism becomes almost a religion. The whole
force of the most energetic geniuses of the time in philosophy, economics, and art, concentrates itself on demonstra-
tions and reminders that morality and law are only
conventions, fallible and continually obsolescing. Trage-
dies in which the heroes are bandits, and comedies in
which law-abiding and conventionally moral folk are compelled to satirize themselves by outraging the conscience
of the spectators every time they do their duty, appear
simultaneously with economic treatises entitled "What is
Property? Theft!" and with histories of "The Conflict between Religion and Science."

Now this is not a healthy state of things. The advantages
of living in society are proportionate, not to the freedom
of the individual from a code, but to the complexity and
subtlety of the code he is prepared not only to accept
but to uphold as a matter of such vital importance that a

lawbreaker at large is hardly to be tolerated on any plea. Such an attitude becomes impossible when the only men who can make themselves heard and remembered throughout the world spend all their energy in raising our gorge against current law, current morality, current respectability, and legal property. The ordinary man, uneducated in social theory even when he is schooled in Latin verse, cannot be set against all the laws of his country and yet persuaded to regard law in the abstract as vitally necessary to society. Once he is brought to repudiate the laws and institutions he knows, he will repudiate the very conception of law and the very groundwork of institutions, ridiculing human rights, extolling brainless methods as "historical," and tolerating nothing except pure empiricism in conduct, with dynamite as the basis of politics and vivisection as the basis of science. That is hideous; but what is to be done? Here am I, for instance, by class a respectable man, by common sense a hater of waste and disorder, by intellectual constitution legally minded to the verge of pedantry, and by temperament apprehensive and economically disposed to the limit of old-maidishness; yet I am, and have always been, and shall now always be, a revolutionary writer, because our laws make law impossible; our liberties destroy all freedom; our property is organized robbery; our morality is an impudent hypocrisy; our wisdom is administered by inexperienced or malexperienced dupes, our power wielded by cowards and weaklings, and our honor false in all its points. I am an enemy of the existing order for good reasons; but that does not make my attacks any less encouraging or helpful to people who are its enemies for bad reasons. The existing order may shriek that if I tell the truth about it, some foolish person may drive it to become still worse by trying to assassinate it. I cannot help that, even if I could see what worse it could do than it is already doing. And the disadvantage of that worst even from its own point of view is that society, with all its prisons and bayonets and whips and ostracisms and starvations, is powerless in the face of the Anarchist who is prepared to sacrifice his own life in the battle with it. Our natural safety from the cheap and devastating explosives which every Russian student can make, and every Russian grenadier has learnt to handle in Manchuria, lies in the fact that brave and resolute men, when they are rascals, will not risk their skins for the good of humanity, and, when they are sympathetic enough to care for humanity, abhor murder, and never commit it until their consciences are outraged beyond endurance. The remedy is, then, simply not to outrage their consciences.

Do not be afraid that they will not make allowances. All men make very large allowances indeed before they stake their own lives in a war to the death with society. Nobody demands or expects the millennium. But there are two things that must be set right, or we shall perish, like Rome, of soul atrophy disguised as empire.

The first is, that the daily ceremony of dividing the wealth of the country among its inhabitants shall be so conducted that no crumb shall go to any able-bodied adults who are not producing by their personal exertions not only a full equivalent for what they take, but a surplus sufficient to provide for their superannuation and pay back the debt due for their nurture.

The second is that the deliberate infliction of malicious injuries which now goes on under the name of punishment be abandoned; so that the thief, the ruffian, the gambler, and the beggar, may without inhumanity be handed over to the law, and made to understand that a State which is too humane to punish will also be too thrifty to waste the life of honest men in watching or restraining dishonest ones. That is why we do not imprison dogs. We even take our chance of their first bite. But if a dog delights to bark and bite, it goes to the lethal chamber. That seems to me sensible. To allow the dog to expiate his bite by a period of torment, and then let him loose in a much more savage condition (for the chain makes a dog savage) to bite again and expiate again, having meanwhile spent a great deal of human life and happiness in the task of chaining and feeding and tormenting him, seems to me idiotic and superstitious. Yet that is what we do to men who bark and bite and steal. It would be far more sensible to put up with their vices, as we put up with their illnesses, until they give more trouble than they are worth, at which point we should, with many apologies and expressions of sympathy, and some generosity in complying with their last wishes, place them in the lethal chamber and get rid of them. Under no circumstances should they be allowed to expiate their misdeeds by a manufactured penalty, to subscribe to a charity, or to compensate the victims. If there is to be no punishment there can be no forgiveness. We shall never have real moral responsibility until everyone knows that his deeds are irrevocable, and that his life depends on his usefulness. Hitherto, alas! humanity has never dared face these hard facts. We frantically scatter conscience money and invent systems of conscience banking, with expiatory penalties, atonements, redemptions, salvations, hospital subscription lists and what not, to enable us to contract-out of the moral code. Not content with the old scapegoat and sacrificial lamb, we deify human saviors, and pray to miraculous virgin intercessors. We attribute mercy to the inexorable; soothe our consciences after committing murder by throwing ourselves on the bosom of divine love; and shrink even from our own gallows because we are forced to admit that it, at least, is irrevocable—as if one hour of imprisonment were not as irrevocable as any execution!

If a man cannot look evil in the face without illusion, he will never know what it really is, or combat it effectually. The few men who have been able (relatively) to do this have been called cynics, and have sometimes had an abnormal share of evil in themselves, corresponding to the abnormal strength of their minds; but they have never done mischief unless they intended to do it. That is why great scoundrels have been beneficent rulers whilst amiable and privately harmless monarchs have ruined their countries by trusting to the hocus-pocus of innocence and guilt, reward and punishment, virtuous indignation and pardon, instead of standing up to the facts without either malice or mercy. Major Barbara stands up to Bill Walker in that way, with the result that the ruffian who cannot get hated, has to hate himself. To relieve this agony he tries to get punished; but the Salvationist whom he tries to provoke is as merciless as Barbara, and only prays for him. Then he tries to pay, but can get nobody to take his money. His doom is the doom of Cain, who, failing to find either a savior, a policeman, or an almoner to help him to pretend that his brother's blood no longer cried from the ground, had to live and die a murderer. Cain took care not to commit another murder, unlike our railway shareholders (I am one) who kill and maim shunters by hundreds to save the cost of automatic couplings, and make atonement by annual subscriptions to deserving charities. Had Cain been allowed to pay off his score, he might possibly have killed Adam and Eve for the mere sake of a second luxurious reconciliation with God afterwards. Bodger, you may depend on it, will go on to the end of his life poisoning people with bad whisky, because he can always depend on the Salvation Army or the Church of England to negotiate a redemption for him in consideration of a trifling percentage of his profits.

There is a third condition too, which must be fulfilled before the great teachers of the world will cease to scoff at its religions. Creeds must become intellectually honest. At present there is not a single credible established religion in the world. That is perhaps the most stupendous fact in the whole world-situation. This play of mine, Major Barbara, is, I hope, both true and inspired; but whoever says that it all happened, and that faith in it and understanding of it consist in believing that it is a record of an actual occurrence, is, to speak according to Scripture, a fool and a liar, and is hereby solemnly denounced and cursed as such by me, the author, to all posterity.

London, June 1906.

Major Barbara

Act I

(It is after dinner on a January night, in the library in LADY BRITOMART UNDERSHAFT'*s house in Wilton Crescent. A large and comfortable settee is in the middle of the room, upholstered in dark leather. A person sitting on it (it is vacant at present) would have, on his right,* LADY BRITOMART'*s writing-table, with the lady herself busy at it; a smaller writing-table behind him on his left; the door behind him on* LADY BRITOMART'*s side; and a window with a window-seat directly on his left. Near the window is an armchair.*

LADY BRITOMART *is a woman of fifty or thereabouts, well dressed and yet careless of her dress, well bred and quite reckless of her breeding, well mannered and yet appallingly outspoken and indifferent to the opinion of her interlocutors, amiable and yet peremptory, arbitrary, and high-tempered to the last bearable degree, and withal a very typical managing matron of the upper class, treated as a naughty child until she grew into a scolding mother, and finally settling down with plenty of practical ability and worldly experience, limited in the oddest way with domestic and class limitations, conceiving the universe exactly as if it were a large house in Wilton Crescent, though handling her corner of it very effectively on that assumption, and being quite enlightened and liberal as to the books in the library, the pictures on the walls, the music in the portfolios, and the articles in the papers.*

Her son, STEPHEN, *comes in. He is a gravely correct young man under 25, taking himself very seriously, but still in some awe of his mother, from childish habit and bachelor shyness rather than from any weakness of character.)*

STEPHEN: What's the matter?

LADY BRITOMART: Presently, Stephen.

(STEPHEN *submissively walks to the settee and sits down. He takes up The Speaker.*)

LADY BRITOMART: Dont begin to read, Stephen. I shall require all your attention.

STEPHEN: It was only while I was waiting—

LADY BRITOMART: Dont make excuses, Stephen. (*He puts down The Speaker.*) Now! (*She finishes her writing; rises; and comes to the settee.*) I have not kept you waiting very long, I think.

STEPHEN: Not at all, mother.

LADY BRITOMART: Bring me my cushion. (*He takes the cushion from the chair at the desk and arranges it for her as she sits down on the settee.*) Sit down. (*He sits down and fingers his tie nervously.*) Dont fiddle with your tie, Stephen: there is nothing the matter with it.

STEPHEN: I beg your pardon. (*He fiddles with his watch chain instead.*)

LADY BRITOMART: Now are you attending to me, Stephen?

STEPHEN: Of course, mother.

LADY BRITOMART: No, it's not of course. I want something much more than your everyday matter-of-course attention. I am going to speak to you very seriously, Stephen. I wish you would let that chain alone.

STEPHEN (*hastily relinquishing the chain*): Have I done anything to annoy you, mother? If so, it was quite unintentional.

LADY BRITOMART (*astonished*): Nonsense! (*With some remorse.*) My poor boy, did you think I was angry with you?

STEPHEN: What is it, then, mother? You are making me very uneasy.

LADY BRITOMART (*squaring herself at him rather aggressively*): Stephen: may I ask how soon you intend to realize that you are a grown-up man, and that I am only a woman?

STEPHEN (*amazed*): Only a—

LADY BRITOMART: Dont repeat my words, please: it is a most aggravating habit. You must learn to face life seriously, Stephen. I really cannot bear the whole burden of our family affairs any longer. You must advise me: you must assume the responsibility.

STEPHEN: I!

LADY BRITOMART: Yes, you, of course. You were 24 last June. Youve been at Harrow and Cambridge. Youve been to India and Japan. You must know a lot of things, now; unless you have wasted your time most scandalously. Well, advise me.

STEPHEN (*much perplexed*):   You know I have never interfered in the household—

LADY BRITOMART: No: I should think not. I dont want you to order the dinner.

STEPHEN: I mean in our family affairs.

LADY BRITOMART: Well, you must interfere now; for they are getting quite beyond me.

STEPHEN (*troubled*):   I have thought sometimes that perhaps I ought; but really, mother, I know so little about them; and what I do know is so painful—it is so impossible to mention some things to you— (*he stops, ashamed*).

LADY BRITOMART: I suppose you mean your father.

STEPHEN (*almost inaudibly*):   Yes.

LADY BRITOMART: My dear: we cant go on all our lives not mentioning him. Of course you were quite right not to open the subject until I asked you to; but you are old enough now to be taken into my confidence, and to help me to deal with him about the girls.

STEPHEN: But the girls are all right. They are engaged.

LADY BRITOMART (*complacently*):   Yes: I have made a very good match for Sarah. Charles Lomax will be a millionaire at 35. But that is ten years ahead; and in the meantime his trustees cannot under the terms of his father's will allow him more than £800 a year.

STEPHEN: But the will says also that if he increases his income by his own exertions, they may double the increase.

LADY BRITOMART: Charles Lomax's exertions are much

more likely to decrease his income than to increase it.
Sarah will have to find at least another £800 a year for
the next ten years; and even then they will be as poor
as church mice. And what about Barbara? I thought
Barbara was going to make the most brilliant career of
all of you. And what does she do? Joins the Salvation
Army; discharges her maid; lives on a pound a week;
and walks in one evening with a professor of Greek
whom she has picked up in the street, and who pretends
to be a Salvationist, and actually plays the big drum for
her in public because he has fallen head over ears in
love with her.

STEPHEN: I was certainly rather taken aback when I heard
they were engaged. Cusins is a very nice fellow, certainly: nobody would ever guess that he was born in
Australia; but—

LADY BRITOMART: Oh, Adolphus Cusins will make a
very good husband. After all, nobody can say a word
against Greek: it stamps a man at once as an educated
gentleman. And my family, thank Heaven, is not a pig-
headed Tory one. We are Whigs, and believe in liberty.
Let snobbish people say what they please: Barbara shall
marry, not the man they like, but the man *I* like.

STEPHEN: Of course I was thinking only of his income.
However, he is not likely to be extravagant.

LADY BRITOMART: Dont be too sure of that, Stephen. I
know your quiet, simple, refined, poetic people like
Adolphus—quite content with the best of everything!
They cost more than your extravagant people, who are
always as mean as they are second rate. No: Barbara
will need at least £2000 a year. You see it means two
additional households. Besides, my dear, you must
marry soon. I dont approve of the present fashion of
philandering bachelors and late marriages; and I am trying to arrange something for you.

STEPHEN: It's very good of you, mother; but perhaps I
had better arrange that for myself.

LADY BRITOMART: Nonsense! you are much too young
to begin matchmaking: you would be taken in by some

pretty little nobody. Of course I dont mean that you are
not to be consulted: you know that as well as I do.
(STEPHEN *closes his lips and is silent.*) Now dont sulk,
Stephen.

STEPHEN: I am not sulking, mother. What has all this
got to do with—with—with my father?

LADY BRITOMART: My dear Stephen: where is the money
to come from? It is easy enough for you and the other
children to live on my income as long as we are in the
same house; but I cant keep four families in four separate houses. You know how poor my father is: he has
barely seven thousand a year now; and really, if he were
not the Earl of Stevenage, he would have to give up
society. He can do nothing for us. He says, naturally
enough, that it is absurd that he should be asked to
provide for the children of a man who is rolling in
money. You see, Stephen, your father must be fabu-
lously wealthy, because there is always a war going on
somewhere.

STEPHEN: You need not remind me of that, mother. I
have hardly ever opened a newspaper in my life without
seeing our name in it. The Undershaft torpedo! The
Undershaft quick firers! The Undershaft ten inch! the
Undershaft disappearing rampart gun! the Undershaft
submarine! and now the Undershaft aerial battleship! At
Harrow they called me the Woolwich Infant. At Cambridge it was the same. A little brute at King's who
was always trying to get up revivals, spoilt my Bible—
your first birthday present to me—by writing under my
name, "Son and heir to Undershaft and Lazarus, Death
and Destruction Dealers: address, Christendom and
Judea." But that was not so bad as the way I was
kowtowed to everywhere because my father was making
millions by selling cannons.

LADY BRITOMART: It is not only the cannons, but the war
loans that Lazarus arranges under cover of giving credit
for the cannons. You know, Stephen, it's perfectly scan-
dalous. Those two men, Andrew Undershaft and Lazarus, positively have Europe under their thumbs. That is

why your father is able to behave as he does. He is above the law. Do you think Bismarck or Gladstone or Disraeli could have openly defied every social and moral obligation all their lives as your father has? They simply wouldnt have dared. I asked Gladstone to take it up. I asked The Times to take it up. I asked the Lord Chamberlain to take it up. But it was just like asking them to declare war on the Sultan. They wouldnt. They said they couldnt touch him. I believe they were afraid.

STEPHEN: What could they do? He does not actually break the law.

LADY BRITOMART: Not break the law! He is always breaking the law. He broke the law when he was born: his parents were not married.

STEPHEN: Mother! Is that true?

LADY BRITOMART: Of course it's true: that was why we separated.

STEPHEN: He married without letting you know this!

LADY BRITOMART (*rather taken aback by this inference*): Oh no. To do Andrew justice, that was not the sort of thing he did. Besides, you know the Undershaft motto: Unashamed. Everybody knew.

STEPHEN: But you said that was why you separated.

LADY BRITOMART: Yes, because he was not content with being a foundling himself: he wanted to disinherit you for another foundling. That was what I couldnt stand.

STEPHEN (*ashamed*): Do you mean for—for—for—

LADY BRITOMART: Dont stammer, Stephen. Speak distinctly.

STEPHEN: But this is so frightful to me, mother. To have to speak to you about such things!

LADY BRITOMART: It's not pleasant for me, either, especially if you are still so childish that you must make it worse by a display of embarrassment. It is only in the middle classes, Stephen, that people get into a state of dumb helpless horror when they find that there are wicked people in the world. In our class, we have to decide what is to be done with wicked people; and nothing should disturb our self-possession. Now ask your question properly.

STEPHEN: Mother: you have no consideration for me. For Heaven's sake either treat me as a child, as you always do, and tell me nothing at all; or tell me everything and let me take it as best I can.

LADY BRITOMART: Treat you as a child! What do you mean? It is most unkind and ungrateful of you to say such a thing. You know I have never treated any of you as children. I have always made you my companions and friends, and allowed you perfect freedom to do and say whatever you liked, so long as you liked what I could approve of.

STEPHEN (*desperately*):   I daresay we have been the very imperfect children of a very perfect mother; but I do beg you to let me alone for once, and tell me about this horrible business of my father wanting to set me aside for another son.

LADY BRITOMART (*amazed*):   Another son! I never said anything of the kind. I never dreamt of such a thing. This is what comes of interrupting me.

STEPHEN: But you said—

LADY BRITOMART (*cutting him short*):   Now be a good boy, Stephen, and listen to me patiently. The Undershafts are descended from a foundling in the parish of St. Andrew Undershaft in the city. That was long ago, in the reign of James the First. Well, this foundling was adopted by an armorer and gun-maker. In the course of time the foundling succeeded to the business; and from some notion of gratitude, or some vow or something, he adopted another foundling, and left the business to him. And that foundling did the same. Ever since that, the cannon business has always been left to an adopted foundling named Andrew Undershaft.

SHEPHEN: But did they never marry? Were there no legitimate sons?

LADY BRITOMART: Oh yes: they married just as your father did; and they were rich enough to buy land for their own children and leave them well provided for. But they always adopted and trained some foundling to succeed them in the business; and of course they always quarrelled with their wives furiously over it. Your father was adopted in that way; and he pretends to consider himself bound to keep up the tradition and adopt somebody to leave the business to. Of course I was not going to stand that. There may have been some reason for it when the Undershafts could only marry women in their own class, whose sons were not fit to govern great estates. But there could be no excuse for passing over my son.

STEPHEN (*dubiously*): I am afraid I should make a poor hand of managing a cannon foundry.

LADY BRITOMART: Nonsense! you could easily get a manager and pay him a salary.

STEPHEN: My father evidently had no great opinion of my capacity.

LADY BRITOMART: Stuff, child! you were only a baby: it had nothing to do with your capacity. Andrew did it on principle, just as he did every perverse and wicked thing on principle. When my father remonstrated, Andrew actually told him to his face that history tells us of only two successful institutions: one the Undershaft firm, and the other the Roman Empire under the Antonines. That was because the Antonine emperors all adopted their successors. Such rubbish! The Stevenages are as good as the Antonines, I hope; and you are a Stevenage. But that was Andrew all over. There you have the man! Always clever and unanswerable when he was defending nonsense and wickedness: always awkward and sullen when he had to behave sensibly and decently!

STEPHEN: Then it was on my account that your home life was broken up, mother. I am sorry.

LADY BRITOMART: Well, dear, there were other differences. I really cannot bear an immoral man. I am not a Pharisee, I hope; and I should not have minded his merely doing wrong things: we are none of us perfect. But your father didnt exactly do wrong things: he said them and thought them: that was what was so dreadful. He really had a sort of religion of wrongness. Just as one doesnt mind men practising immorality so long as they own that they are in the wrong by preaching morality; so I couldnt forgive Andrew for preaching immorality while he practised morality. You would all have grown up without principles, without any knowledge of right and wrong, if he had been in the house. You know, my dear, your father was a very attractive man in some ways. Children did not dislike him; and he took advantage of it to put the wickedest ideas into their heads, and make them quite unmanageable. I did not dislike him myself: very far from it; but nothing can bridge over moral disagreement.

STEPHEN: All this simply bewilders me, mother. People may differ about matters of opinion, or even about religion; but how can they differ about right and wrong? Right is right; and wrong is wrong; and if a man cannot distinguish them properly, he is either a fool or a rascal: thats all.

LADY BRITOMART (*touched*): Thats my own boy (*she pats his cheek*)! Your father never could answer that: he used to laugh and get out of it under cover of some affectionate nonsense. And now that you understand the situation, what do you advise me to do?

STEPHEN: Well, what can you do?

LADY BRITOMART: I must get the money somehow.

STEPHEN: We cannot take money from him. I had rather go and live in some cheap place like Bedford Square or even Hampstead than take a farthing of his money.

LADY BRITOMART: But after all, Stephen, our present income comes from Andrew.

STEPHEN (*shocked*): I never knew that.

LADY BRITOMART: Well, you surely didnt suppose your grandfather had anything to give me. The Stevenages could not do everything for you. We gave you social position. Andrew had to contribute something. He had a very good bargain, I think.

STEPHEN (*bitterly*): We are utterly dependent on him and his cannons, then?

LADY BRITOMART: Certainly not: the money is settled. But he provided it. So you see it is not a question of taking money from him or not: it is simply a question of how much. I dont want any more for myself.

STEPHEN: Nor do I.

LADY BRITOMART: But Sarah does; and Barbara does. That is, Charles Lomax and Adolphus Cusins will cost them more. So I must put my pride in my pocket and ask for it, I suppose. That is your advice, Stephen, is it not?

STEPHEN: No.

LADY BRITOMART (*sharply*): Stephen!

STEPHEN: Of course if you are determined—

LADY BRITOMART: I am not determined: I ask your advice; and I am waiting for it. I will not have all the responsibility thrown on my shoulders.

STEPHEN (*obstinately*): I would die sooner than ask him for another penny.

LADY BRITOMART (*resignedly*): You mean that *I* must ask him. Very well, Stephen: it shall be as you wish. You will be glad to know that your grandfather concurs. But he thinks I ought to ask Andrew to come here and see the girls. After all, he must have some natural affection for them.

STEPHEN: Ask him here!!!

LADY BRITOMART: Do not repeat my words, Stephen. Where else can I ask him?

STEPHEN: I never expected you to ask him at all.

LADY BRITOMART: Now dont tease, Stephen. Come! you see that it is necessary that he should pay us a visit, dont you?

STEPHEN (*reluctantly*): I suppose so, if the girls cannot do without his money.

LADY BRITOMART: Thank you, Stephen: I knew you would give me the right advice when it was properly explained to you. I have asked your father to come this evening. (STEPHEN *bounds from his seat.*) Dont jump, Stephen: it fidgets me.

STEPHEN (*in utter consternation*): Do you mean to say that my father is coming here to-night—that he may be here at any moment?

LADY BRITOMART (*looking at her watch*): I said nine. (*He gasps. She rises.*) Ring the bell, please. (STEPHEN *goes to the smaller writing table; presses a button on it; and sits at it with his elbows on the table and his head in his hands, outwitted and overwhelmed.*) It is ten minutes to nine yet; and I have to prepare the girls. I asked Charles Lomax and Adolphus to dinner on purpose that they might be here. Andrew had better see them in case he should cherish any delusions as to their being capable of supporting their wives. (*The butler enters:* LADY BRITOMART *goes behind the settee to speak to him.*) Morrison: go up to the drawingroom and tell everybody to come down here at once. (MORRISON *withdraws.* LADY BRITOMART *turns to* STEPHEN.) Now remember, Stephen: I shall need all your countenance and authority. (*He rises and tries to recover some vestige of these attributes.*) Give me a chair, dear. (*He pushes a chair forward from the wall to where she stands, near the smaller writing table. She sits down; and he goes to the arm-chair, into which he throws himself.*) 1 dont know how Barbara will take it. Ever since they made her a major in the Salvation Army she has developed a propensity to have her own way and order people about which quite cows me sometimes. It's not ladylike: I'm sure I dont know where she picked it up. Anyhow, Barbara shant bully me; but still it's just as well that your father should be here before she has time to refuse to meet him or make a fuss. Dont look nervous, Stephen; it will only encourage Barbara to make difficulties. *I* am nervous enough, goodness knows; but I dont shew it.

(SARAH *and* BARBARA *come in with their respective young men,* CHARLES LOMAX *and* ADOLPHUS CUSINS. SARAH *is slender, bored, and mundane.* BARBARA *is robuster, jollier, much more energetic.* SARAH *is fashionably dressed:* BARBARA *is in Salvation Army uniform.* LOMAX, *a young man about town, is like many other young men about town. He is afflicted with a frivolous sense of humor which plunges him at the most inopportune moments into paroxysms of imperfectly suppressed laughter.* CUSINS *is a spectacled student, slight,*

*thin haired, and sweet voiced, with a more complex
form of* LOMAX's *complaint. His sense of humor is intellectual and subtle, and is complicated by an appalling
temper. The lifelong struggle of a benevolent temperament and a high conscience against impulses of inhu-
man ridicule and fierce impatience has set up a chronic
strain which has visibly wrecked his constitution. He
is a most implacable, determined, tenacious, intolerant
person who by mere force of character presents himself
as—and indeed actually is—considerate, gentle, explan-
atory, even mild and apologetic, capable possibly of
murder, but not of cruelty or coarseness. By the operation of some instinct which is not merciful enough to
blind him with the illusions of love, he is obstinately
bent on marrying* BARBARA. LOMAX *likes* SARAH *and
thinks it will be rather a lark to marry her. Consequently he has not attempted to resist* LADY BRITO-
MART's *arrangements to that end.*

*All four look as if they had been having a good deal
of fun in the drawingroom. The girls enter first, leaving
the swains outside.* SARAH *comes to the settee.* BAR-
BARA *comes in after her and stops at the door.*)

BARBARA: Are Cholly and Dolly to come in?

LADY BRITOMART (*forcibly*):   Barbara: I will not have
Charles called Cholly: the vulgarity of it positively
makes me ill.

BARBARA: It's all right, mother. Cholly is quite correct
nowadays. Are they to come in?

LADY BRITOMART: Yes, if they will behave themselves.

BARBARA (*through the door*):   Come in, Dolly, and behave yourself.

(BARBARA *comes to her mother's writing table.* CUSINS
enters smiling, and wanders towards LADY
BRITOMART.)

SARAH (*calling*):   Come in, Cholly. (LOMAX *enters, con-
trolling his features very imperfectly, and places himself
vaguely between* SARAH *and* BARBARA.)

LADY BRITOMART (*peremptorily*):   Sit down, all of you. (*They sit.* CUSINS *crosses to the window and seats himself there.* LOMAX *takes a chair.* BARBARA *sits at the writing table and* SARAH *on the settee.*) I dont in the least know what you are laughing at, Adolphus. I am surprised at you, though I expected nothing better from Charles Lomax.

CUSINS (*in a remarkably gentle voice*):   Barbara has been trying to teach me the West Ham Salvation March.

LADY BRITOMART: I see nothing to laugh at in that; nor should you if you are really converted.

CUSINS (*sweetly*):   You were not present. It was really funny, I believe.

LOMAX: Ripping.

LADY BRITOMART: Be quiet, Charles. Now listen to me, children. Your father is coming here this evening. (*General stupefaction.*)

LOMAX (*remonstrating*):   Oh I say!

LADY BRITOMART: You are not called on to say anything, Charles.

SARAH: Are you serious, mother?

LADY BRITOMART: Of course I am serious. It is on your account, Sarah, and also on Charles's. (*Silence.* CHARLES *looks painfully unworthy.*) I hope you are not going to object, Barbara.

BARBARA: I! why should I? My father has a soul to be saved like anybody else. Hes quite welcome as far as I am concerned.

LOMAX (*still remonstrant*):   But really, don't you know! Oh I say!

LADY BRITOMART (*frigidly*):   What do you wish to convey, Charles?

LOMAX: Well, you must admit that this is a bit thick.

LADY BRITOMART (*turning with ominous suavity to* CUSINS):   Adolphus: you are a professor of Greek. Can you translate Charles Lomax's remarks into reputable English for us?

CUSINS (*cautiously*):   If I may say so, Lady Brit, I think Charles has rather happily expressed what we all feel.

Homer, speaking of Autolycus, uses the same phrase. πυκινὸν δόμον ἐλθεῖν means a bit thick.

LOMAX (*handsomely*): Not that I mind, you know, if Sarah dont.

LADY BRITOMART (*crushingly*): Thank you. Have I your permission, Adolphus, to invite my own husband to my own house?

CUSINS (*gallantly*): You have my unhesitating support in everything you do.

LADY BRITOMART: Sarah: have you nothing to say?

SARAH: Do you mean that he is coming regularly to live here?

LADY BRITOMART: Certainly not. The spare room is ready for him if he likes to stay for a day or two and see a little more of you; but there are limits.

SARAH: Well, he cant eat us, I suppose. *I* don't mind.

LOMAX (*chuckling*): I wonder how the old man will take it.

LADY BRITOMART: Much as the old woman will, no doubt, Charles.

LOMAX (*abashed*): I didn't mean—at least—

LADY BRITOMART: You didnt think, Charles. You never do; and the result is, you never mean anything. And now please attend to me, children. Your father will be quite a stranger to us.

LOMAX: I suppose he hasnt seen Sarah since she was a little kid.

LADY BRITOMART: Not since she was a little kid, Charles, as you express it with that elegance of diction and refinement of thought that seem never to desert you. Accordingly—er— (*impatiently*) Now I have forgotten what I was going to say. That comes of your provoking me to be sarcastic, Charles. Adolphus: will you kindly tell me where I was.

CUSINS (*sweetly*): You were saying that as Mr. Undershaft has not seen his children since they were babies, he will form his opinion of the way you have brought them up from their behavior to-night, and that therefore you wish us all to be particularly careful to conduct ourselves well, especially Charles.

LOMAX: Look here: Lady Brit didn't say that.

LADY BRITOMART (*vehemently*):   I did, Charles. Adolphus's recollection is perfectly correct. It is most important that you should be good; and I do beg you for once not to pair off into opposite corners and giggle and whisper while I am speaking to your father.

BARBARA: All right, mother. We'll do you credit.

LADY BRITOMART: Remember, Charles, that Sarah will want to feel proud of you instead of ashamed of you.

LOMAX: Oh I say! theres nothing to be exactly proud of, dont you know.

LADY BRITOMART: Well, try and look as if there was.

(MORRISON, *pale and dismayed, breaks into the room in unconcealed disorder.*)

MORRISON: Might I speak a word to you, my lady?

LADY BRITOMART: Nonsense! Shew him up.

MORRISON: Yes, my lady. (*He goes.*)

LOMAX: Does Morrison know who it is?

LADY BRITOMART: Of course. Morrison has always been with us.

LOMAX: It must be a regular corker for him, dont you know.

LADY BRITOMART: Is this a moment to get on my nerves, Charles, with your outrageous expressions?

LOMAX: But this is something out of the ordinary, really—

MORRISON (*at the door*):   The—er—Mr. Undershaft. (*He retreats in confusion.*)

(ANDREW UNDERSHAFT *comes in. All rise.* LADY BRITOMART *meets him in the middle of the room behind the settee.*

ANDREW *is, on the surface, a stoutish, easygoing elderly man, with kindly patient manners, and an engaging simplicity of character. But he has a watchful, deliberate, waiting, listening face, and formidable reserves of power, both bodily and mental, in his capacious chest and long head. His gentleness is partly that of a strong man who has learnt by experience that his natural grip hurts ordinary people unless he handles them very carefully, and partly the mellowness of age and success. He is also a little shy in his present very delicate situation.)*

LADY BRITOMART: Good evening, Andrew.

UNDERSHAFT: How d'ye do, my dear.

LADY BRITOMART: You look a good deal older.

UNDERSHAFT (*apologetically*):   I am somewhat older. (*With a touch of courtship.*) Time has stood still with you.

LADY BRITOMART (*promptly*):   Rubbish! This is your family.

UNDERSHAFT (*surprised*):   Is it so large? I am sorry to say my memory is failing very badly in some things.

(*He offers his hand with paternal kindness to* LOMAX.)

LOMAX (*jerkily shaking his hand*):   Ahdedoo.

UNDERSHAFT: I can see you are my eldest. I am very glad to meet you again, my boy.

LOMAX (*remonstrating*):   No but look here dont you know— (*Overcome.*) Oh I say!

LADY BRITOMART (*recovering from momentary speechlessness*):   Andrew: do you mean to say that you dont remember how many children you have?

UNDERSHAFT: Well, I am afraid I—. They have grown so much—er. Am I making any ridiculous mistake? I may as well confess: I recollect only one son. But so many things have happened since, of course—er—

LADY BRITOMART (*decisively*):   Andrew: you are talking nonsense. Of course you have only one son.

UNDERSHAFT: Perhaps you will be good enough to introduce me, my dear.

LADY BRITOMART: That is Charles Lomax, who is engaged to Sarah.

UNDERSHAFT: My dear sir, I beg your pardon.

LOMAX: Notatall. Delighted, I assure you.

LADY BRITOMART: This is Stephen.

UNDERSHAFT (*bowing*):   Happy to make your acquaintance,

Mr. Stephen. Then (*going to* CUSINS) you must be my
son. (*Taking* CUSINS' *hands in his.*) How are you, my
young friend? (*To* LADY BRITOMART.) He is very like you,
my love.

CUSINS: You flatter me, Mr. Undershaft. My name is
Cusins: engaged to Barbara. (*Very explicitly.*) That is
Major Barbara Undershaft, of the Salvation Army. That
is Sarah, your second daughter. This is Stephen Undershaft, your son.

UNDERSHAFT: My dear Stephen, I beg your pardon.

STEPHEN: Not at all.

UNDERSHAFT: Mr. Cusins: I am much indebted to you
for explaining so precisely. (*Turning to* SARAH.) Barbara, my dear—

SARAH (*prompting him*): Sarah.

UNDERSHAFT: Sarah, of course. (*They shake hands. He
goes over to* BARBARA.) Barbara—I am right this time,
I hope.

BARBARA: Quite right. (*They shake hands.*)

LADY BRITOMART (*resuming command*): Sit down, all
of you. Sit down, Andrew. (*She comes forward and
sits on the settee.* CUSINS *also brings his chair forward on her left.* BARBARA *and* STEPHEN *resume their
seats.* LOMAX *gives his chair to* SARAH *and goes for
another.*)

UNDERSHAFT: Thank you, my love.

LOMAX (*conversationally, as he brings a chair forward
between the writing table and the settee, and offers it
to* UNDERSHAFT): Takes you some time to find out exactly where you are, dont it?

UNDERSHAFT (*accepting the chair*): That is not what em-
barrasses me, Mr. Lomax. My difficulty is that if I play
the part of a father, I shall produce the effect of an
intrusive stranger; and if I play the part of a discreet
stranger, I may appear a callous father.

LADY BRITOMART: There is no need for you to play any
part at all, Andrew. You had much better be sincere
and natural.

UNDERSHAFT (*submissively*): Yes, my dear: I daresay that

will be best. (*Making himself comfortable.*) Well, here I am. Now what can I do for you all?

LADY BRITOMART: You need not do anything, Andrew. You are one of the family. You can sit with us and enjoy yourself.

(LOMAX'S *too long suppressed mirth explodes in agonized neighings.*)

LADY BRITOMART (*outraged*): Charles Lomax: if you can behave yourself, behave yourself. If not, leave the room.

LOMAX: I'm awfully sorry, Lady Brit; but really, you know, upon my soul! (*He sits on the settee between* LADY BRITOMART *and* UNDERSHAFT, *quite overcome.*)

BARBARA: Why dont you laugh if you want to, Cholly? It's good for your inside.

LADY BRITOMART: Barbara: you have had the education of a lady. Please let your father see that; and dont talk like a street girl.

UNDERSHAFT: Never mind me, my dear. As you know, I am not a gentleman; and I was never educated.

LOMAX (*encouragingly*): Nobody'd know it, I assure you. You look all right, you know.

CUSINS: Let me advise you to study Greek, Mr. Undershaft. Greek scholars are privileged men. Few of them know Greek; and none of them know anything else; but their position is unchallengeable. Other languages are the qualifications of waiters and commercial travellers: Greek is to a man of position what the hallmark is to silver.

BARBARA: Dolly: dont be insincere. Cholly: fetch your concertina and play something for us.

LOMAX (*doubtfully to* UNDERSHAFT): Perhaps that sort of thing isnt in your line, eh?

UNDERSHAFT: I am particularly fond of music.

LOMAX (*delighted*): Are you? Then I'll get it. (*He goes upstairs for the instrument.*)

UNDERSHAFT: Do you play, Barbara?

BARBARA: Only the tambourine. But Cholly's teaching me the concertina.

UNDERSHAFT: Is Cholly also a member of the Salvation Army?

BARBARA: No: he says it's bad form to be a dissenter. But I dont despair of Cholly. I made him come yesterday to a meeting at the dock gates, and took the collection in his hat.

LADY BRITOMART: It is not my doing, Andrew. Barbara is old enough to take her own way. She has no father to advise her.

BARBARA: Oh yes she has. There are no orphans in the Salvation Army.

UNDERSHAFT: Your father there has a great many children and plenty of experience, eh?

BARBARA (*looking at him with quick interest and nodding*): Just so. How did you come to understand that? (LOMAX *is heard at the door trying the concertina.*)

LADY BRITOMART: Come in, Charles. Play us something at once.

LOMAX: Righto! (*He sits down in his former place, and preludes.*)

UNDERSHAFT: One moment, Mr. Lomax. I am rather interested in the Salvation Army. Its motto might be my own: Blood and Fire.

LOMAX (*shocked*): But not your sort of blood and fire, you know.

UNDERSHAFT: My sort of blood cleanses: my sort of fire purifies.

BARBARA: So do ours. Come down to-morrow to my shelter—the West Ham shelter—and see what we're doing. We're going to march to a great meeting in the Assembly Hall at Mile End. Come and see the shelter and then march with us: it will do you a lot of good. Can you play anything?

UNDERSHAFT: In my youth I earned pennies, and even shillings occasionally, in the streets and in public house parlors by my natural talent for stepdancing. Later on, I became a member of the Undershaft orchestral society, and performed passably on the tenor trombone.

LOMAX (*scandalized*): Oh I say!

BARBARA: Many a sinner has played himself into heaven on the trombone, thanks to the Army.

LOMAX (*to* BARBARA, *still rather shocked*): Yes; but what about the cannon business, dont you know? (*To* UN-DERSHAFT.) Getting into heaven is not exactly in your line, is it?

LADY BRITOMART: Charles!!!

LOMAX: Well; but it stands to reason, dont it? The cannon business may be necessary and all that: we cant get on without cannons; but it isnt right, you know. On the other hand, there may be a certain amount of tosh about the Salvation Army—I belong to the Established Church myself—but still you cant deny that it's religion; and you cant go against religion, can you? At least unless youre downright immoral, dont you know.

UNDERSHAFT: You hardly appreciate my position, Mr. Lomax—

LOMAX (*hastily*):   I'm not saying anything against you personally, you know.

UNDERSHAFT: Quite so, quite so. But consider for a moment. Here I am, a manufacturer of mutilation and murder. I find myself in a specially amiable humor just now because, this morning, down at the foundry, we blew twenty-seven dummy soldiers into fragments with a gun which formerly destroyed only thirteen.

LOMAX (*leniently*):   Well, the more destructive war becomes, the sooner it will be abolished, eh?

UNDERSHAFT: Not at all. The more destructive war becomes the more fascinating we find it. No, Mr. Lomax: I am obliged to you for making the usual excuse for my trade; but I am not ashamed of it. I am not one of those men who keep their morals and their business in watertight compartments. All the spare money my trade rivals spend on hospitals, cathedrals and other receptacles for conscience money, I devote to experiments and researches in improved methods of destroying life and property. I have always done so; and I always shall. Therefore your Christmas card moralities of peace on earth and goodwill among men are of no use to me.

Your Christianity, which enjoins you to resist not evil, and to turn the other cheek, would make me a bankrupt. My morality—my religion—must have a place for cannons and torpedoes in it.

STEPHEN (*coldly—almost sullenly*): You speak as if there were half a dozen moralities and religions to choose from, instead of one true morality and one true religion.

UNDERSHAFT: For me there is only one true morality; but it might not fit you, as you do not manufacture aerial battleships. There is only one true morality for every man; but every man has not the same true morality.

LOMAX (*overtaxed*): Would you mind saying that again? I didnt quite follow it.

CUSINS: It's quite simple. As Euripides says, one man's meat is another man's poison morally as well as physically.

UNDERSHAFT: Precisely.

LOMAX: Oh, that. Yes, yes, yes. True. True.

STEPHEN: In other words, some men are honest and some are scoundrels.

BARBARA: Bosh. There are no scoundrels.

UNDERSHAFT: Indeed? Are there any good men?

BARBARA: No. Not one. There are neither good men nor scoundrels: there are just children of one Father; and the sooner they stop calling one another names the better. You neednt talk to me: I know them. Ive had scores of them through my hands: scoundrels, criminals, infidels, philanthropists, missionaries, county councillors, all sorts. Theyre all just the same sort of sinner; and theres the same salvation ready for them all.

UNDERSHAFT: May I ask have you ever saved a maker of cannons?

BARBARA: No. Will you let me try?

UNDERSHAFT: Well, I will make a bargain with you. If I go to see you to-morrow in your Salvation Shelter, will you come the day after to see me in my cannon works?

BARBARA: Take care. It may end in your giving up the cannons for the sake of the Salvation Army.

UNDERSHAFT: Are you sure it will not end in your giving up the Salvation Army for the sake of the cannons?

BARBARA: I will take my chance of that.

UNDERSHAFT: And I will take my chance of the other. (*They shake hands on it.*) Where is your shelter?

BARBARA: In West Ham. At the sign of the cross. Ask anybody in Canning Town. Where are your works?

UNDERSHAFT: In Perivale St. Andrews. At the sign of the sword. Ask anybody in Europe.

LOMAX: Hadnt I better play something?

BARBARA: Yes. Give us Onward, Christian Soldiers.

LOMAX: Well, that's rather a strong order to begin with, dont you know. Suppose I sing Thourt passing hence, my brother. It's much the same tune.

BARBARA: It's too melancholy. You get saved, Cholly; and youll pass hence, my brother, without making such a fuss about it.

LADY BRITOMART: Really, Barbara, you go on as if religion were a pleasant subject. Do have some sense of propriety.

UNDERSHAFT: I do not find it an unpleasant subject, my dear. It is the only one that capable people really care for.

LADY BRITOMART (*looking at her watch*): Well, if you are determined to have it, I insist on having it in a proper and respectable way. Charles: ring for prayers. (*General amazement.* STEPHEN *rises in dismay.*)

LOMAX (*rising*): Oh I say!

UNDERSHAFT (*rising*): I am afraid I must be going.

LADY BRITOMART: You cannot go now, Andrew: it would be most improper. Sit down. What will the servants think?

UNDERSHAFT: My dear: I have conscientious scruples. May I suggest a compromise? If Barbara will conduct a little service in the drawingroom, with Mr. Lomax as organist, I will attend it willingly. I will even take part, if a trombone can be procured.

LADY BRITOMART: Dont mock, Andrew.

UNDERSHAFT (*shocked—to* BARBARA): You dont think I am mocking, my love, I hope.

BARBARA: No, of course not; and it wouldnt matter if you were: half the Army came to their first meeting for a lark. (*Rising.*) Come along. Come, Dolly, Come, Cholly. (*She goes out with* UNDERSHAFT, *who opens the door for her.* CUSINS *rises.*)

LADY BRITOMART: I will not be disobeyed by everybody. Adolphus: sit down. Charles: you may go. You are not fit for prayers: you cannot keep your countenance.

LOMAX: Oh I say! (*He goes out.*)

LADY BRITOMART (*continuing*): But you, Adolphus, can behave yourself if you choose to. I insist on your staying.

CUSINS: My dear Lady Brit: there are things in the family prayer book that I couldn't bear to hear you say.

LADY BRITOMART: What things, pray?

CUSINS: Well, you would have to say before all the servants that we have done things we ought not to have done, and left undone things we ought to have done, and that there is no health in us. I cannot bear to hear you doing yourself such an injustice, and Barbara such an injustice. As for myself, I flatly deny it: I have done my best. I shouldnt dare to marry Barbara—I couldnt look you in the face—if it were true. So I must go to the drawingroom.

LADY BRITOMART (*offended*): Well, go. (*He starts for the door.*) And remember this, Adolphus (*he turns to listen*): I have a very strong suspicion that you went to the Salvation Army to worship Barbara and nothing else. And I quite appreciate the very clever way in which you systematically humbug me. I have found you out. Take care Barbara doesnt. Thats all.

CUSINS (*with unruffled sweetness*): Dont tell on me. (*He goes out.*)

LADY BRITOMART: Sarah: if you want to go, go. Anything's better than to sit there as if you wished you were a thousand miles away.

SARAH (*languidly*): Very well, mamma. (*She goes.*)

(LADY BRITOMART, *with a sudden flounce, gives way to a little gust of tears.*)

STEPHEN *(going to her)*: Mother: what's the matter?

LADY BRITOMART *(swishing away her tears with her hand-kerchief)*: Nothing. Foolishness. You can go with him, too, if you like, and leave me with the servants.

STEPHEN: Oh, you mustnt think that, mother. I—I dont like him.

LADY BRITOMART: The others do. That is the injustice of a woman's lot. A woman has to bring up her children; and that means to restrain them, to deny them things they want, to set them tasks, to punish them when they do wrong, to do all the unpleasant things. And then the father, who has nothing to do but pet them and spoil them, comes in when all her work is done and steals their affection from her.

STEPHEN: He has not stolen our affection from you. It is only curiosity.

LADY BRITOMART *(violently)*: I wont be consoled, Stephen. There is nothing the matter with me. *(She rises and goes towards the door.)*

STEPHEN: Where are you going, mother?

LADY BRITOMART: To the drawingroom, of course. *(She goes out. Onward, Christian Soldiers, on the concertina, with tambourine accompaniment, is heard when the door opens.)* Are you coming, Stephen?

STEPHEN: No. Certainly not. *(She goes. He sits down on the settee, with compressed lips and an expression of strong dislike.)*

END OF ACT I

Act II

(*The yard of the West Ham shelter of the Salvation Army is a cold place on a January morning. The building itself, an old warehouse, is newly whitewashed. Its gabled end projects into the yard in the middle, with a door on the ground floor, and another in the loft above it without any balcony or ladder, but with a pulley rigged over it for hoisting sacks. Those who come from this central gable end into the yard have the gateway leading to the street on their left, with a stone horse-trough just beyond it, and, on the right, a penthouse shielding a table from the weather. There are forms at the table; and on them are seated a man and a woman, both much down on their luck, finishing a meal of bread (one thick slice each, with margarine and golden syrup) and diluted milk.*

The man, a workman out of employment, is young, agile, a talker, a poser, sharp enough to be capable of anything in reason except honesty or altruistic considerations of any kind. The woman is a commonplace old bundle of poverty and hard-worn humanity. She looks sixty and probably is forty-five. If they were rich people, gloved and muffed and well wrapped up in furs and overcoats, they would be numbed and miserable; for it is a grindingly cold, raw, January day; and a glance at the background of grimy warehouses and leaden sky visible over the whitewashed walls of the yard would drive any idle rich person straight to the Mediterranean. But these two, being no more troubled with visions of the Mediterranean than of the moon, and being compelled to keep more of their clothes in the pawnshop,

69

and less on their persons, in winter than in summer, are not depressed by the cold: rather are they stung into vivacity, to which their meal has just now given an almost jolly turn. The man takes a pull at his mug, and then gets up and moves about the yard with his hands deep in his pockets, occasionally breaking into a stepdance.)

THE WOMAN: Feel better arter your meal, sir?

THE MAN: No. Call that a meal! Good enough for you, praps; but wot is it to me, an intelligent workin man.

THE WOMAN: Workin man! Wot are you?

THE MAN: Painter.

THE WOMAN (*sceptically*): Yus, I dessay.

THE MAN: Yus, you dessay! I know. Every loafer that cant do nothink calls isself a painter. Well, I'm a real painter: grainer, finisher, thirty-eight bob a week when I can get it.

THE WOMAN: Then why dont you go and get it?

THE MAN: I'll tell you why. Fust: I'm intelligent—fffff! it's rotten cold here (*he dances a step or two*)—yes: intelligent beyond the station o life into which it has pleased the capitalists to call me; and they dont like a man that sees through em. Second, an intelligent bein needs a doo share of appiness; so I drink somethink cruel when I get the chawnce. Third, I stand by my class and do as little as I can so's to leave arf the job for me fellow workers. Fourth, I'm fly enough to know wots inside the law and wots outside it; and inside it I do as the capitalists do: pinch wot I can lay me ands on. In a proper state of society I am sober, industrious and honest: in Rome, so to speak, I do as the Romans do. Wots the consequence? When trade is bad—and it's rotten bad just now—and the employers az to sack arf their men, they generally start on me.

THE WOMAN: Whats your name?

THE MAN: Price. Bronterre O'Brien Price. Usually called Snobby Price, for short.

THE WOMAN: Snobby's a carpenter, aint it? You said you was a painter.

PRICE: Not that kind of snob, but the genteel sort. I'm too uppish, owing to my intelligence, and my father being a Chartist and a reading, thinking man: a stationer, too. I'm none of your common hewers of wood and drawers of water; and dont you forget it. (*He returns to his seat at the table, and takes up his mug.*) Wots your name?

THE WOMAN: Rummy Mitchens, sir.

PRICE (*quaffing the remains of his milk to her*): Your elth, Miss Mitchens.

RUMMY (*correcting him*): Missis Mitchens.

PRICE: Wot! Oh Rummy, Rummy! Respectable married woman, Rummy, gittin rescued by the Salvation Army by pretendin to be a bad un. Same old game! -

RUMMY: What am I to do? I cant starve. Them Salvation lasses is dear good girls; but the better you are, the worse they likes to think you were before they rescued you. Why shouldnt they av a bit o credit, poor loves? theyre worn to rags by their work. And where would they get the money to rescue us if we was to let on we're no worse than other people? You know what ladies and gentlemen are.

PRICE: Thievin swine! Wish I ad their job, Rummy, all the same. Wot does Rummy stand for? Pet name praps?

RUMMY: Short for Romola.

PRICE: For wot!?

RUMMY: Romola. It was out of a new book. Somebody me mother wanted me to grow up like.

PRICE: We're companions in misfortune, Rummy. Both on us got names that nobody cawnt pronounce. Consequently I'm Snobby and youre Rummy because Bill and Sally wasnt good enough for our parents. Such is life!

RUMMY: Who saved you, Mr. Price? Was it Major Barbara?

PRICE: No: I come here on my own. I'm goin to be Bronterre O'Brien Price, the converted painter. I know wot they like. I'll tell em how I blasphemed and gambled and wopped my poor old mother—

RUMMY (*shocked*): Used you to beat your mother?

PRICE: Not likely. She used to beat me. No matter: you

come and listen to the converted painter, and youll hear how she was a pious woman that taught me me prayers at er knee, an how I used to come home drunk and drag her out o bed be er snow white airs, an lam into er with the poker.

RUMMY: Thats whats so unfair to us women. Your confessions is just as big lies as ours: you dont tell what you really done no more than us; but you men can tell your lies right out at the meetins and be made much of for it; while the sort o confessions we az to make az to be whispered to one lady at a time. It aint right, spite of all their piety.

PRICE: Right! Do you spose the Army'd be allowed if it went and did right? Not much. It combs our air and makes us good little blokes to be robbed and put upon. But I'll play the game as good as any of em. I'll see somebody struck by lightnin, or hear a voice sayin "Snobby Price: where will you spend eternity?" I'll ave a time of it, I tell you.

RUMMY: You wont be let drink, though.

PRICE: I'll take it out in gorspellin, then. I dont want to drink if I can get fun enough any other way.

(JENNY HILL, *a pale, overwrought, pretty Salvation lass of 18, comes in through the yard gate, leading* PETER SHIRLEY, *a half hardened, half worn-out elderly man, weak with hunger.*)

JENNY (*supporting him*): Come! pluck up. I'll get you something to eat. Youll be all right then.

PRICE (*rising and hurrying officiously to take the old man off* JENNY'S *hands*): Poor old man! Cheer up, brother: youll find rest and peace and appiness ere. Hurry up with the food, miss: e's fair done. (JENNY *hurries into the shelter.*) Ere, buck up, daddy! shes fetchin y'a thick slice o breadn treacle, an a mug o skyblue. (*He seats him at the corner of the table.*)

RUMMY (*gaily*): Keep up your old art! Never say die!

SHIRLEY: I'm not an old man. I'm only 46. I'm as good as ever I was. The grey patch come in my hair before

I was thirty. All it wants is three pennorth o hair dye: am I to be turned on the streets to starve for it? Holy God! I've worked ten to twelve hours a day since I was thirteen, and paid my way all through; and now am I to be thrown into the gutter and my job given to a young man that can do it no better than me because Ive black hair that goes white at the first change?

PRICE (*cheerfully*):   No good jawrin about it. Youre ony a jumped-up, jerked-off, orspittle-turned-out incurable of an ole workin man: who cares about you? Eh? Make the thievin swine give you a meal: theyve stole many a one from you. Get a bit o your own back. (JENNY *returns with the usual meal*.) There you are, brother. Awsk a blessin an tuck that into you.

SHIRLEY (*looking at it ravenously but not touching it, and crying like a child*):   I never took anything before.

JENNY (*petting him*):   Come, come! the Lord sends it to you: he wasnt above taking bread from his friends; and why should you be? Besides, when we find you a job you can pay us for it if you like.

SHIRLEY (*eagerly*):   Yes, yes: thats true. I can pay you back: its only a loan. (*Shivering.*) Oh Lord! oh Lord! (*He turns to the table and attacks the meal ravenously.*)

JENNY: Well, Rummy, are you more comfortable now?

RUMMY: God bless you, lovey! youve fed my body and saved my soul, havent you? (JENNY, *touched, kisses her*.) Sit down and rest a bit: you must be ready to drop.

JENNY: Ive been going hard since morning. But theres more work than we can do. I mustnt stop.

RUMMY: Try a prayer for just two minutes. Youll work all the better after.

JENNY (*her eyes lighting up*):   Oh isnt it wonderful how a few minutes prayer revives you! I was quite lightheaded at twelve o'clock, I was so tired; but Major Barbara just sent me to pray for five minutes; and I was able to go on as if I had only just begun. (*To* PRICE.) Did you have a piece of bread?

PRICE (*with unction*):   Yes, miss; but Ive got the piece

that I value more; and thats the peace that passeth hall hannerstennin.

RUMMY (*fervently*):   Glory Hallelujah!

(BILL WALKER, *a rough customer of about 25, appears at the yard gate and looks malevolently at* JENNY.)

JENNY: That makes me so happy. When you say that, I feel wicked for loitering here. I must get to work again.

(*She is hurrying to the shelter, when the new-comer moves quickly up to the door and intercepts her. His manner is so threatening that she retreats as he comes at her truculently, driving her down the yard.*)

BILL: I know you. Youre the one that took away my girl. Youre the one that set er agen me. Well, I'm goin to av er out. Not that I care a curse for her or you: see? But I'll let er know; and I'll let you know. I'm goin to give er a doin thatll teach er to cut away from me. Now in with you and tell er to come out afore I come in and kick er out. Tell er Bill Walker wants er. She'll know what that means; and if she keeps me waitin itll be worse. You stop to jaw back at me; and I'll start on you; d'ye hear? Theres your way. In you go. (*He takes her by the arm and slings her towards the door of the shelter. She falls on her hand and knee.* RUMMY *helps her up again.*)

PRICE (*rising, and venturing irresolutely towards* BILL): Easy there, mate. She aint doin you no arm.

BILL: Who are you callin mate? (*Standing over him threateningly.*) Youre goin to stand up for her, are you? Put up your ands.

RUMMY (*running indignantly to him to scold him*):   Oh, you great brute— (*He instantly swings his left hand back against her face. She screams and reels back to the trough, where she sits down, covering her bruised face with her hands and rocking herself and moaning with pain.*)

JENNY (*going to her*):   Oh God forgive you! How could you strike an old woman like that?

BILL (*seizing her by the hair so violently that she also screams, and tearing her away from the old woman*): You Gawd forgive me again and I'll Gawd forgive you one on the jaw thatll stop you prayin for a week. (*Holding her and turning fiercely on* PRICE.) Av you anything to say agen it? Eh?

PRICE (*intimidated*): No, matey: she aint anything to do with me.

BILL: Good job for you! I'd put two meals into you and fight you with one finger after, you starved cur. (*To* JENNY.) Now are you goin to fetch out Mog Habbijam; or am I to knock your face off you and fetch her myself?

JENNY (*writhing in his grasp*): Oh please someone go in and tell Major Barbara— (*she screams again as he wrenches her head down; and* PRICE *and* RUMMY *flee into the shelter*).

BILL: You want to go in and tell your Major of me, do you?

JENNY: Oh please dont drag my hair. Let me go.

BILL: Do you or dont you? (*She stifles a scream.*) Yes or no.

JENNY: God give me strength—

BILL (*striking her with his fist in the face*): Go and shew her that, and tell her if she wants one like it to come and interfere with me. (JENNY, *crying with pain, goes into the shed. He goes to the form and addresses the old man.*) Here: finish your mess; and get out o my way.

SHIRLEY (*springing up and facing him fiercely, with the mug in his hand*): You take a liberty with me, and I'll smash you over the face with the mug and cut your eye out. Aint you satisfied—young whelps like you—with takin the bread out o the mouths of your elders that have brought you up and slaved for you, but you must come shovin and cheekin and bullyin in here, where the bread o charity is sickenin in our stummicks?

BILL (*contemptuously, but backing a little*): Wot good are you, you old palsy mug? Wot good are you?

SHIRLEY: As good as you and better. I'll do a day's work

agen you or any fat young soaker of your age. Go and
take my job at Horrockses, where I worked for ten year.
They want young men there: they cant afford to keep
men over forty-five. Theyre very sorry—give you a
character and happy to help you to get anything suited
to your years—sure a steady man wont be long out of
a job. Well, let em try you. Theyll find the differ. What
do you know? Not as much as how to beeyave yourself—layin your dirty fist across the mouth of a respectable woman!

BILL: Dont provoke me to lay it acrost yours: d'ye hear?

SHIRLEY (*with blighting contempt*):   Yes: you like an old
man to hit, dont you, when youve finished with the
women. I aint seen you hit a young one yet.

BILL (*stung*):   You lie, you old soupkitchener, you. There
was a young man here. Did I offer to hit him or did I
not?

SHIRLEY: Was he starvin or was he not? Was he a man
or only a crosseyed thief an a loafer? Would you hit
my son-in-law's brother?

BILL: Who's he?

SHIRLEY: Todger Fairmile o Balls Pond. Him that won
£20 off the Japanese wrastler at the music hall by
standin out 17 minutes 4 seconds agen him.

BILL (*sullenly*):   I'm no music hall wrastler. Can he box?

SHIRLEY: Yes: an you cant.

BILL: Wot! I cant, cant I? Wots that you say (*threatening
him*)?

SHIRLEY (*not budging an inch*):   Will you box Todger
Fairmile if I put him on to you? Say the word.

BILL (*subsiding with a slouch*):   I'll stand up to any man
alive, if he was ten Todger Fairmiles. But I dont set up
to be a perfessional.

SHIRLEY (*looking down on him with unfathomable disdain*):   You box! Slap an old woman with the back o
your hand! You hadnt even the sense to hit her where
a magistrate couldnt see the mark of it, you silly young
lump of conceit and ignorance. Hit a girl in the jaw and
ony make her cry! If Todger Fairmile'd done it, she

wouldnt a got up inside o ten minutes, no more than you would if he got on to you. Yah! I'd set about you myself if I had a week's feedin in me instead o two months starvation. (*He returns to the table to finish his meal.*)

BILL (*following him and stooping over him to drive the taunt in*): You lie! you have the bread and treacle in you that you come here to beg.

SHIRLEY (*bursting into tears*): Oh God! it's true: I'm only an old pauper on the scrap heap. (*Furiously.*) But youll come to it yourself; and then youll know. Youll come to it sooner than a teetotaller like me, fillin yourself with gin at this hour o the mornin!

BILL: I'm no gin drinker, you old liar; but when I want to give my girl a bloomin good idin I like to av a bit o devil in me: see? An here I am, talkin to a rotten old blighter like you sted o givin her wot for. (*Working himself into a rage.*) I'm goin in there to fetch her out. (*He makes vengefully for the shelter door.*)

SHIRLEY: Youre goin to the station on a stretcher, more likely; and theyll take the gin and the devil out of you there when they get you inside. You mind what youre about: the major here is the Earl o Stevenage's grand-daughter.

BILL (*checked*): Garn!

SHIRLEY: Youll see.

BILL (*his resolution oozing*): Well, I aint done nothin to er.

SHIRLEY: Spose she said you did! who'd believe you?

BILL (*very uneasy, skulking back to the corner of the penthouse*): Gawd! theres no jastice in this country. To think wot them people can do! I'm as good as er.

SHIRLEY: Tell her so. Its just what a fool like you would do.

(BARBARA, *brisk and businesslike, comes from the shelter with a note book, and addresses herself to* SHIRLEY. BILL, *cowed, sits down in the corner on a form, and turns his back on them.*)

BARBARA: Good morning.

SHIRLEY (*standing up and taking off his hat*): Good morning, miss.

BARBARA: Sit down: make yourself at home. (*He hesitates, but she puts a friendly hand on his shoulder and makes him obey.*) Now then! since youve made friends with us, we want to know all about you. Names and addresses and trades.

SHIRLEY: Peter Shirley. Fitter. Chucked out two months ago because I was too old.

BARBARA (*not at all surprised*): Youd pass still. Why didnt you dye your hair?

SHIRLEY: I did. Me age come out at a coroner's inquest on me daughter.

BARBARA: Steady?

SHIRLEY: Teetotaller. Never out of a job before. Good worker. And sent to the knackers like an old horse!

BARBARA: No matter: if you did your part God will do his.

SHIRLEY (*suddenly stubborn*): My religion's no concern of anybody but myself.

BARBARA (*guessing*): *I* know. Secularist?

SHIRLEY (*hotly*): Did I offer to deny it?

BARBARA: Why should you? My own father's a Secularist, I think. Our Father—yours and mine—fulfils himself in many ways; and I daresay he knew what he was about when he made a Secularist of you. So buck up, Peter! we can always find a job for a steady man like you. (SHIRLEY, *disarmed, touches his hat. She turns from him to* BILL.) Whats your name?

BILL (*insolently*): Wots that to you?

BARBARA (*calmly making a note*): Afraid to give his name. Any trade?

BILL: Who's afraid to give his name? (*Doggedly, with a sense of heroically defying the House of Lords in the person of* LORD STEVENAGE.) If you want to bring a charge agen me, bring it. (*She waits, unruffled.*) My name's Bill Walker.

BARBARA (*as if the name were familiar: trying to remem-*

ber how):   Bill Walker? (*Recollecting.*) Oh, I know: youre the man that Jenny Hill was praying for inside just now. (*She enters his name in her note book.*)

BILL: Who's Jenny Hill? And what call has she to pray for me?

BARBARA: I dont know. Perhaps it was you that cut her lip.

BILL (*defiantly*):   Yes, it was me that cut her lip. I aint afraid o you.

BARBARA: How could you be, since youre not afraid of God? Youre a brave man, Mr. Walker. It takes some pluck to do our work here; but none of us dare lift our hand against a girl like that, for fear of her father in heaven.

BILL (*sullenly*):   I want none o your cantin jaw. I suppose you think I come here to beg from you, like this damaged lot here. Not me. I dont want your bread and scrape and catlap. I dont believe in your Gawd, no more than you do yourself.

BARBARA (*sunnily apologetic and ladylike, as on a new footing with him*):   Oh, I beg your pardon for putting your name down, Mr. Walker. I didnt understand. I'll strike it out.

BILL (*taking this as a slight, and deeply wounded by it*):   Eah! you let my name alone. Aint it good enough to be in your book?

BARBARA (*considering*):   Well, you see, theres no use putting down your name unless I can do something for you, is there? Whats your trade?

BILL (*still smarting*):   Thats no concern o yours.

BARBARA: Just so. (*Very businesslike.*) I'll put you down as (*writing*) the man who—struck—poor little Jenny Hill—in the mouth.

BILL (*rising threateningly*):   See here. Ive ad enough o this.

BARBARA (*quite sunny and fearless*):   What did you come to us for?

BILL: I come for my girl, see? I come to take her out o this and to break er jawr for her.

BARBARA (*complacently*):   You see I was right about your trade. (BILL, *on the point of retorting furiously, finds himself, to his great shame and terror, in danger of crying instead. He sits down again suddenly.*) Whats her name?

BILL (*dogged*):   Er name's Mog Abbijam: thats wot her name is.

BARBARA: Oh, she's gone to Canning Town, to our barracks there.

BILL (*fortified by his resentment of* MOG'S *perfidy*):   Is she? (*Vindictively.*) Then *I*'m goin to Kennintahn arter her. (*He crosses to the gate; hesitates; finally comes back at* BARBARA.) Are you lyin to me to get shut o me?

BARBARA: I dont want to get shut of you. I want to keep you here and save your soul. Youd better stay: youre going to have a bad time today, Bill.

BILL: Who's goin to give it to me? You, praps.

BARBARA: Someone you dont believe in. But youll be glad afterwards.

BILL (*slinking off*):   I'll go to Kennintahn to be out o the reach o your tongue. (*Suddenly turning on her with intense malice.*) And if I dont find Mog there, I'll come back and do two years for you, selp me Gawd if I don't!

BARBARA (*a shade kindlier, if possible*):   It's no use, Bill. Shes got another bloke.

BILL: Wot!

BARBARA: One of her own converts. He fell in love with her when he saw her with her soul saved, and her face clean, and her hair washed.

BILL (*surprised*):   Wottud she wash it for, the carroty slut? It's red.

BARBARA: It's quite lovely now, because she wears a new look in her eyes with it. It's a pity youre too late. The new bloke has put your nose out of joint, Bill.

BILL: I'll put his nose out o joint for him. Not that I care a curse for her, mind that. But I'll teach her to drop me as if I was dirt. And I'll teach him to meddle with my judy. Wots iz bleedin name?

BARBARA: Sergeant Todger Fairmile.

SHIRLEY (*rising with grim joy*):   I'll go with him, miss. I want to see them two meet. I'll take him to the infirmary when it's over.

BILL (*to* SHIRLEY, *with undissembled misgiving*):   Is that im you was speakin on?

SHIRLEY: Thats him.

BILL: Im that wrastled in the music all?

SHIRLEY: The competitions at the National Sportin Club was worth nigh a hundred a year to him. Hes gev em up now for religion; so hes a bit fresh for want of the exercise he was accustomed to. Hell be glad to see you. Come along.

BILL: Wots is weight?

SHIRLEY: Thirteen four. (BILL'S *last hope expires.*)

BARBARA: Go and talk to him, Bill. He'll convert you.

SHIRLEY: He'll convert your head into a mashed potato.

BILL (*sullenly*):   I aint afraid of him. I aint afraid of ennybody. But he can lick me. Shes done me. (*He sits down moodily on the edge of the horse trough.*)

SHIRLEY: You aint goin. I thought not. (*He resumes his seat.*)

BARBARA (*calling*):   Jenny!

JENNY (*appearing at the shelter door with a plaster on the corner of her mouth*):   Yes, Major.

BARBARA: Send Rummy Mitchens out to clear away here.

JENNY: I think shes afraid.

BARBARA (*her resemblance to her mother flashing out for a moment*):   Nonsense! she must do as shes told.

JENNY (*calling into the shelter*):   Rummy: the Major says you must come.

(JENNY *comes to* BARBARA, *purposely keeping on the side next* BILL, *lest he should suppose that she shrank from him or bore malice.*)

BARBARA: Poor little Jenny! Are you tired? (*Looking at the wounded cheek.*) Does it hurt?

JENNY: No; it's all right now. It was nothing.

BARBARA (*critically*):   It was as hard as he could hit, I expect. Poor Bill! You dont feel angry with him, do you?

JENNY: Oh no, no, no: indeed I dont, Major, bless his poor heart! (BARBARA *kisses her; and she runs away merrily into the shelter.* BILL *writhes with an agonizing return of his new and alarming symptoms, but says nothing.* RUMMY MITCHENS *comes from the shelter.*)

BARBARA (*going to meet* RUMMY):   Now Rummy, bustle. Take in those mugs and plates to be washed; and throw the crumbs about for the birds.

(RUMMY *takes the three plates and mugs; but* SHIRLEY *takes back his mug from her, as there is still some milk left in it.*)

RUMMY: There aint any crumbs. This aint a time to waste good bread on birds.

PRICE (*appearing at the shelter door*):   Gentleman come to see the shelter, Major. Says hes your father.

BARBARA: All right. Coming. (SNOBBY *goes back into the shelter, followed by* BARBARA.)

RUMMY (*stealing across to* BILL *and addressing him in a subdued voice, but with intense conviction*):   I'd av the lor of you, you flat eared pignosed potwalloper, if she'd let me. Youre no gentleman, to hit a lady in the face. (BILL, *with greater things moving in him, takes no notice.*)

SHIRLEY (*following her*):   Here! in with you and dont get yourself into more trouble by talking.

RUMMY (*with hauteur*):   I aint ad the pleasure o being hintroduced to you, as I can remember. (*She goes into the shelter with the plates.*)

SHIRLEY: Thats the—

BILL (*savagely*):   Dont you talk to me, d'ye hear. You lea me alone, or I'll do you a mischief. I'm not dirt under your feet, anyway.

SHIRLEY (*calmly*):   Dont you be afeerd. You aint such prime company that you need expect to be sought after.

(*He is about to go into the shelter when* BARBARA *comes out, with* UNDERSHAFT *on her right.*)

BARBARA: Oh there you are, Mr. Shirley! (*Between them.*) This is my father: I told you he was a Secularist, didnt I? Perhaps youll be able to comfort one another.

UNDERSHAFT (*startled*): A Secularist! Not the least in the world: on the contrary, a confirmed mystic.

BARBARA: Sorry, I'm sure. By the way, papa, what is your religion—in case I have to introduce you again?

UNDERSHAFT: My religion? Well, my dear, I am a Millionaire. That is my religion.

BARBARA: Then I'm afraid you and Mr. Shirley wont be able to comfort one another after all. You're not a Millionaire, are you, Peter?

SHIRLEY: No; and proud of it.

UNDERSHAFT (*gravely*): Poverty, my friend, is not a thing to be proud of.

SHIRLEY (*angrily*): Who made your millions for you? Me and my like. Whats kep us poor? Keepin you rich. I wouldnt have your conscience, not for all your income.

UNDERSHAFT: I wouldnt have your income, not for all your conscience, Mr. Shirley. (*He goes to the penthouse and sits down on a form.*)

BARBARA (*stopping* SHIRLEY *adroitly as he is about to retort*): You wouldnt think he was my father, would you, Peter? Will you go into the shelter and lend the lasses a hand for a while: we're worked off our feet.

SHIRLEY (*bitterly*): Yes: I'm in their debt for a meal, aint I?

BARBARA: Oh, not because youre in their debt; but for love of them, Peter, for love of them. (*He cannot understand, and is rather scandalized.*) There! dont stare at me. In with you; and give that conscience of yours a holiday (*bustling him into the shelter*).

SHIRLEY (*as he goes in*): Ah! it's a pity you never was trained to use your reason, miss. Youd have been a very taking lecturer on Secularism.

(BARBARA *turns to her father.*)

UNDERSHAFT: Never mind me, my dear. Go about your work; and let me watch it for a while.

BARBARA: All right.

UNDERSHAFT: For instance, whats the matter with that out-patient over there?

BARBARA (*looking at* BILL, *whose attitude has never changed, and whose expression of brooding wrath has deepened*): Oh, we shall cure him in no time. Just watch. (*She goes over to* BILL *and waits. He glances up at her and casts his eyes down again, uneasy, but grimmer than ever.*) It would be nice to just stamp on Mog Habbijam's face, wouldnt it, Bill?

BILL (*starting up from the trough in consternation*):   It's a lie: I never said so. (*She shakes her head.*) Who told you wot was in my mind?

BARBARA: Only your new friend.

BILL: Wot new friend?

BARBARA: The devil, Bill. When he gets round people they get-miserable, just like you.

BILL (*with a heartbreaking attempt at devil-may-care cheerfulness*): I aint miserable. (*He sits down again, and stretches his legs in an attempt to seem indifferent.*)

BARBARA: Well, if youre happy, why dont you look happy, as we do?

BILL (*his legs curling back in spite of him*): I'm appy enough, I tell you. Why dont you lea me alown? Wot av I done to you? I aint smashed your face, av I?

BARBARA (*softly: wooing his soul*):   It's not me thats getting at you, Bill.

BILL: Who else is it?

BARBARA: Somebody that doesnt intend you to smash women's faces, I suppose. Somebody or something that wants to make a man of you.

BILL (*blustering*):   Make a man o me! Aint I a man? eh? aint I a man? Who sez I'm not a man?

BARBARA: Theres a man in you somewhere, I suppose. But why did he let you hit poor little Jenny Hill? That wasnt very manly of him, was it?

BILL (*tormented*):   Av- done with it, I tell you. Chack it. I'm sick of your Jenny Ill and er silly little face.

BARBARA: Then why do you keep thinking about it? Why does it keep coming up against you in your mind? Youre not getting converted, are you?

BILL (*with conviction*): Not ME. Not likely. Not arf.

BARBARA: Thats right, Bill. Hold out against it. Put out your strength. Dont lets get you cheap. Todger Fairmile said he wrestled for three nights against his Salvation harder than he ever wrestled with the Jap at the music hall. He gave in to the Jap when his arm was going to break. But he didnt give in to his salvation until his heart was going to break. Perhaps youll escape that. You havnt any heart, have you?

BILL: Wot d'ye mean? Wy aint I got a art the same as ennybody else?

BARBARA: A man with a heart wouldnt have bashed poor little Jenny's face, would he?

BILL (*almost crying*): Ow, will you lca mc alown? Av I ever offered to meddle with you, that you come naggin and provowkin me lawk this? (*He writhes convulsively from his eyes to his toes.*)

BARBARA (*with a steady soothing hand on his arm and a gentle voice that never lets him go*): It's your soul thats hurting you, Bill, and not me. Weve been through it all ourselves. Come with us, Bill. (*He looks wildly round.*) To brave manhood on earth and eternal glory in heaven. (*He is on the point of breaking down.*) Come. (*A drum is heard in the shelter; and* BILL, *with a gasp, escapes from the spell as* BARBARA *turns quickly.* ADOLPHUS *enters from the shelter with a big drum.*) Oh! there you are, Dolly. Let me introduce a new friend of mine, Mr. Bill Walker. This is my bloke, Bill: Mr. Cusins. (CUSINS *salutes with his drumstick.*)

BILL: Goin to marry im?

BARBARA: Yes.

BILL (*fervently*): Gord elp im! Gawd elp im!

BARBARA: Why? Do you think he wont be happy with me?

BILL: Ive only ad to stand it for a mornin: e'll av to stand it for a lifetime.

CUSINS: That is a frightful reflection, Mr. Walker. But I cant tear myself away from her

BILL: Well, I can. (*To* BARBARA.) Eah! do you know where I'm going to, and wot I'm goin to do?

BARBARA: Yes: youre going to heaven; and youre coming back here before the week's out to tell me so.

BILL: You lie. I'm going to Kennintahn, to spit in Todger Fairmile's eye. I bashed Jenny Ill's face; and now I'll get me own face bashed and come back and shew it to er. E'll it me ardern I it er. Thatll make us square. (*To* ADOLPHUS.) Is that fair or is it not? Youre a genlmn: you oughter know.

BARBARA: Two black eyes wont make one white one, Bill.

BILL: I didnt ast you. Cawnt you never keep your mahth shut? I ast the genlmn.

CUSINS (*reflectively*): Yes: I think youre right, Mr. Walker. Yes: I should do it. Its curious: its exactly what an ancient Greek would have done.

BARBARA: But what good will it do?

CUSINS: Well, it will give Mr. Fairmile some exercise; and it will satisfy Mr. Walker's soul.

BILL: Rot! there aint no sach a thing as a soul. Ah kin you tell wether Ive a soul or not? You never seen it.

BARBARA: Ive seen it hurting you when you went against it.

BILL (*with compressed aggravation*): If you was my girl and took the word out o me mahth lawk thet, I'd give you suthink youd feel urtin, so I would. (*To* ADOLPHUS.) You take my tip, mate. Stop er jawr; or youll die afore your time. (*With intense expression.*) Wore aht: thets wot youll be: wore aht. (*He goes away through the gate.*)

CUSINS (*looking after him*): I wonder!

BARBARA: Dolly! (*indignant, in her mother's manner.*)

CUSINS: Yes, my dear, it's very wearing to be in love with you. If it lasts, I quite think I shall die young.

BARBARA: Should you mind?

CUSINS: Not at all. (*He is suddenly softened, and kisses her over the drum, evidently not for the first time, as people cannot kiss over a big drum without practice.* UNDERSHAFT *coughs.*)

BARBARA: It's all right, papa, weve not forgotten you. Dolly: explain the place to papa: I havnt time. (*She goes busily into the shelter.*)

(UNDERSHAFT *and* ADOLPHUS *now have the yard to themselves.* UNDERSHAFT, *seated on a form, and still keenly attentive, looks hard at* ADOLPHUS. ADOLPHUS *looks hard at him.*)

UNDERSHAFT: I fancy you guess something of what is in my mind, Mr. Cusins. (CUSINS *flourishes his drumsticks as if in the act of beating a lively rataplan, but makes no sound.*) Exactly so. But suppose Barbara finds you out!

CUSINS: You know, I do not admit that I am imposing on Barbara. I am quite genuinely interested in the views of the Salvation Army. The fact is, I am a sort of collector of religions; and the curious thing is that I find I can believe them all. By the way, have you any religion?

UNDERSHAFT: Yes.

CUSINS: Anything out of the common?

UNDERSHAFT: Only that there are two things necessary to Salvation.

CUSINS (*disappointed, but polite*): Ah, the Church Catechism. Charles Lomax also belongs to the Established Church.

UNDERSHAFT: The two things are—

CUSINS: Baptism and—

UNDERSHAFT: No. Money and gunpowder.

CUSINS (*surprised, but interested*): That is the general opinion of our governing classes. The novelty is in hearing any man confess it.

UNDERSHAFT: Just so.

CUSINS: Excuse me: is there any place in your religion for honor, justice, truth, love, mercy and so forth?

UNDERSHAFT: Yes: they are the graces and luxuries of a rich, strong, and safe life.

CUSINS: Suppose one is forced to choose between them and money or gunpowder?

UNDERSHAFT: Choose money and gunpowder; for without enough of both you cannot afford the others.

CUSINS: That is your religion?

UNDERSHAFT: Yes.

(The cadence of this reply makes a full close in the conversation. CUSINS *twists his face dubiously and contemplates* UNDERSHAFT. UNDERSHAFT *contemplates him.)*

CUSINS: Barbara wont stand that. You will have to choose between your religion and Barbara.

UNDERSHAFT: So will you, my friend. She will find out that that drum of yours is hollow.

CUSINS: Father Undershaft: you are mistaken: I am a sincere Salvationist. You do not understand the Salvation Army. It is the army of joy, of love, of courage: it has banished the fear and remorse and despair of the old hell-ridden evangelical sects: it marches to fight the devil with trumpet and drum, with music and dancing, with banner and palm, as becomes a sally from heaven by its happy garrison. It picks the waster out of the public house and makes a man of him: it finds a worm wriggling in a back kitchen, and lo! a woman! Men and women of rank too, sons and daughters of the Highest. It takes the poor professor of Greek, the most artificial and self-suppressed of human creatures, from his meal of roots, and lets loose the rhapsodist in him; reveals the true worship of Dionysos to him; sends him down the public street drumming dithyrambs *(he plays a thundering flourish on the drum).*

UNDERSHAFT: You will alarm the shelter.

CUSINS: Oh, they are accustomed to these sudden ecstasies of piety. However, if the drum worries you— *(he pockets the drumsticks; unhooks the drum; and stands it on the ground opposite the gateway).*

UNDERSHAFT: Thank you.

CUSINS: You remember what Euripides says about your money and gunpowder?

UNDERSHAFT: No.

CUSINS (*declaiming*):

> One and another
> In money and guns may outpass his brother;
> And men in their millions float and flow
> And seethe with a million hopes as leaven;
> And they win their will; or they miss their will;
> And their hopes are dead or are pined for still;
> But whoe'er can know
> As the long days go
> That to live is happy, has found his heaven.

My translation: what do you think of it?

UNDERSHAFT: I think, my friend, that if you wish to know, as the long days go, that to live is happy, you must first acquire money enough for a decent life, and power enough to be your own master.

CUSINS: You are damnably discouraging. (*He resumes his declamation.*)

> Is it so hard a thing to see
> That the spirit of God—whate'er it be—
> The Law that abides and changes not, ages long,
> The Eternal and Nature-born: these things be strong?
> What else is Wisdom? What of Man's endeavor,
> Or God's high grace so lovely and so great?
> To stand from fear set free? to breathe and wait?
> To hold a hand uplifted over Fate?
> And shall not Barbara be loved for ever?

UNDERSHAFT: Euripides mentions Barbara, does he?

CUSINS: It is a fair translation. The word means Loveliness.

UNDERSHAFT: May I ask—as Barbara's father—how much a year she is to be loved for ever on?

CUSINS: As Barbara's father, that is more your affair than mine. I can feed her by teaching Greek: that is about all.

UNDERSHAFT: Do you consider it a good match for her?

CUSINS (*with polite obstinacy*): Mr. Undershaft: I am in many ways a weak, timid, ineffectual person; and my

health is far from satisfactory. But whenever I feel that
I must have anything, I get it, sooner or later. I feel
that way about Barbara. I dont like marriage: I feel
intensely afraid of it; and I dont know what I shall do
with Barbara or what she will do with me. But I feel
that I and nobody else must marry her. Please regard
that as settled.—Not that I wish to be arbitrary; but
why should I waste your time in discussing what is
inevitable?

UNDERSHAFT: You mean that you will stick at nothing:
not even the conversion of the Salvation Army to the
worship of Dionysos.

CUSINS: The business of the Salvation Army is to save,
not to wrangle about the name of the pathfinder. Dionysos or another: what does it matter?

UNDERSHAFT (*rising and approaching him*): Professor
Cusins: you are a young man after my own heart.

CUSINS: Mr. Undershaft: you are, as far as I am able to
gather, a most infernal old rascal; but you appeal very
strongly to my sense of ironic humor.

(UNDERSHAFT *mutely offers his hand. They shake.*)

UNDERSHAFT (*suddenly concentrating himself*): And now
to business.

CUSINS: Pardon me. We were discussing religion. Why
go back to such an uninteresting and unimportant subject as business?

UNDERSHAFT: Religion is our business at present, because it is through religion alone that we can win
Barbara.

CUSINS: Have you, too, fallen in love with Barbara?

UNDERSHAFT: Yes, with a father's love.

CUSINS: A father's love for a grown-up daughter is the
most dangerous of all infatuations. I apologize for mentioning my own pale, coy, mistrustful fancy in the same
breath with it.

UNDERSHAFT: Keep to the point. We have to win her;
and we are neither of us Methodists.

CUSINS: That doesnt matter. The power Barbara wields

here—the power that wields Barbara herself—is not
Calvinism, not Presbyterianism, not Methodism—

UNDERSHAFT: Not Greek Paganism either, eh?

CUSINS: I admit that. Barbara is quite original in her
religion.

UNDERSHAFT (*triumphantly*): Aha! Barbara Undershaft
would be. Her inspiration comes from within herself.

CUSINS: How do you suppose it got there?

UNDERSHAFT (*in towering excitement*): It is the Undershaft inheritance. I shall hand on my torch to my
daughter. She shall make my converts and preach my
gospel—

CUSINS: What! Money and gunpowder!

UNDERSHAFT: Yes, money and gunpowder; freedom and
power; command of life and command of death.

CUSINS (*urbanely: trying to bring him down to earth*): This
is extremely interesting, Mr. Undershaft. Of course you
know that you are mad.

UNDERSHAFT (*with redoubled force*): And you?

CUSINS: Oh, mad as a hatter. You are welcome to my
secret since I have discovered yours. But I am astonished. Can a madman make cannons?

UNDERSHAFT: Would anyone else than a madman make
them? And now (*with surging energy*) question for question. Can a sane man translate Euripides?

CUSINS: No.

UNDERSHAFT (*seizing him by the shoulder*): Can a sane
woman make a man of a waster or a woman of a worm?

CUSINS (*reeling before the storm*): Father Colossus—
Mammoth Millionaire—

UNDERSHAFT (*pressing him*): Are there two mad people
or three in this Salvation shelter to-day?

CUSINS: You mean Barbara is as mad as we are!

UNDERSHAFT (*pushing him lightly off and resuming his
equanimity suddenly and completely*): Pooh, Professor! let us call things by their proper names. I am a
millionaire; you are a poet; Barbara is a savior of souls.
What have we three to do with the common mob of
slaves and idolaters? (*He sits down again with a shrug
of contempt for the mob.*)

CUSINS: Take care! Barbara is in love with the common people. So am I. Have you never felt the romance of that love?

UNDERSHAFT (*cold and sardonic*): Have you ever been in love with Poverty, like St. Francis? Have you ever been in love with Dirt, like St. Simeon? Have you ever been in love with disease and suffering, like our nurses and philanthropists? Such passions are not virtues, but the most unnatural of all the vices. This love of the common people may please an earl's granddaughter and a university professor; but I have been a common man and a poor man; and it has no romance for me. Leave it to the poor to pretend that poverty is a blessing: leave it to the coward to make a religion of his cowardice by preaching humility: we know better than that. We three must stand together above the common people: how else can we help their children to climb up beside us? Barbara must belong to us, not to the Salvation Army.

CUSINS: Well, I can only say that if you think you will get her away from the Salvation Army by talking to her as you have been talking to me, you dont know Barbara.

UNDERSHAFT: My friend: I never ask for what I can buy.

CUSINS (*in a white fury*): Do I understand you to imply that you can buy Barbara?

UNDERSHAFT: No; but I can buy the Salvation Army.

CUSINS: Quite impossible.

UNDERSHAFT: You shall see. All religious organizations exist by selling themselves to the rich.

CUSINS: Not the Army. That is the Church of the poor.

UNDERSHAFT: All the more reason for buying it.

CUSINS: I dont think you quite know what the Army does for the poor.

UNDERSHAFT: Oh yes I do. It draws their teeth: that is enough for me—as a man of business—

CUSINS: Nonsense. It makes them sober—

UNDERSHAFT: I prefer sober workmen. The profits are larger.

CUSINS: —honest—

UNDERSHAFT: Honest workmen are the most economical.

CUSINS: —attached to their homes—

UNDERSHAFT: So much the better: they will put up with anything sooner than change their shop.

CUSINS: —happy—

UNDERSHAFT: An invaluable safeguard against revolution.

CUSINS: —unselfish—

UNDERSHAFT: Indifferent to their own interests, which suits me exactly.

CUSINS: —with their thoughts on heavenly things—

UNDERSHAFT (*rising*): And not on Trade Unionism nor Socialism. Excellent.

CUSINS (*revolted*): You really are an infernal old rascal.

UNDERSHAFT (*indicating* PETER SHIRLEY, *who has just come from the shelter and strolled dejectedly down the yard between them*): And this is an honest man!

SHIRLEY: Yes; and what av I got by it? (*he passes on bitterly and sits on the form, in the corner of the penthouse*).

(SNOBBY PRICE, *beaming sanctimoniously,* and JENNY HILL, *with a tambourine full of coppers, come from the shelter and go to the drum, on which* JENNY *begins to count the money.*)

UNDERSHAFT (*replying to* SHIRLEY): Oh, your employers must have got a good deal by it from first to last. (*He sits on the table, with one foot on the side form.* CUSINS, *overwhelmed, sits down on the same form nearer the shelter.* BARBARA *comes from the shelter to the middle of the yard. She is excited and a little overwrought.*)

BARBARA: Weve just had a splendid experience meeting at the other gate in Cripps's lane. Ive hardly ever seen them so much moved as they were by your confession, Mr. Price.

PRICE: I could almost be glad of my past wickedness if I could believe that it would elp to keep hathers stright.

BARBARA: So it will, Snobby. How much, Jenny?

JENNY: Four and tenpence, Major.

BARBARA: Oh Snobby, if you had given your poor

mother just one more kick, we should have got the
whole five shillings!

PRICE: If she heard you say that, miss, she'd be sorry I
didnt. But I'm glad. Oh what a joy it will be to her
when she hears I'm saved!

UNDERSHAFT: Shall I contribute the odd twopence, Barbara? The millionaire's mite, eh? (*He takes a couple of
pennies from his pocket.*)

BARBARA: How did you make that twopence?

UNDERSHAFT: As usual. By selling cannons, torpedoes,
submarines, and my new patent Grand Duke hand
grenade.

BARBARA: Put it back in your pocket. You cant buy your
Salvation here for twopence: you must work it out.

UNDERSHAFT: Is twopence not enough? I can afford a
little more, if you press me.

BARBARA: Two million millions would not be enough.
There is bad blood on your hands; and nothing but good
blood can cleanse them. Money is no use. Take it away.
(*She turns to* CUSINS.) Dolly: you must write another
letter for me to the papers. (*He makes a wry face.*) Yes:
I know you dont like it; but it must be done. The starvation this winter is beating us: everybody is unemployed.
The General says we must close this shelter if we cant
get more money. I force the collections at the meetings
until I am ashamed: dont I, Snobby?

PRICE: It's a fair treat to see you work it, Miss. The way
you got them up from three-and-six to four-and-ten with
that hymn, penny by penny and verse by verse, was a
caution. Not a Cheap Jack on Mile End Waste could
touch you at it.

BARBARA: Yes; but I wish we could do without it. I am
getting at last to think more of the collection than of
the people's souls. And what are those hatfuls of pence
and halfpence? We want thousands! tens of thousands!
hundreds of thousands! I want to convert people, not to
be always begging for the Army in a way I'd die sooner
than beg for myself.

UNDERSHAFT (*in profound irony*): Genuine unselfishness
is capable of anything, my dear.

BARBARA (*unsuspectingly, as she turns away to take the money from the drum and put it in a cash bag she carries*):   Yes, isnt it? (UNDERSHAFT *looks sardonically at* CUSINS.)

CUSINS (*aside to* UNDERSHAFT):   Mephistopheles! Machiavelli!

BARBARA (*tears coming into her eyes as she ties the bag and pockets it*):   How are we to feed them? I cant talk religion to a man with bodily hunger in his eyes. (*Almost breaking down.*) It's frightful.

JENNY (*running to her*):   Major, dear—

BARBARA (*rebounding*):   No, dont comfort me. It will be all right. We shall get the money.

UNDERSHAFT: How?

JENNY: By praying for it, of course. Mrs. Baines says she prayed for it last night; and she has never prayed for it in vain: never once. (*She goes to the gate and looks out into the street.*)

BARBARA (*who has dried her eyes and regained her composure*):   By the way, dad, Mrs. Baines has come to march with us to our big meeting this afternoon; and she is very anxious to meet you, for some reason or other. Perhaps she'll convert you.

UNDERSHAFT: I shall be delighted, my dear.

JENNY (*at the gate: excitedly*):   Major! Major! heres that man back again.

BARBARA: What man?

JENNY: The man that hit me. Oh, I hope hes coming back to join us.

(BILL WALKER, *with frost on his jacket, comes through the gate, his hands deep in his pockets and his chin sunk between his shoulders, like a cleaned-out gambler. He halts between* BARBARA *and the drum.*)

BARBARA: Hullo, Bill! Back already!

BILL (*nagging at her*):   Bin talkin ever sence, av you?

BARBARA: Pretty nearly. Well, has Todger paid you out for poor Jenny's jaw?

BILL: No he aint.

BARBARA: I thought your jacket looked a bit snowy.

BILL: So it is snowy. You want to know where the snow come from, dont you?

BARBARA: Yes.

BILL: Well, it come from off the ground in Parkinses Corner in Kennintahn. It got rubbed off be my shoulders: see?

BARBARA: Pity you didnt rub some off with your knees, Bill! That would have done you a lot of good.

BILL (*with sour mirthless humor*): I was saving another man's knees at the time. E was kneelin on my ed, so e was.

JENNY: Who was kneeling on your head?

BILL: Todger was. E was prayin for me: prayin comfortable with me as a carpet. So was Mog. So was the ole bloomin meetin. Mog she sez "O Lord break is stubborn spirit; but dont urt is dear art." That was wot she said. "Don't urt is dear art"! An er bloke—thirteen stun four!—kneelin wiv all is weight on me. Funny, aint it?

JENNY: Oh no. We're so sorry, Mr. Walker.

BARBARA (*enjoying it frankly*): Nonsense! of course it's funny. Served you right, Bill! You must have done something to him first.

BILL (*doggedly*): I did wot I said I'd do. I spit in is eye. E looks up at the sky and sez, "O that I should be fahnd worthy to be spit upon for the gospel's sake!" e sez; an Mog sez "Glory Allelloolier!"; and then e called me Brother, an dahned me as if I was a kid and e was me mother washin me a Setterda nawt. I adnt just no show wiv im at all. Arf the street prayed; an the tother arf larfed fit to split theirselves. (*To* BARBARA.) There! are you settisfawd nah?

BARBARA (*her eyes dancing*): Wish I'd been there, Bill.

BILL: Yes: youd a got in a hextra bit o talk on me, wouldnt you?

JENNY: I'm so sorry, Mr. Walker.

BILL (*fiercely*): Dont you go bein sorry for me: youve no call. Listen ere. I broke your jawr.

JENNY: No, it didnt hurt me: indeed it didnt, except for a moment. It was only that I was frightened.

BILL: I dont want to be forgive be you, or be ennybody. Wot I did I'll pay for. I tried to get me own jawr broke to settisfaw you—

JENNY (*distressed*): Oh no—

BILL (*impatiently*): Tell y'I did: cawnt you listen to wots bein told you? All I got be it was bein made a sight of in the public street for me pains. Well, if I cawnt settisfaw you one way, I can another. Listen ere! I ad two quid saved agen the frost; and Ive a pahnd of it left. A mate o mine last week ad words with the judy e's goin to marry. E give er wot-for; an e's bin fined fifteen bob. E ad a right to it er because they was goin to be marrid; but I adnt no right to it you; so put anather fawv bob on an call it a pahnd's worth. (*He produces a sovereign.*) Eres the money. Takc it; and lets av no more o your forgivin an prayin and your Major jawrin me. Let wot I done be done and paid for; and let there be a end of it.

JENNY: Oh, I couldnt take it, Mr. Walker. But if you would give a shilling or two to poor Rummy Mitchens! you really did hurt her; and shes old.

BILL (*contemptuously*): Not likely. I'd give her anather as soon as look at er. Let her av the lawr o me as she threatened! She aint forgiven me: not mach. Wot I done to er is not on me mawnd—wot she (*indicating* BARBARA) might call on me conscience—no more than stickin a pig. It's this Christian game o yours that I wont av played agen me: this bloomin forgivin an naggin an jawrin that makes a man that sore that iz lawf's a burdn to im. I wont av it, I tell you; so take your money and stop throwin your silly bashed face hup agen me.

JENNY: Major: may I take a little of it for the Army?

BARBARA: No: the Army is not to be bought. We want your soul, Bill; and we'll takc nothing less.

BILL (*bitterly*): I know. It aint enough. Me an me few shillins is not good enough for you. Youre a earl's grendorter, you are. Nothin less than a underd pahnd for you.

UNDERSHAFT: Come, Barbara! you could do a great deal of good with a hundred pounds. If you will set this gentleman's mind at ease by taking his pound, I will give the other ninety-nine. (BILL, *astounded by such opulence, instinctively touches his cap.*)

BARBARA: Oh, youre too extravagant, papa. Bill offers twenty pieces of silver. All you need offer is the other ten. That will make the standard price to buy anybody who's for sale. I'm not; and the Army's not. (*To* BILL.) Youll never have another quiet moment, Bill, until you come round to us. You cant stand out against your salvation.

BILL (*sullenly*): I cawnt stend aht agen music-all wrastlers and artful tongued women. Ive offered to pay. I can do no more. Take it or leave it. There it is. (*He throws the sovereign on the drum, and sits down on the horse-trough. The coin fascinates* SNOBBY PRICE, *who takes an early opportunity of dropping his cap on it.*)

(MRS. BAINES *comes from the shelter. She is dressed as a Salvation Army Commissioner. She is an earnest looking woman of about 40, with a caressing, urgent voice, and an appealing manner.*)

BARBARA: This is my father, Mrs. Baines. (UNDERSHAFT *comes from the table, taking his hat off with marked civility.*) Try what you can do with him. He wont listen to me, because he remembers what a fool I was when I was a baby. (*She leaves them together and chats with* JENNY.)

MRS. BAINES: Have you been shewn over the shelter, Mr. Undershaft? You know the work we're doing, of course.

UNDERSHAFT (*very civilly*): The whole nation knows it, Mrs. Baines.

MRS. BAINES: No, sir: the whole nation does not know it, or we should not be crippled as we are for want of money to carry our work through the length and breadth of the land. Let me tell you that there would have been rioting this winter in London but for us.

UNDERSHAFT: You really think so?

MRS. BAINES: I know it. I remember 1886, when you rich gentlemen hardened your hearts against the cry of the poor. They broke the windows of your clubs in Pall Mall.

UNDERSHAFT (*gleaming with approval of their method*):   And the Mansion House Fund went up next day from thirty thousand pounds to seventy-nine thousand! I remember quite well.

MRS. BAINES: Well, wont you help me to get at the people? They wont break windows then. Come here, Price. Let me shew you to this gentleman (PRICE *comes to be inspected*). Do you remember the window breaking?

PRICE: My ole father thought it was the revolution, maam.

MRS. BAINES: Would you break windows now?

PRICE: Oh no maam. The windows of eaven av bin opened to me. I know now that the rich man is a sinner like myself.

RUMMY (*appearing above at the loft door*):   Snobby Price!

SNOBBY: Wot is it?

RUMMY: Your mother's askin for you at the other gate in Crippses Lane. She's heard about your confession (PRICE *turns pale*).

MRS. BAINES: Go, Mr. Price; and pray with her.

JENNY: You can go through the shelter, Snobby.

PRICE (*to* MRS. BAINES):   I couldnt face her now, maam, with all the weight of my sins fresh on me. Tell her she'll find her son at ome, waitin for her in prayer.

(*He skulks off through the gate, incidentally stealing the sovereign on his way out by picking up his cap from the drum.*)

MRS. BAINES (*with swimming eyes*):   You see how we take the anger and the bitterness against you out of their hearts, Mr. Undershaft.

UNDERSHAFT: It is certainly most convenient and gratifying to all large employers of labor, Mrs. Baines.

MRS. BAINES: Barbara: Jenny: I have good news: most wonderful news. (JENNY *runs to her.*) My prayers have been answered. I told you they would, Jenny, didn't I?

JENNY: Yes, yes.

BARBARA (*moving nearer to the drum*): Have we got money enough to keep the shelter open?

MRS. BAINES: I hope we shall have enough to keep all the shelters open. Lord Saxmundham has promised us five thousand pounds—

BARBARA: Hooray!

JENNY: Glory!

MRS. BAINES: —if—

BARBARA: "If!" If what?

MRS. BAINES: —if five other gentlemen will give a thousand each to make it up to ten thousand.

BARBARA: Who is Lord Saxmundham? I never heard of him.

UNDERSHAFT (*who has pricked up his ears at the peer's name, and is now watching* BARBARA *curiously*): A new creation, my dear. You have heard of Sir Horace Bodger?

BARBARA: Bodger! Do you mean the distiller? Bodger's whisky!

UNDERSHAFT: That is the man. He is one of the greatest of our public benefactors. He restored the cathedral at Hakington. They made him a baronet for that. He gave half a million to the funds of his party: they made him a baron for that.

SHIRLEY: What will they give him for the five thousand?

UNDERSHAFT: There is nothing left to give him. So the five thousand, I should think, is to save his soul.

MRS. BAINES: Heaven grant it may! Oh Mr. Undershaft, you have some very rich friends. Cant you help us towards the other five thousand? We are going to hold a great meeting this afternoon at the Assembly Hall in the Mile End Road. If I could only announce that one gentleman had come forward to support Lord Saxmundham, others would follow. Dont you know somebody? couldnt you? wouldnt you? (*her eyes fill with tears*) oh,

think of those poor people, Mr. Undershaft: think of
how much it means to them, and how little to a great
man like you.

UNDERSHAFT (*sardonically gallant*):   Mrs. Baines: you
are irresistible. I cant disappoint you; and I cant deny
myself the satisfaction of making Bodger pay up. You
shall have your five thousand pounds.

MRS. BAINES: Thank God!

UNDERSHAFT: You dont thank me?

MRS. BAINES: Oh sir, dont try to be cynical: dont be
ashamed of being a good man. The Lord will bless
you abundantly; and our prayers will be like a strong
fortification round you all the days of your life. (*With
a touch of caution.*) You will let me have the cheque
to shew at the meeting, wont you? Jenny: go in and
fetch a pen and ink. (JENNY *runs to the shelter door.*)

UNDERSHAFT: Do not disturb Miss Hill: I have a fountain
pen. (JENNY *halts. He sits at the table and writes the
cheque.* CUSINS *rises to make more room for him. They
all watch him silently.*)

BILL (*cynically, aside to* BARBARA, *his voice and accent
horribly debased*):   Wot prawce Selvytion nah?

BARBARA: Stop. (UNDERSHAFT *stops writing: they all
turn to her in surprise.*) Mrs. Baines: are you really
going to take this money?

MRS. BAINES (*astonished*):   Why not, dear?

BARBARA: Why not! Do you know what my father is?
Have you forgotten that Lord Saxmundham is Bodger
the whisky man? Do you remember how we implored
the County Council to stop him from writing Bodger's
Whisky in letters of fire against the sky; so that the poor
drink-ruined creatures on the embankment could not
wake up from their snatches of sleep without being re-
minded of their deadly thirst by that wicked sky sign?
Do you know that the worst thing I have had to fight
here is not the devil, but Bodger, Bodger, Bodger, with
his whisky, his distilleries, and his tied houses? Are you
going to make our shelter another tied house for him,
and ask me to keep it?

BILL: Rotten drunken whisky it is too.

MRS. BAINES: Dear Barbara: Lord Saxmundham has a soul to be saved like any of us. If heaven has found the way to make a good use of his money, are we to set ourselves up against the answer to our prayers?

BARBARA: I know he has a soul to be saved. Let him come down here; and I'll do my best to help him to his salvation. But he wants to send his cheque down to buy us, and go on being as wicked as ever.

UNDERSHAFT (*with a reasonableness which* CUSINS *alone perceives to be ironical*):   My dear Barbara: alcohol is a very necessary article. It heals the sick—

BARBARA: It does nothing of the sort.

UNDERSHAFT: Well, it assists the doctor: that is perhaps a less questionable way of putting it. It makes life bearable to millions of people who could not endure their existence if they were quite sober. It enables Parliament to do things at eleven at night that no sane person would do at eleven in the morning. Is it Bodger's fault that this inestimable gift is deplorably abused by less than one per cent of the poor? (*He turns again to the table; signs the cheque; and crosses it.*)

MRS. BAINES: Barbara: will there be less drinking or more if all those poor souls we are saving come tomorrow and find the doors of our shelters shut in their faces? Lord Saxmundham gives us the money to stop drinking—to take his own business from him.

CUSINS (*impishly*):   Pure self-sacrifice on Bodger's part, clearly! Bless dear Bodger! (BARBARA *almost breaks down as* ADOLPHUS, *too, fails her.*)

UNDERSHAFT (*tearing out the cheque and pocketing the book as he rises and goes past* CUSINS *to* MRS. BAINES):   I also, Mrs. Baines, may claim a little disinterestedness. Think of my business! think of the widows and orphans! the men and lads torn to pieces with shrapnel and poisoned with lyddite (MRS. BAINES *shrinks; but he goes on remorsely*)! the oceans of blood, not one drop of which is shed in a really just cause! the ravaged crops! the peaceful peasants forced,

women and men, to till their fields under the fire of
opposing armies on pain of starvation! the bad blood of
the fierce little cowards at home who egg on others to
fight for the gratification of their national vanity! All
this makes money for me: I am never richer, never
busier than when the papers are full of it. Well, it is
your work to preach peace on earth and goodwill to
men. (MRS. BAINES'S *face lights up again.*) Every
convert you make is a vote against war. (*Her lips move
in prayer.*) Yet I give you this money to help you to
hasten my own commercial ruin. (*He gives her the
cheque.*)

CUSINS (*mounting the form in an ecstasy of mischief*):
The millennium will be inaugurated by the unselfishness
of Undershaft and Bodger. Oh be joyful! (*He takes the
drumsticks from his pockets and flourishes them.*)

MRS. BAINES (*taking the cheque*):   The longer I live the
more proof I see that there is an Infinite Goodness that
turns everything to the work of salvation sooner or later.
Who would have thought that any good could have
come out of war and drink? And yet their profits are
brought today to the feet of salvation to do its blessed
work. (*She is affected to tears.*)

JENNY (*running to MRS. BAINES and throwing her arms
round her*):   Oh dear! how blessed, how glorious it all
is!

CUSINS (*in a convulsion of irony*):   Let us seize this unspeakable moment. Let us march to the great meeting
at once. Excuse me just an instant. (*He rushes into
the shelter. JENNY takes her tambourine from the drum
head.*)

MRS. BAINES: Mr. Undershaft: have you ever seen a
thousand people fall on their knees with one impulse
and pray? Come with us to the meeting. Barbara shall
tell them that the Army is saved, and saved through
you.

CUSINS (*returning impetuously from the shelter with a flag
and a trombone, and coming between MRS. BAINES and
UNDERSHAFT*):   You shall carry the flag down the first

street, Mrs. Baines (*he gives her the flag*). Mr. Undershaft is a gifted trombonist: he shall intone an Olympian diapason to the West Ham Salvation March. (*Aside to* UNDERSHAFT, *as he forces the trombone on him.*) Blow, Machiavelli, blow.

UNDERSHAFT (*aside to him, as he takes the trombone*): The trumpet in Zion! (CUSINS *rushes to the drum, which he takes up and puts on.* UNDERSHAFT *continues, aloud*) I will do my best. I could vamp a bass if I knew the tune.

CUSINS: It is a wedding chorus from one of Donizetti's operas; but we have converted it. We convert everything to good here, including Bodger. You remember the chorus. "For thee immense rejoicing—immenso giubilo—immenso giubilo." (*With drum obbligato.*) Rum tum ti tum tum, tum tum ti ta—

BARBARA: Dolly: you are breaking my heart.

CUSINS: What is a broken heart more or less here? Dionysos Undershaft has descended. I am possessed.

MRS. BAINES: Come, Barbara: I must have my dear Major to carry the flag with me.

JENNY: Yes, yes, Major darling.

CUSINS (*snatches the tambourine out of* JENNY'S *hand and mutely offers it to* BARBARA).

BARBARA (*coming forward a little as she puts the offer behind her with a shudder, whilst* CUSINS *recklessly tosses the tambourine back to* JENNY *and goes to the gate*): I cant come.

JENNY: Not come!

MRS. BAINES (*with tears in her eyes*):   Barbara: do you think I am wrong to take the money?

BARBARA (*impulsively going to her and kissing her*):   No, no: God help you, dear, you must: you are saving the Army. Go; and may you have a great meeting!

JENNY: But arnt you coming?

BARBARA: No. (*She begins taking off the silver S brooch from her collar.*)

MRS. BAINES: Barbara: what are you doing?

JENNY: Why are you taking your badge off? You cant be going to leave us, Major.

BARBARA (*quietly*):   Father: come here.

UNDERSHAFT (*coming to her*):   My dear! (*Seeing that she is going to pin the badge on his collar, he retreats to the penthouse in some alarm.*)

BARBARA (*following him*):   Dont be frightened. (*She pins the badge on and steps back towards the table, shewing him to the others.*) There! It's not much for £5000, is it?

MRS. BAINES: Barbara: if you wont come and pray with us, promise me you will pray for us.

BARBARA: I cant pray now. Perhaps I shall never pray again.

MRS. BAINES: Barbara!

JENNY: Major!

BARBARA (*almost delirious*):   I cant bear any more. Quick march!

CUSINS (*calling to the procession in the street outside*):   Off we go. Play up, there! Immenso giubilo. (*He gives the time with his drum; and the band strikes up the march, which rapidly becomes more distant as the procession moves briskly away.*)

MRS. BAINES: I must go, dear. Youre overworked: you will be all right tomorrow. We'll never lose you. Now Jenny: step out with the old flag. Blood and Fire!

(*She marches out through the gate with her flag.*)

JENNY: Glory Hallelujah! (*flourishing her tambourine and marching*).

UNDERSHAFT (*to CUSINS, as he marches out past him easing the slide of his trombone*).   "My ducats and my daughter"!

CUSINS (*follwing him out*):   Money and gunpowder!

BARBARA: Drunkenness and Murder! My God: why hast thou forsaken me?

(*She sinks on the form with her face buried in her hands. The march passes away into silence. BILL WALKER steals across to her.*)

BILL (*taunting*):   Wot prawce Selvytion nah?

SHIRLEY: Dont you hit her when shes down.

BILL: She it me wen aw wiz dahn. Waw shouldnt I git
a bit o me own back?

BARBARA (*raising her head*):   I didnt take your money,
Bill. (*She crosses the yard to the gate and turns her
back on the two men to hide her face from them.*)

BILL (*sneering after her*):   Naow, it warnt enough for
you. (*Turning to the drum, he misses the money.*)
Ellow! If you aint took it summun else az. Weres it
gorn? Blame me if Jenny Ill didnt take it arter all!

RUMMY (*screaming at him from the loft*):   You lie, you
dirty blackguard! Snobby Price pinched it off the drum
wen e took ap iz cap. I was ap ere all the time an see
im do it.

BILL: Wot! Stowl maw money! Waw didnt you call thief
on him, you silly old mucker you?

RUMMY: To serve you aht for ittin me acrost the fice.
It's cost y'pahnd, that az. (*Raising a pæan of squalid
triumph.*) I done you. I'm even with you. Ive ad it aht
o y— (BILL *snatches up* SHIRLEY'S *mug and hurls it at
her. She slams the loft door and vanishes. The mug
smashes against the door and falls in fragments.*)

BILL (*beginning to chuckle*):   Tell us, ole man, wot
o'clock this mornin was it wen im as they call Snobby
Prawce was sived?

BARBARA (*turning to him more composedly, and with un-
spoiled sweetness*):   About half past twelve, Bill. And
he pinched your pound at a quarter to two. *I* know.
Well, you cant afford to lose it. I'll send it to you.

BILL (*his voice and accent suddenly improving*):   Not if I
was to starve for it. *I* aint to be bought.

SHIRLEY: Aint you? Youd sell yourself to the devil for a
pint o beer; ony there aint no devil to make the offer.

BILL (*unshamed*):   So I would, mate, and often av, cheerful. But she cawnt buy me. (*Approaching* BARBARA.)
You wanted my soul, did you? Well, you aint got it.

BARBARA: I nearly got it, Bill. But weve sold it back to
you for ten thousand pounds.

SHIRLEY: And dear at the money!

BARBARA: No, Peter: it was worth more than money.

BILL (*salvationproof*): It's no good: you cawnt get rahnd me nah. I dont blieve in it; and Ive seen today that I was right. (*Going.*) So long, old soupkitchener! Ta, ta, Major Earl's Grendorter! (*Turning at the gate.*) Wot prawce Selvytion nah? Snobby Prawce! Ha! ha!

BARBARA (*offering her hand*): Goodbye, Bill.

BILL (*taken aback, half plucks his cap off; then shoves it on again defiantly*): Git aht. (BARBARA *drops her hand, discouraged. He has a twinge of remorse.*) But thets aw rawt, you knaow. Nathink pasnl. Naow mellice. So long, Judy. (*He goes.*)

BARBARA: No malice. So long, Bill.

SHIRLEY (*shaking his head*): You make too much of him, Miss, in your innocence.

BARBARA (*going to him*): Peter: I'm like you now. Cleaned out, and lost my job.

SHIRLEY: Youve youth an hope. Thats two better than me.

BARBARA: I'll get you a job, Peter. Thats hope for you: the youth will have to be enough for me. (*She counts her money.*) I have just enough left for two teas at Lockharts, a Rowton doss for you, and my tram and bus home. (*He frowns and rises with offended pride. She takes his arm.*) Dont be proud, Peter: it's sharing between friends. And promise me youll talk to me and not let me cry. (*She draws him towards the gate.*)

SHIRLEY: Well, I'm not accustomed to talk to the like of you—

BARBARA (*urgently*): Yes, yes: you must talk to me. Tell me about Tom Paine's books and Bradlaugh's lectures. Come along.

SHIRLEY: Ah, if you would only read Tom Paine in the proper spirit, Miss! (*They go out through the gate together.*)

END OF ACT II

Act III

(*Next day after lunch* LADY BRITOMART *is writing in the library in Wilton Crescent.* SARAH *is reading in the armchair near the window.* BARBARA, *in ordinary dress, pale and brooding, is on the settee.* CHARLES LOMAX *enters. Coming forward between the settee and the writing table, he starts on seeing* BARBARA *fashionably attired and in low spirits.*)

LOMAX: Youve left off your uniform!

(BARBARA *says nothing; but an expression of pain passes over her face.*)

LADY BRITOMART (*warning him in low tones to be careful*):   Charles!

LOMAX (*much concerned, sitting down sympathetically on the settee beside* BARBARA):   I'm awfully sorry, Barbara. You know I helped you all I could with the concertina and so forth. (*Momentously.*) Still, I have never shut my eyes to the fact that there is a certain amount of tosh about the Salvation Army. Now the claims of the Church of England—

LADY BRITOMART: Thats enough, Charles. Speak of something suited to your mental capacity.

LOMAX: But surely the Church of England is suited to all our capacities.

BARBARA (*pressing his hand*):   Thank you for your sympathy, Cholly. Now go and spoon with Sarah.

LOMAX (*rising and going to* SARAH):   How is my ownest today?

SARAH: I wish you wouldnt tell Cholly to do things, Bar-

109

bara. He always comes straight and does them. Cholly: we're going to the works at Perivale St. Andrews this afternoon.

LOMAX: What works?

SARAH: The cannon works.

LOMAX: What! Your governor's shop!

SARAH: Yes.

LOMAX: Oh I say!

(CUSINS *enters in poor condition. He also starts visibly when he sees* BARBARA *without her uniform.*)

BARBARA: I expected you this morning, Dolly. Didnt you guess that?

CUSINS (*sitting down beside her*): I'm sorry. I have only just breakfasted.

SARAH: But weve just finished lunch.

BARBARA: Have you had one of your bad nights?

CUSINS: No: I had rather a good night: in fact, one of the most remarkable nights I have ever passed.

BARBARA: The meeting?

CUSINS: No: after the meeting.

LADY BRITOMART: You should have gone to bed after the meeting. What were you doing?

CUSINS: Drinking.

LADY BRITOMART:	Adolphus!
SARAH:	Dolly!
BARBARA:	Dolly!
LOMAX:	Oh I say!

LADY BRITOMART: What were you drinking, may I ask?

CUSINS: A most devilish kind of Spanish burgundy, warranted free from added alcohol: a Temperance burgundy in fact. Its richness in natural alcohol made any addition superfluous.

BARBARA: Are you joking, Dolly?

CUSINS (*patiently*): No. I have been making a night of it with the nominal head of this household: that is all.

LADY BRITOMART: Andrew made you drunk!

CUSINS: No: he only provided the wine. I think it was

Dionysos who made me drunk. (*To* BARBARA.) I told you I was possessed.

LADY BRITOMART: Youre not sober yet. Go home to bed at once.

CUSINS: I have never before ventured to reproach you, Lady Brit; but how could you marry the Prince of Darkness?

LADY BRITOMART: It was much more excusable to marry him than to get drunk with him. That is a new accomplishment of Andrew's, by the way. He usent to drink.

CUSINS: He doesnt now. He only sat there and completed the wreck of my moral basis, the rout of my convictions, the purchase of my soul. He cares for you, Barbara. That is what makes him so dangerous to me.

BARBARA: That has nothing to do with it, Dolly. There are larger loves and diviner dreams than the fireside ones. You know that, dont you?

CUSINS: Yes: that is our understanding. I know it. I hold to it. Unless he can win me on that holier ground he may amuse me for a while; but he can get no deeper hold, strong as he is.

BARBARA: Keep to that; and the end will be right. Now tell me what happened at the meeting?

CUSINS: It was an amazing meeting. Mrs. Baines almost died of emotion. Jenny Hill went stark mad with hysteria. The Prince of Darkness played his trombone like a madman: its brazen roarings were like the laughter of the damned. 117 conversions took place then and there. They prayed with the most touching sincerity and gratitude for Bodger, and for the anonymous donor of the £5000. Your father would not let his name be given.

LOMAX: That was rather fine of the old man, you know. Most chaps would have wanted the advertisement.

CUSINS: He said all the charitable institutions would be down on him like kites on a battle field if he gave his name.

LADY BRITOMART: Thats Andrew all over. He never does a proper thing without giving an improper reason for it.

CUSINS: He convinced me that I have all my life been doing improper things for proper reasons.

LADY BRITOMART: Adolphus: now that Barbara has left the Salvation Army, you had better leave it too. I will not have you playing that drum in the streets.

CUSINS: Your orders are already obeyed, Lady Brit.

BARBARA: Dolly: were you ever really in earnest about it? Would you have joined if you had never seen me?

CUSINS (*disingenuously*):   Well—er—well, possibly, as a collector of religions—

LOMAX (*cunningly*):   Not as a drummer, though, you know. You are a very clearheaded brainy chap, Cholly; and it must have been apparent to you that there is a certain amount of tosh about—

LADY BRITOMART: Charles: if you must drivel, drivel like a grown-up man and not like a schoolboy.

LOMAX (*out of countenance*):   Well, drivel is drivel, dont you know, whatever a man's age.

LADY BRITOMART: In good society in England, Charles, men drivel at all ages by repeating silly formulas with an air of wisdom. Schoolboys make their own formulas out of slang, like you. When they reach your age, and get political private secretaryships and things of that sort, they drop slang and get their formulas out of The Spectator or The Times. You had better confine yourself to The Times. You will find that there is a certain amount of tosh about The Times; but at least its language is reputable.

LOMAX (*overwhelmed*):   You are so awfully strong-minded, Lady Brit—

LADY BRITOMART: Rubbish! (MORRISON *comes in*.) What is it?

MORRISON: If you please, my lady, Mr. Undershaft has just drove up to the door.

LADY BRITOMART: Well, let him in. (MORRISON *hesitates*.) Whats the matter with you?

MORRISON: Shall I announce him, my lady; or is he at home here, so to speak, my lady?

LADY BRITOMART: Announce him.

MORRISON: Thank you, my lady. You wont mind my asking, I hope. The occasion is in a manner of speaking new to me.

LADY BRITOMART: Quite right. Go and let him in.

MORRISON: Thank you, my lady. (*He withdraws.*)

LADY BRITOMART: Children: go and get ready. (SARAH *and* BARBARA *go upstairs for their out-of-door wraps.*) Charles: go and tell Stephen to come down here in five minutes: you will find him in the drawing room. (CHARLES *goes.*) Adolphus: tell them to send round the carriage in about fifteen minutes. (ADOLPHUS *goes.*)

MORRISON (*at the door*):   Mr. Undershaft.

(UNDERSHAFT *comes in.* MORRISON *goes out.*)

UNDERSHAFT: Alone! How fortunate!

LADY BRITOMART (*rising*):   Dont be sentimental, Andrew. Sit down. (*She sits on the settee: he sits beside her, on her left. She comes to the point before he has time to breathe.*) Sarah must have £800 a year until Charles Lomax comes into his property. Barbara will need more, and need it permanently, because Adolphus hasnt any property.

UNDERSHAFT (*resignedly*):   Yes, my dear: I will see to it. Anything else? for yourself, for instance?

LADY BRITOMART: I want to talk to you about Stephen.

UNDERSHAFT (*rather wearily*):   Dont, my dear. Stephen doesnt interest me.

LADY BRITOMART: He does interest me. He is our son.

UNDERSHAFT: Do you really think so? He has induced us to bring him into the world; but he chose his parents very incongruously, I think. I see nothing of myself in him, and less of you.

LADY BRITOMART: Andrew: Stephen is an excellent son, and a most steady, capable, highminded young man. You are simply trying to find an excuse for disinheriting him.

UNDERSHAFT: My dear Biddy: the Undershaft tradition disinherits him. It would be dishonest of me to leave the cannon foundry to my son.

LADY BRITOMART: It would be most unnatural and improper of you to leave it anyone else, Andrew. Do you suppose this wicked and immoral tradition can be kept up for ever? Do you pretend that Stephen could not carry on the foundry just as well as all the other sons of the big business houses?

UNDERSHAFT: Yes: he could learn the office routine without understanding the business, like all the other sons; and the firm would go on by its own momentum until the real Undershaft—probably an Italian or a German—would invent a new method and cut him out.

LADY BRITOMART: There is nothing that any Italian or German could do that Stephen could not do. And Stephen at least has breeding.

UNDERSHAFT: The son of a foundling! nonsense!

LADY BRITOMART: My son, Andrew! And even you may have good blood in your veins for all you know.

UNDERSHAFT: True. Probably I have. That is another argument in favor of a foundling.

LADY BRITOMART: Andrew: dont be aggravating. And dont be wicked. At present you are both.

UNDERSHAFT: This conversation is part of the Undershaft tradition, Biddy. Every Undershaft's wife has treated him to it ever since the house was founded. It is mere waste of breath. If the tradition be ever broken it will be for an abler man than Stephen.

LADY BRITOMART (*pouting*): Then go away.

UNDERSHAFT (*deprecatory*): Go away!

LADY BRITOMART: Yes: go away. If you will do nothing for Stephen, you are not wanted here. Go to your foundling, whoever he is; and look after him.

UNDERSHAFT: The fact is, Biddy—

LADY BRITOMART: Dont call me Biddy. I dont call you Andy.

UNDERSHAFT: I will not call my wife Britomart: it is not good sense. Seriously, my love, the Undershaft tradition has landed me in a difficulty. I am getting on in years; and my partner Lazarus has at last made a stand and insisted that the succession must be settled one way or the other; and of course he is quite right. You see, I havnt found a fit successor yet.

LADY BRITOMART (*obstinately*):   There is Stephen.

UNDERSHAFT: Thats just it: all the foundlings I can find are exactly like Stephen.

LADY BRITOMART: Andrew!!

UNDERSHAFT: I want a man with no relations and no schooling: that is, a man who would be out of the running altogether if he were not a strong man. And I cant find him. Every blessed foundling nowadays is snapped up in his infancy by Barnardo homes, or School Board officers, or Boards of Guardians; and if he shews the least ability, he is fastened on by schoolmasters; trained to win scholarships like a racehorse; crammed with secondhand ideas; drilled and disciplined in docility and what they call good taste; and lamed for life so that he is fit for nothing but teaching. If you want to keep the foundry in the family, you had better find an eligible foundling and marry him to Barbara.

LADY BRITOMART: Ah! Barbara! Your pet! You would sacrifice Stephen to Barbara.

UNDERSHAFT: Cheerfully. And you, my dear, would boil Barbara to make soup for Stephen.

LADY BRITOMART: Andrew: this is not a question of our likings and dislikings: it is a question of duty. It is your duty to make Stephen your successor.

UNDERSHAFT: Just as much as it is your duty to submit to your husband. Come, Biddy! these tricks of the governing class are of no use with me. I am one of the governing class myself; and it is waste of time giving tracts to a missionary. I have the power in this matter; and I am not to be humbugged into using it for your purposes.

LADY BRITOMART: Andrew: you can talk my head off; but you cant change wrong into right. And your tie is all on one side. Put it straight.

UNDERSHAFT (*disconcerted*):   It wont stay unless it's pinned— (*he fumbles at it with childish grimaces*).

(STEPHEN *comes in.*)

STEPHEN (*at the door*): I beg your pardon (*about to retire*).

LADY BRITOMART: No: come in, Stephen. (STEPHEN *comes forward to his mother's writing table.*)

UNDERSHAFT (*not very cordially*): Good afternoon.

STEPHEN (*coldly*): Good afternoon.

UNDERSHAFT (*to* LADY BRITOMART): He knows all about the tradition, I suppose?

LADY BRITOMART: Yes. (*To* STEPHEN.) It is what I told you last night, Stephen.

UNDERSHAFT (*sulkily*): I understand you want to come into the cannon business.

STEPHEN: *I* go into trade! Certainly not.

UNDERSHAFT (*opening his eyes, greatly eased in mind and manner*): Oh! in that case—!

LADY BRITOMART: Cannons are not trade, Stephen. They are enterprise.

STEPHEN: I have no intention of becoming a man of business in any sense. I have no capacity for business and no taste for it. I intend to devote myself to politics.

UNDERSHAFT (*rising*): My dear boy: this is an immense relief to me. And I trust it may prove an equally good thing for the country. I was afraid you would consider yourself disparaged and slighted. (*He moves towards* STEPHEN *as if to shake hands with him.*)

LADY BRITOMART (*rising and interposing*): Stephen: I cannot allow you to throw away an enormous property like this.

STEPHEN (*stiffly*): Mother: there must be an end of treating me as a child, if you please. (LADY BRITOMART *recoils, deeply wounded by his tone.*) Until last night I did not take your attitude seriously, because I did not think you meant it seriously. But I find now that you left me in the dark as to matters which you should have explained to me years ago. I am extremely hurt and offended. Any further discussion of my intentions had better take place with my father, as between one man and another.

LADY BRITOMART: Stephen! (*She sits down again; and her eyes fill with tears.*)

UNDERSHAFT (*with grave compassion*): You see, my dear, it is only the big men who can be treated as children.

STEPHEN: I am sorry, mother, that you have forced me—

UNDERSHAFT (*stopping him*): Yes, yes, yes, yes: thats all right, Stephen. She wont interfere with you any more: your independence is achieved: you have won your latchkey. Dont rub it in; and above all, dont apologize. (*He resumes his seat.*) Now what about your future, as between one man and another—I beg your pardon, Biddy: as between two men and a woman.

LADY BRITOMART (*who has pulled herself together strongly*): I quite understand, Stephen. By all means go your own way if you feel strong enough. (STEPHEN *sits down magisterially in the chair at the writing table with an air of affirming his majority.*)

UNDERSHAFT: It is settled that you do not ask for the succession to the cannon business.

STEPHEN: I hope it is settled that I repudiate the cannon business.

UNDERSHAFT: Come, come! dont be so devilishly sulky: it's boyish. Freedom should be generous. Besides, I owe you a fair start in life in exchange for disinheriting you. You cant become prime minister all at once. Havnt you a turn for something? What about literature, art and so forth?

STEPHEN: I have nothing of the artist about me, either in faculty or character, thank Heaven!

UNDERSHAFT: A philosopher, perhaps? Eh?

STEPHEN: I make no such ridiculous pretension.

UNDERSHAFT: Just so. Well, there is the army, the navy, the Church, the Bar. The Bar requires some ability. What about the Bar?

STEPHEN: I have not studied law. And I am afraid I have not the necessary push—I believe that is the name barristers give to their vulgarity—for success in pleading.

UNDERSHAFT: Rather a difficult case, Stephen. Hardly anything left but the stage, is there? (STEPHEN *makes*

an impatient movement.) Well, come! is there anything
you know or care for?

STEPHEN (*rising and looking at him steadily*):   I know the
difference between right and wrong.

UNDERSHAFT (*hugely tickled*):   You dont say so! What!
no capacity for business, no knowledge of law, no sympathy with art, no pretension to philosophy; only a
simple knowledge of the secret that has puzzled all
the philosophers, baffled all the lawyers, muddled all
the men of business, and ruined most of the artists: the
secret of right and wrong. Why, man, youre a genius,
a master of masters, a god! At twenty-four, too!

STEPHEN (*keeping his temper with difficulty*):   You are
pleased to be facetious. I pretend to nothing more than
any honorable English gentleman claims as his birthright
(*he sits down angrily*).

UNDERSHAFT: Oh, thats everybody's birthright. Look at
poor little Jenny Hill, the Salvation lassie! she would
think you were laughing at her if you asked her to stand
up in the street and teach grammar or geography or
mathematics or even drawingroom dancing; but it never
occurs to her to doubt that she can teach morals and
religion. You are all alike, you respectable people. You
cant tell me the bursting strain of a ten-inch gun, which
is a very simple matter; but you all think you can tell
me the bursting strain of a man under temptation. You
darent handle high explosives; but youre all ready to
handle honesty and truth and justice and the whole duty
of man, and kill one another at that game. What a
country! what a world!

LADY BRITOMART (*uneasily*):   What do you think he had
better do, Andrew?

UNDERSHAFT: Oh, just what he wants to do. He knows
nothing; and he thinks he knows everything. That points
clearly to a political career. Get him a private secretaryship to someone who can get him an Under Secretaryship; and then leave him alone. He will find his natural
and proper place in the end on the Treasury bench.

STEPHEN (*springing up again*):   I am sorry, sir, that you

force me to forget the respect due to you as my father. I am an Englishman; and I will not hear the Government of my country insulted. (*He thrusts his hands in his pockets, and walks angrily across to the window*.)

UNDERSHAFT (*with a touch of brutality*):   The government of your country! *I* am the government of your country: I, and Lazarus. Do you suppose that you and half a dozen amateurs like you, sitting in a row in that foolish gabble shop, can govern Undershaft and Lazarus? No, my friend: you will do what pays us. You will make war when it suits us, and keep peace when it doesnt. You will find out that trade requires certain measures when we have decided on those measures. When I want anything to keep my dividends up, you will discover that my want is a national need. When other people want something to keep my dividends down, you will call out the police and military. And in return you shall have the support and applause of my newspapers, and the delight of imagining that you are a great statesman. Government of your country! Be off with you, my boy, and play with your caucuses and leading articles and historic parties and great leaders and burning questions and the rest of your toys. *I* am going back to my counting house to pay the piper and call the tune.

STEPHEN (*actually smiling, and putting his hand on his father's shoulder with indulgent patronage*):   Really, my dear father, it is impossible to be angry with you. You don't know how absurd all this sounds to me. You are very properly proud of having been industrious enough to make money; and it is greatly to your credit that you have made so much of it. But it has kept you in circles where you are valued for your money and deferred to for it, instead of in the doubtless very old-fashioned and behind-the-times public school and university where I formed my habits of mind. It is natural for you to think that money governs England; but you must allow me to think I know better.

UNDERSHAFT: And what does govern England, pray?

STEPHEN: Character, father, character.

UNDERSHAFT: Whose character? Yours or mine?

STEPHEN: Neither yours nor mine, father, but the best elements in the English national character.

UNDERSHAFT: Stephen: Ive found your profession for you. Youre a born journalist. I'll start you with a high-toned weekly review. There!

(STEPHEN *goes to the smaller writing table and busies himself with his letters.*

SARAH, BARBARA, LOMAX, *and* CUSINS *come in ready for walking.* BARBARA *crosses the room to the window and looks out.* CUSINS *drifts amiably to the armchair, and* LOMAX *remains near the door, whilst* SARAH *comes to her mother.*)

SARAH: Go and get ready, mamma: the carriage is waiting. (LADY BRITOMART *leaves the room.*)

UNDERSHAFT (*to* SARAH): Good day, my dear. Good afternoon, Mr. Lomax.

LOMAX (*vaguely*): Ahdedoo.

UNDERSHAFT (*to* CUSINS): Quite well after last night, Euripides, eh?

CUSINS: As well as can be expected.

UNDERSHAFT: Thats right. (*To* BARBARA.) So you are coming to see my death and devastation factory, Barbara?

BARBARA (*at the window*): You came yesterday to see my salvation factory. I promised you a return visit.

LOMAX (*coming forward between* SARAH *and* UNDERSHAFT): Youll find it awfully interesting. Ive been through the Woolwich Arsenal; and it gives you a ripping feeling of security, you know, to think of the lot of beggars we could kill if it came to fighting. (*To* UNDERSHAFT, *with sudden solemnity.*) Still, it must be rather an awful reflection for you, from the religious point of view as it were. Youre getting on, you know, and all that.

SARAH: You dont mind Cholly's imbecility, papa, do you?

LOMAX (*much taken aback*): Oh I say!

UNDERSHAFT: Mr. Lomax looks at the matter in a very proper spirit, my dear.

LOMAX: Just so. Thats all I meant, I assure you.

SARAH: Are you coming, Stephen?

STEPHEN: Well, I am rather busy—er— (*Magnanimously.*) Oh well, yes: I'll come. That is, if there is room for me.

UNDERSHAFT: I can take two with me in a little motor I am experimenting with for field use. You wont mind its being rather unfashionable. It's not painted yet; but it's bullet proof.

LOMAX (*appalled at the prospect of confronting Wilton Crescent in an unpainted motor*): Oh I say!

SARAH: The carriage for me, thank you. Barbara doesnt mind what shes seen in.

LOMAX: I say, Dolly old chap: do you really mind the car being a guy? Because of course if you do I'll go in it. Still—

CUSINS: I prefer it.

LOMAX: Thanks awfully, old man. Come, Sarah. (*He hurries out to secure his seat in the carriage.* SARAH *follows him.*)

CUSINS (*moodily walking across to* LADY BRITOMART'S *writing table*): Why are we two coming to this Works Department of Hell? that is what I ask myself.

BARBARA: I have always thought of it as a sort of pit where lost creatures with blackened faces stirred up smoky fires and were driven and tormented by my father? Is it like that, dad?

UNDERSHAFT (*scandalized*): My dear! It is a spotlessly clean and beautiful hillside town.

CUSINS: With a Methodist chapel? Oh do say theres a Methodist chapel.

UNDERSHAFT: There are two: a Primitive one and a sophisticated one. There is even an Ethical Society; but it is not much patronized, as my men are all strongly religious. In the High Explosives Sheds they object to the presence of Agnostics as unsafe.

CUSINS: And yet they dont object to you!

BARBARA: Do they obey all your orders?

UNDERSHAFT: I never give them any orders. When I speak to one of them it is "Well, Jones, is the baby doing well? and has Mrs. Jones made a good recovery?" "Nicely, thank you, sir." And thats all.

CUSINS: But Jones has to be kept in order. How do you maintain discipline among your men?

UNDERSHAFT: I dont. They do. You see, the one thing Jones wont stand is any rebellion from the man under him, or any assertion of social equality between the wife of the man with 4 shillings a week less than himself, and Mrs. Jones! Of course they all rebel against me, theoretically. Practically, every man of them keeps the man just below him in his place. I never meddle with them. I never bully them. I dont even bully Lazarus. I say that certain things are to be done; but I dont order anybody to do them. I dont say, mind you, that there is no ordering about and snubbing and even bullying. The men snub the boys and order them about; the carmen snub the sweepers; the artisans snub the unskilled laborers; the foremen drive and bully both the laborers and artisans; the assistant engineers find fault with the foremen; the chief engineers drop on the assistants; the departmental managers worry the chiefs; and the clerks have tall hats and hymnbooks and keep up the social tone by refusing to associate on equal terms with anybody. The result is a colossal profit, which comes to me.

CUSINS (revolted): You really are a—well, what I was saying yesterday.

BARBARA: What was he saying yesterday?

UNDERSHAFT: Never mind, my dear. He thinks I have made you unhappy. Have I?

BARBARA: Do you think I can be happy in this vulgar silly dress? I! who have worn the uniform. Do you understand what you have done to me? Yesterday I had a man's soul in my hand. I set him in the way of life with his face to salvation. But when we took your money he turned back to drunkenness and derision.

(*With intense conviction.*) I will never forgive you that. If I had a child, and you destroyed its body with your explosives—if you murdered Dolly with your horrible guns—I could forgive you if my forgiveness would open the gates of heaven to you. But to take a human soul from me, and turn it into the soul of a wolf! that is worse than any murder.

UNDERSHAFT: Does my daughter despair so easily? Can you strike a man to the heart and leave no mark on him?

BARBARA (*her face lighting up*): Oh, you are right: he can never be lost now: where was my faith?

CUSINS: Oh, clever clever devil!

BARBARA: You may be a devil; but God speaks through you sometimes. (*She takes her father's hands and kisses them.*) You have given me back my happiness: I feel it deep down now, though my spirit is troubled.

UNDERSHAFT: You have learnt something. That always feels at first as if you had lost something.

BARBARA: Well, take me to the factory of death, and let me learn something more. There must be some truth or other behind all this frightful irony. Come, Dolly. (*She goes out.*)

CUSINS: My guardian angel! (*To* UNDERSHAFT.) Avaunt! (*He follows* BARBARA.)

STEPHEN (*quietly, at the writing table*): You must not mind Cusins, father. He is a very amiable good fellow; but he is a Greek scholar and naturally a little eccentric.

UNDERSHAFT: Ah, quite so. Thank you, Stephen. Thank you. (*He goes out.*)

(STEPHEN *smiles patronizingly; buttons his coat responsibly; and crosses the room to the door.* LADY BRITOMART, *dressed for out-of-doors, opens it before he reaches it. She looks round for the others; looks at* STEPHEN; *and turns to go without a word.*)

STEPHEN (*embarrassed*): Mother—

LADY BRITOMART: Dont be apologetic, Stephen. And

dont forget that you have outgrown your mother. (*She goes out.*)

(*Perivale St. Andrews lies between two Middlesex hills, half climbing the northern one. It is an almost smokeless town of white walls, roofs of narrow green slates or red tiles, tall trees, domes, campaniles, and slender chimney shafts, beautifully situated and beautiful in itself. The best view of it is obtained from the crest of a slope about half a mile to the east, where the high explosives are dealt with. The foundry lies hidden in the depths between, the tops of its chimneys sprouting like huge skittles into the middle distance. Across the crest runs a platform of concrete, with a parapet which suggests a fortification, because there is a huge cannon of the obsolete Woolwich Infant pattern peering across it at the town. The cannon is mounted on an experimental gun carriage: possibly the original model of the Undershaft disappearing rampart gun alluded to by* STEPHEN. *The parapet has a high step inside which serves as a seat.*

BARBARA *is leaning over the parapet, looking towards the town. On her right is the cannon; on her left the end of a shed raised on piles, with a ladder of three or four steps up to the door, which opens outwards and has a little wooden landing at the threshold, with a fire bucket in the corner of the landing. The parapet stops short of the shed, leaving a gap which is the beginning of the path down the hill through the foundry to the town. Behind the cannon is a trolley carrying a huge conical bombshell, with a red band painted on it. Further from the parapet, on the same side, is a deck chair, near the door of an office, which, like the sheds, is of the lightest possible construction.*

CUSINS *arrives by the path from the town.*)

BARBARA: Well?
CUSINS: Not a ray of hope. Everything perfect, wonderful, real. It only needs a cathedral to be a heavenly city instead of a hellish one.

BARBARA: Have you found out whether they have done anything for old Peter Shirley.

CUSINS: They have found him a job as gatekeeper and timekeeper. He's frightfully miserable. He calls the timekeeping brainwork, and says he isnt used to it; and his gate lodge is so splendid that hes ashamed to use the rooms, and skulks in the scullery.

BARBARA: Poor Peter!

(STEPHEN *arrives from the town. He carries a field-glass.*)

STEPHEN (*enthusiastically*): Have you two seen the place? Why did you leave us?

CUSINS: I wantcd to see everything I was not intended to see; and Barbara wanted to make the men talk.

STEPHEN: Have you found anything discreditable?

CUSINS: No. They call him Dandy Andy and are proud of his being a cunning old rascal; but it's all horribly, frightfully, immorally, unanswerably perfect.

(SARAH *arrives.*)

SARAH: Heavens! what a place! (*She crosses to the trolley.*) Did you see the nursing home!? (*She sits down on the shell.*)

STEPHEN: Did you see the libraries and schools!?

SARAH: Did you see the ball room and the banqueting chamber in the Town Hall!?

STEPHEN: Have you gone into the insurance fund, the pension fund, the building society, the various applications of co-operation!?

(UNDERSHAFT *comes from the office, with a sheaf of telegrams in his hands.*)

UNDERSHAFT: Well, have you seen everything? I'm sorry I was called away. (*Indicating the telegrams.*) News from Manchuria.

STEPHEN: Good news, I hope.

UNDERSHAFT: Very.

STEPHEN: Another Japanese victory?

UNDERSHAFT: Oh, I dont know. Which side wins does

not concern us here. No: the good news is that the aerial battleship is a tremendous success. At the first trial it has wiped out a fort with three hundred soldiers in it.

CUSINS (*from the platform*):   Dummy soldiers?

UNDERSHAFT: No: the real thing. (CUSINS *and* BARBARA *exchange glances. Then* CUSINS *sits on the step and buries his face in his hands.* BARBARA *gravely lays her hand on his shoulder, and he looks up at her in a sort of whimsical desperation.*) Well, Stephen, what do you think of the place?

STEPHEN: Oh, magnificent. A perfect triumph of organization. Frankly, my dear father, I have been a fool: I had no idea of what it all meant—of the wonderful forethought, the power of organization, the administrative capacity, the financial genius, the colossal capital it represents. I have been repeating to myself as I came through your streets "Peace hath her victories no less renowned than War." I have only one misgiving about it all.

UNDERSHAFT: Out with it.

STEPHEN: Well, I cannot help thinking that all this provision for every want of your workmen may sap their independence and weaken their sense of responsibility. And greatly as we enjoyed our tea at that splendid restaurant—how they gave us all that luxury and cake and jam and cream for threepence I really cannot imagine!— still you must remember that restaurants break up home life. Look at the continent, for instance! Are you sure so much pampering is really good for the men's characters?

UNDERSHAFT: Well you see, my dear boy, when you are organizing civilization you have to make up your mind whether trouble and anxiety are good things or not. If you decide that they are, then, I take it, you simply dont organize civilization; and there you are, with trouble and anxiety enough to make us all angels! But if you decide the other way, you may as well go through with it. However, Stephen, our characters are safe here. A sufficient dose of anxiety is always provided by the fact that we may be blown to smithereens at any moment.

SARAH: By the way, papa, where do you make the explosives?

UNDERSHAFT: In separate little sheds, like that one. When one of them blows up, it costs very little; and only the people quite close to it are killed.

(STEPHEN, *who is quite close to it, looks at it rather scaredly, and moves away quickly to the cannon. At the same moment the door of the shed is thrown abruptly open; and a foreman in overalls and list slippers comes out on the little landing and holds the door open for* LOMAX, *who appears in the doorway.*)

LOMAX (*with studied coolness*): My good fellow: you neednt get into a state of nerves. Nothing's going to happen to you; and I suppose it wouldnt be the end of the world if anything did. A little bit of British pluck is what you want, old chap. (*He descends and strolls across to* SARAH.)

UNDERSHAFT (*to the foreman*): Anything wrong, Bilton?

BILTON (*with ironic calm*): Gentleman walked into the high explosives shed and lit a cigaret, sir: thats all.

UNDERSHAFT: Ah, quite so. (*To* LOMAX.) Do you happen to remember what you did with the match?

LOMAX: Oh come! I'm not a fool. I took jolly good care to blow it out before I chucked it away.

BILTON: The top of it was red hot inside, sir.

LOMAX: Well, suppose it was! I didnt chuck it into any of your messes.

UNDERSHAFT: Think no more of it, Mr. Lomax. By the way, would you mind lending me your matches?

LOMAX (*offering his box*): Certainly.

UNDERSHAFT: Thanks. (*He pockets the matches.*)

LOMAX (*lecturing to the company generally*): You know, these high explosives dont go off like gunpowder, except when theyre in a gun. When theyre spread loose, you can put a match to them without the least risk: they just burn quietly like a bit of paper. (*Warming to the scientific interest of the subject.*) Did you know that, Undershaft? Have you ever tried?

UNDERSHAFT: Not on a large scale, Mr. Lomax. Bilton
will give you a sample of gun cotton when you are
leaving if you ask him. You can experiment with it at
home. (BILTON *looks puzzled.*)

SARAH: Bilton will do nothing of the sort, papa. I sup-
pose it's your business to blow up the Russians and
Japs; but you might really stop short of blowing up poor
Cholly. (BILTON *gives it up and retires into the shed.*)

LOMAX: My ownest, there is no danger. (*He sits beside
her on the shell.*)

(LADY BRITOMART *arrives from the town with a
bouquet.*)

LADY BRITOMART (*coming impetuously between* UN-
DERSHAFT *and the deck chair*):   Andrew: you shouldnt
have let me see this place.

UNDERSHAFT: Why, my dear?

LADY BRITOMART: Never mind why: you shouldnt have:
thats all. To think of all that (*indicating the town*) being
yours! and that you have kept it to yourself all these
years!

UNDERSHAFT: It does not belong to me. I belong to it.
It is the Undershaft inheritance.

LADY BRITOMART: It is not. Your ridiculous cannons and
that noisy banging foundry may be the Undershaft inheritance; but all that plate and linen, all that furniture and
those houses and orchards and gardens belong to us.
They belong to me: they are not a man's business. I
wont give them up. You must be out of your senses to
throw them all away; and if you persist in such folly, I
will call in a doctor.

UNDERSHAFT (*stooping to smell the bouquet*):   Where did
you get the flowers, my dear?

LADY BRITOMART: Your men presented them to me in
your William Morris Labor Church.

CUSINS (*springing up*):   Oh! It needed only that. A Labor
Church!

LADY BRITOMART: Yes, with Morris's words in mosaic
letters ten feet high round the dome. NO MAN IS GOOD

ENOUGH TO BE ANOTHER MAN'S MASTER. The cynicism of it!

UNDERSHAFT: It shocked the men at first, I am afraid. But now they take no more notice of it than of the ten commandments in church.

LADY BRITOMART: Andrew: you are trying to put me off the subject of the inheritance by profane jokes. Well, you shant. I dont ask it any longer for Stephen: he has inherited far too much of your perversity to be fit for it. But Barbara has rights as well as Stephen. Why should not Adolphus succeed to the inheritance? I could manage the town for him; and he can look after the cannons, if they are really necessary.

UNDERSHAFT: I should ask nothing better if Adolphus were a foundling. He is exactly the sort of new blood that is wanted in English business. But hes not a foundling; and theres an end of it.

CUSINS (*diplomatically*): Not quite. (*They all turn and stare at him. He comes from the platform past the shed to* UNDERSHAFT.) I think— Mind! I am not committing myself in any way as to my future course—but I think the foundling difficulty can be got over.

UNDERSHAFT: What do you mean?

CUSINS: Well, I have something to say which is in the nature of a confession.

SARAH:
LADY BRITOMART: } Confession!
BARBARA:
STEPHEN:

LOMAX: Oh I say!

CUSINS: Yes, a confession. Listen, all. Until I met Barbara I thought myself in the main an honorable, truthful man, because I wanted the approval of my conscience more than I wanted anything else. But the moment I saw Barbara, I wanted her far more than the approval of my conscience.

LADY BRITOMART: Adolphus!

CUSINS: It is true. You accused me yourself, Lady Brit, of joining the Army to worship Barbara; and so I did.

She bought my soul like a flower at a street corner; but she bought it for herself.

UNDERSHAFT: What! Not for Dionysos or another?

CUSINS: Dionysos and all the others are in herself. I adored what was divine in her, and was therefore a true worshipper. But I was romantic about her too. I thought she was a woman of the people, and that a marriage with a professor of Greek would be far beyond the wildest social ambitions of her rank.

LADY BRITOMART: Adolphus!!

LOMAX: Oh I say!!!

CUSINS: When I learnt the horrible truth—

LADY BRITOMART: What do you mean by the horrible truth, pray?

CUSINS: That she was enormously rich; that her grandfather was an earl; that her father was the Prince of Darkness—

UNDERSHAFT: Chut!

CUSINS: —and that I was only an adventurer trying to catch a rich wife, then I stooped to deceive her about my birth.

BARBARA: Dolly!

LADY BRITOMART: Your birth! Now Adolphus, dont dare to make up a wicked story for the sake of these wretched cannons. Remember: I have seen photographs of your parents; and the Agent General for South Western Australia knows them personally and has assured me that they are most respectable married people.

CUSINS: So they are in Australia; but here they are outcasts. Their marriage is legal in Australia, but not in England. My mother is my father's deceased wife's sister; and in this island I am consequently a foundling. (*Sensation.*) Is the subterfuge good enough, Machiavelli?

UNDERSHAFT (*thoughtfully*): Biddy: this may be a way out of the difficulty.

LADY BRITOMART: Stuff! A man cant make cannons any the better for being his own cousin instead of his proper self (*she sits down in the deck chair with a bounce that expresses her downright contempt for their casuistry*).

UNDERSHAFT (*to* CUSINS): You are an educated man. That is against the tradition.

CUSINS: Once in ten thousand times it happens that the schoolboy is a born master of what they try to teach him. Greek has not destroyed my mind: it has nourished it. Besides, I did not learn it at an English public school.

UNDERSHAFT: Hm! Well, I cannot afford to be too particular: you have cornered the foundling market. Let it pass. You are eligible, Euripides: you are eligible.

BARBARA (*coming from the platform and interposing between* CUSINS *and* UNDERSHAFT): Dolly: yesterday morning, when Stephen told us all about the tradition, you became very silent; and you have been strange and excited ever since. Were you thinking of your birth then?

CUSINS: When the finger of Destiny suddenly points at a man in the middle of his breakfast, it makes him thoughtful. (BARBARA *turns away sadly and stands near her mother, listening perturbedly.*)

UNDERSHAFT: Aha! You have had your eye on the business, my young friend, have you?

CUSINS: Take care! There is an abyss of moral horror between me and your accursed aerial battleships.

UNDERSHAFT: Never mind the abyss for the present. Let us settle the practical details and leave your final decision open. You know that you will have to change your name. Do you object to that?

CUSINS: Would any man named Adolphus—any man called Dolly!—object to be called something else?

UNDERSHAFT: Good. Now, as to money! I propose to treat you handsomely from the beginning. You shall start at a thousand a year.

CUSINS (*with sudden heat, his spectacles twinkling with mischief*): A thousand! You dare offer a miserable thousand to the son-in-law of a millionaire! No, by Heavens, Machiavelli! you shall not cheat me. You cannot do without me; and I can do without you. I must have two thousand five hundred a year for two years. At the end of that time, if I am a failure, I go. But if

I am a success, and stay on, you must give me the other five thousand.

UNDERSHAFT: What other five thousand?

CUSINS: To make the two years up to five thousand a year. The two thousand five hundred is only half pay in case I should turn out a failure. The third year I must have ten per cent on the profits.

UNDERSHAFT (*taken aback*): Ten per cent! Why, man, do you know what my profits are?

CUSINS: Enormous, I hope: otherwise I shall require twentyfive per cent.

UNDERSHAFT: But, Mr. Cusins, this is a serious matter of business. You are not bringing any capital into the concern.

CUSINS: What! no capital! Is my mastery of Greek no capital? Is my access to the subtlest thought, the loftiest poetry yet attained by humanity, no capital? My character! my intellect! my life! my career! what Barbara calls my soul! are these no capital? Say another word; and I double my salary.

UNDERSHAFT: Be reasonable—

CUSINS (*peremptorily*): Mr. Undershaft: you have my terms. Take them or leave them.

UNDERSHAFT (*recovering himself*): Very well. I note your terms; and I offer you half.

CUSINS (*disgusted*): Half!

UNDERSHAFT (*firmly*): Half.

CUSINS: You call yourself a gentleman; and you offer me half!!

UNDERSHAFT: I do not call myself a gentleman; but I offer you half.

CUSINS: This to your future partner! your successor! your son-in-law!

BARBARA: You are selling your own soul, Dolly, not mine. Leave me out of the bargain, please.

UNDERSHAFT: Come! I will go a step further for Barbara's sake. I will give you three fifths; but that is my last word.

CUSINS: Done!

LOMAX: Done in the eye. Why, *I* only get eight hundred, you know.

CUSINS: By the way, Mac, I am a classical scholar, not an arithmetical one. Is three fifths more than half or less?

UNDERSHAFT: More, of course.

CUSINS: I would have taken two hundred and fifty. How you can succeed in business when you are willing to pay all that money to a University don who is obviously not worth a junior clerk's wages!—well! What will Lazarus say?

UNDERSHAFT: Lazarus is a gentle romantic Jew who cares for nothing but string quartets and stalls at fashionable theatres. He will get the credit of your rapacity in money matters, as he has hitherto had the credit of mine. You are a shark of the first order, Euripides. So much the better for the firm!

BARBARA: Is the bargain closed, Dolly? Does your soul belong to him now?

CUSINS: No: the price is settled: that is all. The real tug of war is still to come. What about the moral question?

LADY BRITOMART: There is no moral question in the matter at all, Adolphus. You must simply sell cannons and weapons to people whose cause is right and just, and refuse them to foreigners and criminals.

UNDERSHAFT (*determinedly*):   No: none of that. You must keep the true faith of an Armorer, or you dont come in here.

CUSINS: What on earth is the true faith of an Armorer?

UNDERSHAFT: To give arms to all men who offer an honest price for them, without respect of persons or principles: to aristocrat and republican, to Nihilist and Tsar, to Capitalist and Socialist, to Protestant and Catholic, to burglar and policeman, to black man white man and yellow man, to all sorts and conditions, all nationalities, all faiths, all follies, all causes and all crimes. The first Undershaft wrote up in his shop IF GOD GAVE THE HAND, LET NOT MAN WITHHOLD THE SWORD. The second wrote up ALL HAVE THE RIGHT TO FIGHT: NONE

HAVE THE RIGHT TO JUDGE. The third wrote up TO MAN THE WEAPON: TO HEAVEN THE VICTORY. The fourth had no literary turn; so he did not write up anything; but he sold cannons to Napoleon under the nose of George the Third. The fifth wrote up PEACE SHALL NOT PREVAIL SAVE WITH A SWORD IN HER HAND. The sixth, my master, was the best of all. He wrote up NOTHING IS EVER DONE IN THIS WORLD UNTIL MEN ARE PREPARED TO KILL ONE ANOTHER IF IT IS NOT DONE. After that, there was nothing left for the seventh to say. So he wrote up, simply, UNASHAMED.

CUSINS: My good Machiavelli, I shall certainly write something up on the wall; only, as I shall write it in Greek, you wont be able to read it. But as to your Armorer's faith, if I take my neck out of the noose of my own morality I am not going to put it into the noose of yours. I shall sell cannons to whom I please and refuse them to whom I please. So there!

UNDERSHAFT: From the moment when you become Andrew Undershaft, you will never do as you please again. Dont come here lusting for power, young man.

CUSINS: If power were my aim I should not come here for it. You have no power.

UNDERSHAFT: None of my own, certainly.

CUSINS: I have more power than you, more will. You do not drive this place: it drives you. And what drives the place?

UNDERSHAFT (*enigmatically*): A will of which I am a part.

BARBARA (*startled*): Father! Do you know what you are saying; or are you laying a snare for my soul?

CUSINS: Dont listen to his metaphysics, Barbara. The place is driven by the most rascally part of society, the money hunters, the pleasure hunters, the military promotion hunters; and he is their slave.

UNDERSHAFT: Not necessarily. Remember the Armorer's Faith. I will take an order from a good man as cheerfully as from a bad one. If you good people prefer preaching and shirking to buying my weapons and fighting the rascals, dont blame me. I can make cannons: I cannot make courage and conviction. Bah! You tire me, Euripides, with your morality mongering. Ask Barbara: she understands. (*He suddenly takes* BARBARA'S *hands, and looks powerfully into her eyes.*) Tell him, my love, what power really means.

BARBARA (*hypnotized*): Before I joined the Salvation Army, I was in my own power; and the consequence was that I never knew what to do with myself. When I joined it, I had not time enough for all the things I had to do.

UNDERSHAFT (*approvingly*): Just so. And why was that, do you suppose?

BARBARA: Yesterday I should have said, because I was in the power of God. (*She resumes her self-possession, withdrawing her hands from his with a power equal to his own.*) But you came and shewed me that I was in the power of Bodger and Undershaft. Today I feel—oh! how can I put into words? Sarah: do you remember the earthquake at Cannes, when we were little children?— how little the surprise of the first shock mattered compared to the dread and horror of waiting for the second? That is how I feel in this place today. I stood on the rock I thought eternal; and without a word of warning it reeled and crumbled under me. I was safe with an infinite wisdom watching me, an army marching to Salvation with me; and in a moment, at a stroke of your pen in a cheque book, I stood alone; and the heavens were empty. That was the first shock of the earthquake: I am waiting for the second.

UNDERSHAFT: Come, come, my daughter! dont make too much of your little tinpot tragedy. What do we do here when we spend years of work and thought and thousands of pounds of solid cash on a new gun or an aerial battleship that turns out just a hairsbreadth wrong after all? Scrap it. Scrap it without wasting another hour or another pound on it. Well, you have made for yourself something that you call a morality or a religion or what not. It doesnt fit the facts. Well, scrap it. Scrap it and

get one that does fit. That is what is wrong with the
world at present. It scraps its obsolete steam engines
and dynamos; but it wont scrap its old prejudices and its
old moralities and its old religions and its old political
constitutions. Whats the result? In machinery it does
very well; but in morals and religion and politics it is
working at a loss that brings it nearer bankruptcy every
year. Dont persist in that folly. If your old religion
broke down yesterday, get a newer and a better one for
tomorrow.

BARBARA: Oh how gladly I would take a better one to
my soul! But you offer me a worse one. (*Turning on
him with sudden vehemence*.) Justify yourself: shew me
some light through the darkness of this dreadful place,
with its beautifully clean workshops, and respectable
workmen, and model homes.

UNDERSHAFT: Cleanliness and respectability do not need
justification, Barbara: they justify themselves. I see no
darkness here, no dreadfulness. In your Salvation shelter
I saw poverty, misery, cold and hunger. You gave them
bread and treacle and dreams of heaven. I give from
thirty shillings a week to twelve thousand a year. They
find their own dreams; but I look after the drainage.

BARBARA: And their souls?

UNDERSHAFT: I save their souls just as I saved yours.

BARBARA (*revolted*): You saved my soul! What do you
mean?

UNDERSHAFT: I fed you and clothed you and housed you.
I took care that you should have money enough to live
handsomely—more than enough; so that you could be
wasteful, careless, generous. That saved your soul from
the seven deadly sins.

BARBARA (*bewildered*): The seven deadly sins!

UNDERSHAFT: Yes, the deadly seven. (*Counting on his
fingers*.) Food, clothing, firing, rent, taxes, respectability and children. Nothing can lift those seven millstones
from Man's neck but money; and the spirit cannot soar
until the millstones are lifted. I lifted them from your
spirit. I enabled Barbara to become Major Barbara; and
I saved her from the crime of poverty.

CUSINS: Do you call poverty a crime?

UNDERSHAFT: The worst of crimes. All the other crimes
are virtues beside it: all the other dishonors are chivalry
itself by comparison. Poverty blights whole cities;
spreads horrible pestilences; strikes dead the very souls
of all who come within sight, sound or smell of it. What
you call crime is nothing: a murder here and a theft
there, a blow now and a curse then: what do they matter? they are only the accidents and illnesses of life:
there are not fifty genuine professional criminals in London. But there are millions of poor people, abject people, dirty people, ill fed, ill clothed people. They poison
us morally and physically: they kill the happiness of
society: they force us to do away with our own liberties
and to organize unnatural cruelties for fear they should
rise against us and drag us down into their abyss. Only
fools fear crime: we all fear poverty. Pah! (*turning on*
BARBARA) you talk of your half-saved ruffian in West
Ham: you accuse me of dragging his soul back to perdi-
tion. Well, bring him to me here; and I will drag his
soul back again to salvation for you. Not by words and
dreams; but by thirtyeight shillings a week, a sound
house in a handsome street, and a permanent job. In
three weeks he will have a fancy waistcoat; in three
months a tall hat and a chapel sitting; before the end of
the year he will shake hands with a duchess at a Primrose League meeting, and join the Conservative Party.

BARBARA: And will he be the better for that?

UNDERSHAFT: You know he will. Dont be a hypocrite,
Barbara. He will be better fed, better housed, better
clothed, better behaved; and his children will be pounds
heavier and bigger. That will be better than an American
cloth mattress in a shelter, chopping firewood, eating
bread and treacle, and being forced to kneel down from
time to time to thank heaven for it: knee drill, I think
you call it. It is cheap work converting starving men
with a Bible in one hand and a slice of bread in the other. I
will undertake to convert West Ham to Mahometanism on
the same terms. Try your hand on my men: their souls
are hungry because their bodies are full.

BARBARA: And leave the east end to starve?

UNDERSHAFT (*his energetic tone dropping into one of bitter and brooding remembrance*): *I* was an east ender. I moralized and starved until one day I swore that I would be a full-fed free man at all costs—that nothing should stop me except a bullet, neither reason nor morals nor the lives of other men. I said "Thou shalt starve ere I starve"; and with that word I became free and great. I was a dangerous man until I had my will: now I am a useful, beneficent, kindly person. That is the history of most self-made millionaires, I fancy. When it is the history of every Englishman we shall have an England worth living in.

LADY BRITOMART: Stop making speeches, Andrew. This is not the place for them.

UNDERSHAFT (*punctured*): My dear: I have no other means of conveying my ideas.

LADY BRITOMART: Your ideas are nonsense. You got on because you were selfish and unscrupulous.

UNDERSHAFT: Not at all. I had the strongest scruples about poverty and starvation. Your moralists are quite unscrupulous about both: they make virtues of them. I had rather be a thief than a pauper. I had rather be a murderer than a slave. I dont want to be either; but if you force the alternative on me, then, by Heaven, I'll choose the braver and more moral one. I hate poverty and slavery worse than any other crimes whatsoever. And let me tell you this. Poverty and slavery have stood up for centuries to your sermons and leading articles: they will not stand up to my machine guns. Dont preach at them: dont reason with them. Kill them.

BARBARA: Killing. Is that your remedy for everything?

UNDERSHAFT: It is the final test of conviction, the only lever strong enough to overturn a social system, the only way of saying Must. Let six hundred and seventy fools loose in the street; and three policemen can scatter them. But huddle them together in a certain house in Westminster; and let them go through certain ceremonies and call themselves certain names until at last they get the courage to kill; and your six hundred and seventy fools become a government. Your pious mob fills up ballot papers and imagines it is governing its masters; but the ballot paper that really governs is the paper that has a bullet wrapped up in it.

CUSINS: That is perhaps why, like most intelligent people, I never vote.

UNDERSHAFT: Vote! Bah! When you vote, you only change the names of the cabinet. When you shoot, you pull down governments, inaugurate new epochs, abolish old orders and set up new. Is that historically true, Mr. Learned Man, or is it not?

CUSINS: It is historically true. I loathe having to admit it. I repudiate your sentiments. I abhor your nature. I defy you in every possible way. Still, it is true. But it ought not to be true.

UNDERSHAFT: Ought, ought, ought, ought, ought! Are you going to spend your life saying ought, like the rest of our moralists? Turn your oughts into shalls, man. Come and make explosives with me. Whatever can blow men up can blow society up. The history of the world is the history of those who had courage enough to embrace this truth. Have you the courage to embrace it, Barbara?

LADY BRITOMART: Barbara, I positively forbid you to listen to your father's abominable wickedness. And you, Adolphus, ought to know better than to go about saying that wrong things are true. What does it matter whether they are true if they are wrong?

UNDERSHAFT: What does it matter whether they are wrong if they are true?

LADY BRITOMART (*rising*): Children: come home instantly. Andrew: I am exceedingly sorry I allowed you to call on us. You are wickeder than ever. Come at once.

BARBARA (*shaking her head*): It's no use running away from wicked people, mamma.

LADY BRITOMART: It is every use. It shews your disapprobation of them.

BARBARA: It does not save them.

LADY BRITOMART: I can see that you are going to disobey me. Sarah: are you coming home or are you not?

SARAH: I daresay it's very wicked of papa to make cannons; but I dont think I shall cut him on that account.

LOMAX (*pouring oil on the troubled waters*): The fact is, you know, there is a certain amount of tosh about this notion of wickedness. It doesnt work. You must look at facts. Not that I would say a word in favor of anything wrong; but then, you see, all sorts of chaps are always doing all sorts of things; and we have to fit them in somehow, dont you know. What I mean is that you cant go cutting everybody; and thats about what it comes to. (*Their rapt attention to his eloquence makes him nervous.*) Perhaps I dont make myself clear.

LADY BRITOMART: You are lucidity itself, Charles. Because Andrew is successful and has plenty of money to give to Sarah, you will flatter him and encourage him in his wickedness.

LOMAX (*unruffled*): Well, where the carcase is, there will the eagles be gathered, dont you know. (*To* UNDERSHAFT.) Eh? What?

UNDERSHAFT: Precisely. By the way, may I call you Charles?

LOMAX: Delighted. Cholly is the usual ticket.

UNDERSHAFT (*to* LADY BRITOMART): Biddy—

LADY BRITOMART (*violently*): Dont dare call me Biddy. Charles Lomax: you are a fool. Adolphus Cusins: you are a Jesuit. Stephen: you are a prig. Barbara: you are a lunatic. Andrew: you are a vulgar tradesman. Now you all know my opinion; and my conscience is clear, at all events (*she sits down again with a vehemence that almost wrecks the chair*).

UNDERSHAFT: My dear: you are the incarnation of morality. (*She snorts.*) Your conscience is clear and your duty done when you have called everybody names. Come, Euripides! it is getting late; and we all want to get home. Make up your mind.

CUSINS: Understand this, you old demon—

LADY BRITOMART: Adolphus!

UNDERSHAFT: Let him alone, Biddy. Proceed, Euripides.

CUSINS: You have me in a horrible dilemma. I want Barbara.

UNDERSHAFT: Like all young men, you greatly exaggerate the difference between one young woman and another.

BARBARA: Quite true, Dolly.

CUSINS: I also want to avoid being a rascal.

UNDERSHAFT (*with biting contempt*): You lust for personal righteousness, for self-approval, for what you call a good conscience, for what Barbara calls salvation, for what I call patronizing people who are not so lucky as yourself.

CUSINS: I do not: all the poet in me recoils from being a good man. But there are things in me that I must reckon with: pity—

UNDERSHAFT: Pity! The scavenger of misery.

CUSINS: Well, love.

UNDERSHAFT: I know. You love the needy and the outcast: you love the oppressed races, the negro, the Indian ryot, the Pole, the Irishman. Do you love the Japanese? Do you love the Germans? Do you love the English?

CUSINS: No. Every true Englishman detests the English. We are the wickedest nation on earth; and our success is a moral horror.

UNDERSHAFT: That is what comes of your gospel of love, is it?

CUSINS: May I not love even my father-in-law?

UNDERSHAFT: Who wants your love, man? By what right do you take the liberty of offering it to me? I will have your due heed and respect, or I will kill you. But your love. Damn your impertinence!

CUSINS (*grinning*): I may not be able to control my affections, Mac.

UNDERSHAFT: You are fencing, Euripides. You are weakening: your grip is slipping. Come! try your last weapon. Pity and love have broken in your hand: forgiveness is still left.

CUSINS: No: forgiveness is a beggar's refuge. I am with you there: we must pay our debts.

UNDERSHAFT: Well said. Come! you will suit me. Remember the words of Plato.

CUSINS (*starting*): Plato! You dare quote Plato to me!

UNDERSHAFT: Plato says, my friend, that society cannot be saved until either the Professors of Greek take to making gunpowder, or else the makers of gunpowder become Professors of Greek.

CUSINS: Oh, tempter, cunning tempter!

UNDERSHAFT: Come! choose, man, choose.

CUSINS: But perhaps Barbara will not marry me if I make the wrong choice.

BARBARA: Perhaps not.

CUSINS (*desperately perplexed*): You hear!

BARBARA: Father: do you love nobody?

UNDERSHAFT: I love my best friend.

LADY BRITOMART: And who is that, pray?

UNDERSHAFT: My bravest enemy. That is the man who keeps me up to the mark.

CUSINS: You know, the creature is really a sort of poet in his way. Suppose he is a great man, after all!

UNDERSHAFT: Suppose you stop talking and make up your mind, my young friend.

CUSINS: But you are driving me against my nature. I hate war.

UNDERSHAFT: Hatred is the coward's revenge for being intimidated. Dare you make war on war? Here are the means: my friend Mr. Lomax is sitting on them.

LOMAX (*springing up*): Oh I say! You dont mean that this thing is loaded, do you? My ownest: come off it.

SARAH (*sitting placidly on the shell*): If I am to be blown up, the more thoroughly it is done the better. Dont fuss, Cholly.

LOMAX (*to* UNDERSHAFT, *strongly remonstrant*): Your own daughter, you know.

UNDERSHAFT: So I see. (*To* CUSINS.) Well, my friend, may we expect you here at six tomorrow morning?

CUSINS (*firmly*): Not on any account. I will see the whole

establishment blown up with its own dynamite before I will get up at five. My hours are healthy, rational hours: eleven to five.

UNDERSHAFT: Come when you please: before a week you will come at six and stay until I turn you out for the sake of your health. (*Calling.*) Bilton! (*He turns to* LADY BRITOMART, *who rises.*) My dear: let us leave these two young people to themselves for a moment. (BILTON *comes from the shed.*) I am going to take you through the gun cotton shed.

BILTON (*barring the way*): You cant take anything explosive in here, sir.

LADY BRITOMART: What do you mean? Are you alluding to me?

BILTON (*unmoved*): No, maam. Mr. Undershaft has the other gentleman's matches in his pocket.

LADY BRITOMART (*abruptly*): Oh! I beg your pardon. (*She goes into the shed.*)

UNDERSHAFT: Quite right, Bilton, quite right: here you are. (*He gives* BILTON *the box of matches.*) Come, Stephen. Come, Charles. Bring Sarah. (*He passes into the shed.*)

(BILTON *opens the box and deliberately drops the matches into the fire-bucket.*)

LOMAX: Oh I say! (BILTON *stolidly hands him the empty box.*) Infernal nonsense! Pure scientific ignorance! (*He goes in.*)

SARAH: Am I all right, Bilton?

BILTON: Youll have to put on list slippers, miss: thats all. Weve got em inside. (*She goes in.*)

STEPHEN (*very seriously to* CUSINS): Dolly, old fellow, think. Think before you decide. Do you feel that you are a sufficiently practical man? It is a huge undertaking, an enormous responsibility. All this mass of business will be Greek to you.

CUSINS: Oh, I think it will be much less difficult than Greek.

STEPHEN: Well, I just want to say this before I leave you

to yourselves. Dont let anything I have said about right
and wrong prejudice you against this great chance in
life. I have satisfied myself that the business is one
of the highest character and a credit to our country.
(*Emotionally.*) I am very proud of my father. I— (*Unable to proceed, he presses* CUSINS' *hand and goes hastily into the shed, followed by* BILTON.)

(BARBARA *and* CUSINS, *left alone together, look at one another silently.*)

CUSINS: Barbara: I am going to accept this offer.

BARBARA: I thought you would.

CUSINS: You understand, dont you, that I had to decide
without consulting you. If I had thrown the burden of
the choice on you, you would sooner or later have despised me for it.

BARBARA: Yes: I did not want you to sell your soul for
me any more than for this inheritance.

CUSINS: It is not the sale of my soul that troubles me: I
have sold it too often to care about that. I have sold it
for a professorship. I have sold it for an income. I have
sold it to escape being imprisoned for refusing to pay
taxes for hangmen's ropes and unjust wars and things
that I abhor. What is all human conduct but the daily
and hourly sale of our souls for trifles? What I am now
selling it for is neither money nor position nor comfort,
but for reality and for power.

BARBARA: You know that you will have no power, and
that he has none.

CUSINS: I know. It is not for myself alone. I want to
make power for the world.

BARBARA: I want to make power for the world too; but
it must be spiritual power.

CUSINS: I think all power is spiritual: these cannons will
not go off by themselves. I have tried to make spiritual
power by teaching Greek. But the world can never be
really touched by a dead language and a dead civilization. The people must have power; and the people can-

not have Greek. Now the power that is made here can be wielded by all men.

BARBARA: Power to burn women's houses down and kill their sons and tear their husbands to pieces.

CUSINS: You cannot have power for good without having power for evil too. Even mother's milk nourishes murderers as well as heroes. This power which only tears men's bodies to pieces has never been so horribly abused as the intellectual power, the imaginative power, the poetic, religious power than can enslave men's souls. As a teacher of Greek I gave the intellectual man weapons against the common man. I now want to give the common man weapons against the intellectual man. I love the common people. I want to arm them against the lawyer, the doctor, the priest, the literary man, the professor, the artist, and the politician, who, once in authority, are the most dangerous, disastrous, and tyrannical of all the fools, rascals, and impostors. I want a democratic power strong enough to force the intellectual oligarchy to use its genius for the general good or else perish.

BARBARA: Is there no higher power than that (*pointing to the shell*)?

CUSINS: Yes: but that power can destroy the higher powers just as a tiger can destroy a man: therefore man must master that power first. I admitted this when the Turks and Greeks were last at war. My best pupil went out to fight for Hellas. My parting gift to him was not a copy of Plato's Republic, but a revolver and a hundred Undershaft cartridges. The blood of every Turk he shot—if he shot any—is on my head as well as on Undershaft's. That act committed me to this place for ever. Your father's challenge has beaten me. Dare I make war on war? I dare. I must. I will. And now, is it all over between us?

BARBARA (*touched by his evident dread of her answer*):   Silly baby Dolly! How could it be?

CUSINS (*overjoyed*):   Then you—you—you— Oh for my drum! (*He flourishes imaginary drumsticks.*)

BARBARA (*angered by his levity*): Take care, Dolly, take care. Oh, if only I could get away from you and from father and from it all! if I could have the wings of a dove and fly away to heaven!

CUSINS: And leave me!

BARBARA: Yes, you, and all the other naughty mischievous children of men. But I cant. I was happy in the Salvation Army for a moment. I escaped from the world into a paradise of enthusiasm and prayer and soul saving; but the moment our money ran short, it all came back to Bodger: it was he who saved our people: he, and the Prince of Darkness, my papa. Undershaft and Bodger: their hands stretch everywhere: when we feed a starving fellow creature, it is with their bread, because there is no other bread; when we tend the sick, it is in the hospitals they endow; if we turn from the churches they build, we must kneel on the stones of the streets they pave. As long as that lasts, there is no getting away from them. Turning our backs on Bodger and Undershaft is turning our backs on life.

CUSINS: I thought you were determined to turn your back on the wicked side of life.

BARBARA: There is no wicked side: life is all one. And I never wanted to shirk my share in whatever evil must be endured, whether it be sin or suffering. I wish I could cure you of middle-class ideas, Dolly.

CUSINS (*gasping*): Middle cl—! A snub! A social snub to me! from the daughter of a foundling!

BARBARA: That is why I have no class, Dolly: I come straight out of the heart of the whole people. If I were middle-class I should turn my back on my father's business; and we should both live in the artistic drawing-room, with you reading the reviews in one corner, and I in the other at the piano, playing Schumann: both very superior persons, and neither of us a bit of use. Sooner than that, I would sweep out the guncotton shed, or be one of Bodger's barmaids. Do you know what would have happened if you had refused papa's offer?

CUSINS: I wonder!

BARBARA: I should have given you up and married the
man who accepted it. After all, my dear old mother has
more sense than any of you. I felt like her when I saw
this place—felt that I must have it—that never, never,
never could I let it go; only she thought it was the
houses and the kitchen ranges and the linen and china,
when it was really all the human souls to be saved: not
weak souls in starved bodies, crying with gratitude for
a scrap of bread and treacle, but fullfed, quarrelsome,
snobbish, uppish creatures, all standing on their little
rights and dignities, and thinking that my father ought
to be greatly obliged to them for making so much
money for him—and so he ought. That is where salvation is really wanted. My father shall never throw it in
my teeth again that my converts were bribed with bread.
(*She is transfigured.*) I have got rid of the bribe of
bread. I have got rid of the bribe of heaven. Let God's
work be done for its own sake: the work he had to
create us to do because it cannot be done except by
living men and women. When I die, let him be in my
debt, not I in his; and let me forgive him as becomes
a woman of my rank.

CUSINS: Then the way of life lies through the factory of
death?

BARBARA: Yes, through the raising of hell to heaven and
of man to God, through the unveiling of an eternal light
in the Valley of The Shadow. (*Seizing him with both
hands.*) Oh, did you think my courage would never
come back? did you believe that I was a deserter? that
I, who have stood in the streets, and taken my people
to my heart, and talked of the holiest and greatest things
with them, could ever turn back and chatter foolishly to
fashionable · people about nothing in a drawingroom?
Never, never, never, never: Major Barbara will die with
the colors. Oh! and I have my dear little Dolly boy still;
and he has found me my place and my work. Glory
Hallelujah! (*She kisses him.*)

CUSINS: My dearest: consider my delicate health. I cannot stand as much happiness as you can.

BARBARA: Yes: it is not easy work being in love with me, is it? But it's good for you. (*She runs to the shed, and calls, childlike*) Mamma! Mamma! (BILTON *comes out of the shed, followed by* UNDERSHAFT.) I want Mamma.

UNDERSHAFT: She is taking off her list slippers, dear. (*He passes on to* CUSINS.) Well? What does she say?

CUSINS: She has gone right up into the skies.

LADY BRITOMART (*coming from the shed and stopping on the steps, obstructing* SARAH, *who follows with* LOMAX. BARBARA *clutches like a baby at her mother's skirt.*) Barbara: when will you learn to be independent and to act and think for yourself? I know as well as possible what that cry of "Mamma, Mamma," means. Always running to me!

SARAH (*touching* LADY BRITOMART'S *ribs with her finger tips and imitating a bicycle horn*): Pip! pip!

LADY BRITOMART (*highly indignant*): How dare you say Pip! pip! to me, Sarah? You are both very naughty children. What do you want, Barbara?

BARBARA: I want a house in the village to live in with Dolly. (*Dragging at the skirt.*) Come and tell me which one to take.

UNDERSHAFT (*to* CUSINS): Six o'clock tomorrow morning, my young friend.

THE END

Pygmalion
(1912)

Preface to Pygmalion

A Professor of Phonetics

As will be seen later on, Pygmalion needs, not a preface, but a sequel, which I have supplied in its due place.

The English have no respect for their language, and will not teach their children to speak it. They spell it so abominably that no man can teach himself what it sounds like. It is impossible for an Englishman to open his mouth without making some other Englishman hate or despise him. German and Spanish are accessible to foreigners: English is not accessible even to Englishmen. The reformer England needs today is an energetic phonetic enthusiast: that is why I have made such a one the hero of a popular play. There have been heroes of that kind crying in the wilderness for many years past. When I became interested in the subject towards the end of the eighteen-seventies, Melville Bell was dead; but Alexander J. Ellis was still a living patriarch, with an impressive head always covered by a velvet skull cap, for which he would apologize to public meetings in a very courtly manner. He and Tito Pagliardini, another phonetic veteran, were men whom it was impossible to dislike. Henry Sweet, then a young man, lacked their sweetness of character: he was about as conciliatory to conventional mortals as Ibsen or Samuel Butler. His great ability as a phonetician (he was, I think, the best of them all at his job) would have entitled him to high official recognition, and perhaps enabled him to popularize his subject, but for his Satanic contempt for all

academic dignitaries and persons in general who thought
more of Greek than of phonetics. Once, in the days when
the Imperial Institute rose in South Kensington, and Joseph
Chamberlain was booming the Empire, I induced the editor of a leading monthly review to commission an article
from Sweet on the imperial importance of his subject.
When it arrived, it contained nothing but a savagely deri-
sive attack on a professor of language and literature whose
chair Sweet regarded as proper to a phonetic expert only.
The article, being libellous, had to be returned as impossible; and I had to renounce my dream of dragging its author
into the limelight. When I met him afterwards, for the
first time for many years, I found to my astonishment that
he, who had been a quite tolerably presentable young man,
had actually managed by sheer scorn to alter his personal
appearance until he had become a sort of walking repudia-
tion of Oxford and all its traditions. It must have been
largely in his own despite that he was squeezed into something called a Readership of phonetics there. The future
of phonetics rests probably with his pupils, who all swore
by him; but nothing could bring the man himself into
any sort of compliance with the university to which he
nevertheless clung by divine right in an intensely Oxonian
way. I daresay his papers, if he has left any, include
some satires that may be published without too destructive
results fifty years hence. He was, I believe, not in the
least an illnatured man: very much the opposite, I should
say; but he would not suffer fools gladly.

Those who knew him will recognize in my third act the
allusion to the patent shorthand in which he used to write
postcards, and which may be acquired from a four and
sixpenny manual published by the Clarendon Press. The
postcards which Mrs Higgins describes are such as I have
received from Sweet. I would decipher a sound which a
cockney would represent by *zerr*, and a Frenchman by
seu, and then write demanding with some heat what on
earth it meant. Sweet, with boundless contempt for my
stupidity, would reply that it not only meant but obviously
was the word Result, as no other word containing that
sound, and capable of making sense with the context, ex-

isted in any language spoken on earth. That less expert mortals should require fuller indications was beyond Sweet's patience. Therefore, though the whole point of his "Current Shorthand" is that it can express every sound in the language perfectly, vowels as well as consonants, and that your hand has to make no stroke except the easy and current ones with which you write m, n, and u, l, p, and q, scribbling them at whatever angle comes easiest to you, his unfortunate determination to make this remarkable and quite legible script serve also as a shorthand reduced it in his own practice to the most inscrutable of cryptograms. His true objective was the provision of a full, accurate, legible script for our noble but ill-dressed language; but he was led past that by his contempt for the popular Pitman system of shorthand, which he called the Pitfall system. The triumph of Pitman was a triumph of business organization: there was a weekly paper to persuade you to learn Pitman: there were cheap textbooks and exercise books and transcripts of speeches for you to copy, and schools where experienced teachers coached you up to the necessary proficiency. Sweet could not organize his market in that fashion. He might as well have been the Sybil who tore up the leaves of prophecy that nobody would attend to. The four and sixpenny manual, mostly in his lithographed handwriting, that was never vulgarly advertized, may perhaps some day be taken up by a syndicate and pushed upon the public as The Times pushed the Encyclopædia Britannica; but until then it will certainly not prevail against Pitman. I have bought three copies of it during my lifetime; and I am informed by the publishers that its cloistered existence is still a steady and healthy one. I actually learned the system two several times; and yet the shorthand in which I am writing these lines is Pitman's. And the reason is, that my secretary cannot transcribe Sweet, having been perforce taught in the schools of Pitman. Therefore, Sweet railed at Pitman as vainly as Thersites railed at Ajax: his raillery, however it may have eased his soul, gave no popular vogue to Current Shorthand.

Pygmalion Higgins is not a portrait of Sweet, to whom

the adventure of Eliza Doolittle would have been impossible; still, as will be seen, there are touches of Sweet in the play. With Higgins's physique and temperament Sweet might have set the Thames on fire. As it was, he impressed himself professionally on Europe to an extent that made his comparative personal obscurity, and the failure of Oxford to do justice to his eminence, a puzzle to foreign specialists in his subject. I do not blame Oxford, because I think Oxford is quite right in demanding a certain social amenity from its nurslings (heaven knows it is not exorbitant in its requirements!); for although I well know how hard it is for a man of genius with a seriously underrated subject to maintain serene and kindly relations with the men who underrate it, and who keep all the best places for less important subjects which they profess without originality and sometimes without much capacity for them, still, if he overwhelms them with wrath and disdain, he cannot expect them to heap honors on him.

Of the later generations of phoneticians I know little. Among them towers the Poet Laureate, to whom perhaps Higgins may owe his Miltonic sympathies, though here again I must disclaim all portraiture. But if the play makes the public aware that there are such people as phoneticians, and that they are among the most important people in England at present, it will serve its turn.

I wish to boast that Pygmalion has been an extremely successful play all over Europe and North America as well as at home. It is so intensely and deliberately didactic, and its subject is esteemed so dry, that I delight in throwing it at the heads of the wiseacres who repeat the parrot cry that art should never be didactic. It goes to prove my contention that art should never be anything else.

Finally, and for the encouragement of people troubled with accents that cut them off from all high employment, I may add that the change wrought by Professor Higgins in the flower-girl is neither impossible nor uncommon. The modern concierge's daughter who fulfils her ambition by playing the Queen of Spain in Ruy Blas at the Théâtre Français is only one of many thousands of men and

women who have sloughed off their native dialects and
acquired a new tongue. But the thing has to be done scien-
tifically, or the last state of the aspirant may be worse than
the first. An honest and natural slum dialect is more tolerable than the attempt of a phonetically untaught person to
imitate the vulgar dialect of the golf club; and I am sorry
to say that in spite of the efforts of our Academy of Dramatic Art, there is still too much sham golfing English on
our stage, and too little of the noble English of Forbes
Robertson.

Pygmalion

Act I

(*Covent Garden at 11.15 p.m. Torrents of heavy summer rain. Cab whistles blowing frantically in all directions. Pedestrians running for shelter into the market and under the portico of St. Paul's Church, where there are already several people, among them a lady and her daughter in evening dress. They are all peering out gloomily at the rain, except one man with his back turned to the rest, who seems wholly preoccupied with a notebook in which he is writing busily.*

The church clock strikes the first quarter.)

THE DAUGHTER (*in the space between the central pillars, close to the one on her left*): I'm getting chilled to the bone. What can Freddy be doing all this time? Hes been gone twenty minutes.

THE MOTHER (*on her daughter's right*): Not so long. But he ought to have got us a cab by this.

A BYSTANDER (*on the lady's right*): He wont get no cab not until half-past eleven, missus, when they come back after dropping their theatre fares.

THE MOTHER: But we must have a cab. We cant stand here until half-past eleven. It's too bad.

THE BYSTANDER: Well, it aint my fault, missus.

THE DAUGHTER: If Freddy had a bit of gumption, he would have got one at the theatre door.

THE MOTHER: What could he have done, poor boy?

THE DAUGHTER: Other people got cabs. Why couldnt he?

(FREDDY *rushes in out of the rain from the Southampton Street side, and comes between them closing a dripping*

159

*umbrella. He is a young man of twenty, in evening
dress, very wet round the ankles.*)

THE DAUGHTER: Well, havnt you got a cab?

FREDDY: Theres not one to be had for love or money.

THE MOTHER: Oh, Freddy, there must be one. You cant
have tried.

THE DAUGHTER: It's too tiresome. Do you expect us to
go and get one ourselves?

FREDDY: I tell you theyre all engaged. The rain was so
sudden: nobody was prepared; and everybody had to
take a cab. Ive been to Charing Cross one way and
nearly to Ludgate Circus the other; and they were all
engaged.

THE MOTHER: Did you try Trafalgar Square?

FREDDY: There wasnt one at Trafalgar Square.

THE DAUGHTER: Did you try?

FREDDY: I tried as far as Charing Cross Station. Did you
expect me to walk to Hammersmith?

THE DAUGHTER: You havnt tried at all.

THE MOTHER: You really are very helpless, Freddy. Go
again; and dont come back until you have found a cab.

FREDDY: I shall simply get soaked for nothing.

THE DAUGHTER: And what about us? Are we to stay here
all night in this draught, with next to nothing on. You
selfish pig—

FREDDY: Oh, very well: I'll go, I'll go. (*He opens his
umbrella and dashes off Strandwards, but comes into
collision with a flower girl, who is hurrying in for shelter, knocking her basket out of her hands. A blinding
flash of lightning, followed instantly by a rattling peal
of thunder, orchestrates the incident.*)

THE FLOWER GIRL: Nah then, Freddy: look wh' y' gowin,
deah.

FREDDY: Sorry (*he rushes off*).

THE FLOWER GIRL (*picking up her scattered flowers and
replacing them in the basket*):   Theres menners f' yer!
Te-oo banches o voylets trod into the mad. (*She sits
down on the plinth of the column, sorting her flowers,
on the lady's right. She is not at all an attractive per-*

*son. She is perhaps eighteen, perhaps twenty, hardly
older. She wears a little sailor hat of black straw that
has long been exposed to the dust and soot of London
and has seldom if ever been brushed. Her hair needs
washing rather badly: its mousy color can hardly be
natural. She wears a shoddy black coat that reaches
nearly to her knees and is shaped to her waist. She has
a brown skirt with a coarse apron. Her boots are much
the worse for wear. She is no doubt as clean as she
can afford to be; but compared to the ladies she is very
dirty. Her features are no worse than theirs; but their
condition leaves something to be desired; and she needs
the services of a dentist).*

THE MOTHER: How do you know that my son's name is
Freddy, pray?

THE FLOWER GIRL: Ow, eez ye-ooa san, is e? Wal, fewd
dan y' de-ooty bawmz a mather should, eed now bettern
to spawl a pore gel's flahrzn than ran awy athaht pyin.
Will ye-oo py me f'them? (*Here, with apologies, this
desperate attempt to represent her dialect without a
phonetic alphabet must be abandoned as unintelligible
outside London*).

THE DAUGHTER: Do nothing of the sort, mother. The
idea!

THE MOTHER: Please allow me, Clara. Have you any
pennies?

THE DAUGHTER: No. Ive nothing smaller than sixpence.

THE FLOWER GIRL (*hopefully*): I can give you change for
a tanner, kind lady.

THE MOTHER (*to* CLARA): Give it to me. (CLARA *parts
reluctantly*). Now (*to the girl*): This is for your flowers.

THE FLOWER GIRL: Thank you kindly, lady.

THE DAUGHTER: Make her give you the change. These
things are only a penny a bunch.

THE MOTHER: Do hold your tongue, Clara. (*To the girl*)
You can keep the change.

THE FLOWER GIRL: Oh, thank you, lady.

THE MOTHER: Now tell me how you know that young
gentleman's name.

THE FLOWER GIRL: I didnt.

THE MOTHER: I heard you call him by it. Dont try to deceive me.

THE FLOWER GIRL (*protesting*): Whos trying to deceive you? I called him Freddy or Charlie same as you might yourself if you was talking to a stranger and wished to be pleasant. (*She sits down beside her basket*).

THE DAUGHTER: Sixpence thrown away! Really, mamma, you might have spared Freddy that. (*She retreats in disgust behind the pillar*).

(*An elderly gentleman of the amiable military type rushes into shelter, and closes a dripping umbrella. He is in the same plight as* FREDDY, *very wet about the ankles. He is in evening dress, with a light overcoat. He takes the place left vacant by the daughter's retirement.*)

THE GENTLEMAN: Phew!

THE MOTHER (*to* THE GENTLEMAN): Oh, sir, is there any sign of its stopping?

THE GENTLEMAN: I'm afraid not. It started worse than ever about two minutes ago (*he goes to the plinth beside the flower girl; puts up his foot on it; and stoops to turn down his trouser ends*).

THE MOTHER: Oh dear! (*She retires sadly and joins her daughter*).

THE FLOWER GIRL (*taking advantage of the military gentleman's proximity to establish friendly relations with him*): If it's worse, it's a sign it's nearly over. So cheer up, Captain; and buy a flower off a poor girl.

THE GENTLEMAN: I'm sorry. I havnt any change.

THE FLOWER GIRL: I can give you change, Captain.

THE GENTLEMAN: For a sovereign? Ive nothing less.

THE FLOWER GIRL: Garn! Oh do buy a flower off me, Captain. I can change half-a-crown. Take this for tuppence.

THE GENTLEMAN: Now dont be troublesome: theres a good girl. (*Trying his pockets*) I really havnt any change—Stop: heres three hapence, if thats any use to you (*he retreats to the other pillar*).

THE FLOWER GIRL (*disappointed, but thinking three half-pence better than nothing*):   Thank you, sir.

THE BYSTANDER (*to the girl*):   You be careful: give him a flower for it. Theres a bloke here behind taking down every blessed word youre saying. (*All turn to the man who is taking notes*).

THE FLOWER GIRL (*springing up terrified*):   I aint done nothing wrong by speaking to the gentleman. Ive a right to sell flowers if I keep off the kerb. (*Hysterically*) I'm a respectable girl: so help me, I never spoke to him except to ask him to buy a flower off me. (*General hubbub, mostly sympathetic to* THE FLOWER GIRL, *but deprecating her excessive sensibility. Cries of* Don't start hollerin. Whos hurting you? Nobody's going to touch you. Whats the good of fussing? Steady on. Easy easy, etc., *come from the elderly staid spectators, who pat her comfortingly. Less patient ones bid her shut her head, or ask her roughly what is wrong with her. A remoter group, not knowing what the matter is, crowd in and increase the noise with question and answer:* Whats the row? Whatshe do? Where is he? A tec taking her down. What! him? Yes: him over there: Took money off the gentleman, etc. THE FLOWER GIRL, *distraught and mobbed, breaks through them to* THE GENTLEMAN, *crying wildly*) Oh, sir, dont let him charge me. You dunno what it means to me. Theyll take away my character and drive me on the streets for speaking to gentlemen. They—

THE NOTE TAKER (*coming forward on her right, the rest crowding after him*):   There, there, there, there! whos hurting you, you silly girl? What do you take me for?

THE BYSTANDER: It's all right: hes a gentleman: look at his boots. (*Explaining to* THE NOTE TAKER) She thought you was a copper's nark, sir.

THE NOTE TAKER (*with quick interest*):   Whats a copper's nark?

THE BYSTANDER (*inapt at definition*):   It's a—well, it's a copper's nark, as you might say. What else would you call it? A sort of informer.

THE FLOWER GIRL (*still hysterical*): I take my Bible oath
I never said a word—

THE NOTE TAKER (*overbearing but good-humored*): Oh,
shut up, shut up. Do I look like a policeman?

THE FLOWER GIRL (*far from reassured*): Then what did
you take down my words for? How do I know whether
you took me down right? You just shew me what youve
wrote about me. (THE NOTE TAKER *opens his book and
holds it steadily under her nose, though the pressure of
the mob trying to read it over his shoulders would upset
a weaker man*). Whats that? That aint proper writing. I
cant read that.

THE NOTE TAKER: I can. (*Reads, reproducing her pronunciation exactly*) "Cheer ap, Keptin; n' baw ya flahr
orf a pore gel."

THE FLOWER GIRL (*much distressed*): It's because I called
him Captain. I meant no harm. (*To* THE GENTLEMAN)
Oh, sir, dont let him lay a charge agen me for a word
like that. You—

THE GENTLEMAN: Charge! I make no charge. (*To* THE
NOTE TAKER) Really, sir, if you are a detective, you
need not begin protecting me against molestation by
young women until I ask you. Anybody could see that
the girl meant no harm.

THE BYSTANDERS GENERALLY (*demonstrating against police espionage*): Course they could. What business is
it of yours? You mind your own affairs. He wants promotion, he does. Taking down people's words! Girl
never said a word to him. What harm if she did? Nice
thing a girl cant shelter from the rain without being
insulted, etc., etc., etc. (*She is conducted by the more
sympathetic demonstrators back to her plinth, where she
resumes her seat and struggles with her emotion.*)

THE BYSTANDER: He aint a tec. Hes a blooming busy-
body: thats what he is. I tell you, look at his boots.

THE NOTE TAKER (*turning on him genially*): And how are
all your people down at Selsey?

THE BYSTANDER (*suspiciously*): Who told you my people
come from Selsey?

THE NOTE TAKER: Never you mind. They did. (*To the girl*) How do you come to be up so far east? You were born in Lisson Grove.

THE FLOWER GIRL (*appalled*): Oh, what harm is there in my leaving Lisson Grove? It wasnt fit for a pig to live in; and I had to pay four-and-six a week. (*In tears*) Oh, boo—hoo—oo—

THE NOTE TAKER: Live where you like; but stop that noise.

THE GENTLEMAN (*to the girl*): Come, come! he cant touch you: you have a right to live where you please.

A SARCASTIC BYSTANDER (*thrusting himself between* THE NOTE TAKER *and* THE GENTLEMAN): Park Lane, for instance. Id like to go into the Housing Question with you, I would.

THE FLOWER GIRL (*subsiding into a brooding melancholy over her basket, and talking very low-spiritedly to herself*): I'm a good girl, I am.

THE SARCASTIC BYSTANDER (*not attending to her*): Do you know where *I* come from?

THE NOTE TAKER (*promptly*): Hoxton.

(*Titterings. Popular interest in* THE NOTE TAKER'*s performance increases.*)

THE SARCASTIC ONE (*amazed*): Well, who said I didnt? Bly me! You know everything, you do.

THE FLOWER GIRL (*still nursing her sense of injury*): Aint no call to meddle with me, he aint.

THE BYSTANDER (*to her*): Of course he aint. Dont you stand it from him. (*To* THE NOTE TAKER) See here: what call have you to know about people what never offered to meddle with you? Wheres your warrant?

SEVERAL BYSTANDERS (*encouraged by this seeming point of law*): Yes: wheres your warrant?

THE FLOWER GIRL: Let him say what he likes. I dont want to have no truck with him.

THE BYSTANDER: You take us for dirt under your feet, dont you? Catch you taking liberties with a gentleman!

THE SARCASTIC BYSTANDER: Yes: tell him where he come from if you want to go fortune-telling.

THE NOTE TAKER: Cheltenham, Harrow, Cambridge, and India.

THE GENTLEMAN: Quite right. (*Great laughter. Reaction in* THE NOTE TAKER's *favor. Exclamations of* He knows all about it. Told him proper. Hear him tell the toff where he come from? etc.). May I ask, sir, do you do this for your living at a music hall?

THE NOTE TAKER: Ive thought of that. Perhaps I shall some day.

(*The rain has stopped; and the persons on the outside of the crowd begin to drop off.*)

THE FLOWER GIRL (*resenting the reaction*): Hes no gentleman, he aint, to interfere with a poor girl.

THE DAUGHTER (*out of patience, pushing her way rudely to the front and displacing* THE GENTLEMAN, *who politely retires to the other side of the pillar*): What on earth is Freddy doing? I shall get pneumonia if I stay in this draught any longer.

THE NOTE TAKER (*to himself, hastily making a note of her pronunciation of "monia"*): Earlscourt.

THE DAUGHTER (*violently*): Will you please keep your impertinent remarks to yourself.

THE NOTE TAKER: Did I say that out loud? I didn't mean to. I beg your pardon. Your mother's Epsom, unmistakeably.

THE MOTHER (*advancing between her daughter and* THE NOTE TAKER): How very curious! I was brought up in Largelady Park, near Epsom.

THE NOTE TAKER (*uproariously amused*): Ha! ha! What a devil of a name! Excuse me. (*To* THE DAUGHTER) You want a cab, do you?

THE DAUGHTER: Dont dare speak to me.

THE MOTHER: Oh please, please, Clara. (*Her daughter repudiates her with an angry shrug and retires haughtily*). We should be so grateful to you, sir, if you found

us a cab. (THE NOTE TAKER *produces a whistle*). Oh,
thank you. (*She joins her daughter*).

(THE NOTE TAKER *blows a piercing blast*.)

THE SARCASTIC BYSTANDER: There! I knowed he was a
plain-clothes copper.

THE BYSTANDER: That ain't a police whistle: thats a
sporting whistle.

THE FLOWER GIRL (*still preoccupied with her wounded
feelings*): Hes no right to take away my character. My
character is the same to me as any lady's.

THE NOTE TAKER: I don't know whether youve noticed
it; but the rain stopped about two minutes ago.

THE BYSTANDER: So it has. Why didnt you say so before? and us losing our time listening to your silliness!
(*He walks off towards the Strand*).

THE SARCASTIC BYSTANDER: I can tell where you come
from. You come from Anwell. Go back there.

THE NOTE TAKER (*helpfully*): Hanwell.

THE SARCASTIC BYSTANDER (*affecting great distinction of
speech*): Thank you, teacher. Haw haw! So long (*he
touches his hat with much respect and strolls off*).

THE FLOWER GIRL: Frightening people like that! How
would he like it himself?

THE MOTHER: It's quite fine now, Clara. We can walk to
a motor bus. Come. (*She gathers her skirts above her
ankles and hurries off towards the Strand*).

THE DAUGHTER: But the cab— (*her mother is out of
hearing*). Oh, how tiresome! (*She follows angrily*).

(*All the rest have gone except* THE NOTE TAKER, THE
GENTLEMAN, *and* THE FLOWER GIRL, *who sits arranging
her basket, and still pitying herself in murmurs.*)

THE FLOWER GIRL: Poor girl! Hard enough for her to live
without being worried and chivied.

THE GENTLEMAN (*returning to his former place on* THE
NOTE TAKER'S *left*): How do you do it, if I may ask?

THE NOTE TAKER: Simply phonetics. The science of
speech. Thats my profession: also my hobby. Happy is

the man who can make a living by his hobby! You can
spot an Irishman or a Yorkshireman by his brogue. *I*
can place any man within six miles. I can place him
within two miles in London. Sometimes within two
streets.

THE FLOWER GIRL: Ought to be ashamed of himself, un-
manly coward!

THE GENTLEMAN: But is there a living in that?

THE NOTE TAKER: Oh yes. Quite a fat one. This is an
age of upstarts. Men begin in Kentish Town with £80
a year, and end in Park Lane with a hundred thousand.
They want to drop Kentish Town; but they give themselves away every time they open their mouths. Now I
can teach them—

THE FLOWER GIRL: Let him mind his own business and
leave a poor girl—

THE NOTE TAKER (*explosively*):   Woman: cease this de-
testable boohooing instantly; or else seek the shelter of
some other place of worship.

THE FLOWER GIRL (*with feeble defiance*):   Ive a right to
be here if I like, same as you.

THE NOTE TAKER: A woman who utters such depressing
and disgusting sounds has no right to be anywhere—no
right to live. Remember that you are a human being
with a soul and the divine gift of articulate speech: that
your native language is the language of Shakespear and
Milton and The Bible; and dont sit there crooning like
a bilious pigeon.

THE FLOWER GIRL (*quite overwhelmed, looking up at him
in mingled wonder and deprecation without daring to
raise her head*):   Ah-ah-ah-ow-ow-ow-oo!

THE NOTE TAKER (*whipping out his book*):   Heavens! what
a sound! (*He writes; then holds out the book and reads,
reproducing her vowels exactly*) Ah-ah-ah-ow-ow-ow-
oo!

THE FLOWER GIRL (*tickled by the performance, and laughing in spite of herself*):   Garn!

THE NOTE TAKER: You see this creature with her kerbstone English: the English that will keep her in the gut-

ter to the end of her days. Well, sir, in three months I could pass that girl off as a duchess at an ambassador's garden party. I could even get her a place as lady's maid or shop assistant, which requires better English. Thats the sort of thing I do for commercial millionaires. And on the profits of it I do genuine scientific work in phonetics, and a little as a poet on Miltonic lines.

THE GENTLEMAN: I am myself a student of Indian dialects; and—

THE NOTE TAKER (*eagerly*): Are you? Do you know Colonel Pickering, the author of Spoken Sanscrit?

THE GENTLEMAN: I am Colonel Pickering. Who are you?

THE NOTE TAKER: Henry Higgins, author of Higgins's Universal Alphabet.

PICKERING (*with enthusiasm*): I came from India to meet you.

HIGGINS: I was going to India to meet you.

PICKERING: Where do you live?

HIGGINS: 27A Wimpole Street. Come and see me tomorrow.

PICKERING: I'm at the Carlton. Come with me now and lets have a jaw over some supper.

HIGGINS: Right you are.

THE FLOWER GIRL (*to* PICKERING, *as he passes her*): Buy a flower, kind gentleman. I'm short for my lodging.

PICKERING: I really havn't any change. I'm sorry (*he goes away*).

HIGGINS (*shocked at the girl's mendacity*): Liar. You said you could change half-a-crown.

THE FLOWER GIRL (*rising in desperation*): You ought to be stuffed with nails, you ought. (*Flinging the basket at his feet*) Take the whole blooming basket for sixpence.

(*The church clock strikes the second quarter.*)

HIGGINS (*hearing in it the voice of God, rebuking him for his Pharisaic want of charity to the poor girl*): A reminder. (*He raises his hat solemnly; then throws a handful of money into the basket and follows* PICKERING).

THE FLOWER GIRL (*picking up a half-crown*): Ah-ow-ooh!

(*Picking up a couple of florins*) Aaah-ow-ooh! (*Picking up several coins*) Aaaaaah-ow-ooh! (*Picking up a half-sovereign*) Aaaaaaaaaaaah-ow-ooh!!!

FREDDY (*springing out of a taxicab*): Got one at last. Hallo! (*To the girl*) Where are the two ladies that were here?

THE FLOWER GIRL: They walked to the bus when the rain stopped.

FREDDY: And left me with a cab on my hands! Damnation!

THE FLOWER GIRL (*with grandeur*): Never you mind, young man. *I'm* going home in a taxi. (*She sails off to the cab. The driver puts his hand behind him and holds the door firmly shut against her. Quite understanding his mistrust, she shews him her handful of money*). Eightpence aint no object to me, Charlie. (*He grins and opens the door*). Angel Court, Drury Lane, round the corner of Micklejohn's oil shop. Lets see how fast you can make her hop it. (*She gets in and pulls the door to with a slam as the taxicab starts*).

FREDDY: Well, I'm dashed!

Act II

(*Next day at 11 a.m.* HIGGINS's *laboratory in Wimpole Street. It is a room on the first floor, looking on the street, and was meant for the drawing-room. The double doors are in the middle of the back wall; and persons entering find in the corner to their right two tall file cabinets at right angles to one another against the walls. In this corner stands a flat writing-table, on which are a phonograph, a laryngoscope, a row of tiny organ pipes with a bellows, a set of lamp chimneys for singeing flames with burners attached to a gas plug in the wall by an indiarubber tube, several tuning-forks of different sizes, a life-size image of half a human head, shewing in section the vocal organs, and a box containing a supply of wax cylinders for the phonograph.*

Further down the room, on the same side, is a fireplace, with a comfortable leather-covered easy-chair at the side of the hearth nearest the door, and a coalscuttle. There is a clock on the mantelpiece. Between the fireplace and the phonograph table is a stand for newspapers.

On the other side of the central door, to the left of the visitor, is a cabinet of shallow drawers. On it is a telephone and the telephone directory. The corner beyond, and most of the side wall, is occupied by a grand piano, with the keyboard at the end furthest from the door, and a bench for the player extending the full length of the keyboard. On the piano is a dessert dish heaped with fruit and sweets, mostly chocolates.

The middle of the room is clear. Besides the easy-chair, the piano bench, and two chairs at the phono-

graph table, there is one stray chair. It stands near the fireplace. On the walls, engravings: mostly Piranesis and mezzotint portraits. No paintings.

PICKERING *is seated at the table, putting down some cards and a tuning-fork which he has been using.* HIGGINS *is standing up near him, closing two or three file drawers which are hanging out. He appears in the morning light as a robust, vital, appetizing sort of man of forty or thereabouts, dressed in a professional-looking black frock-coat with a white linen collar and black silk tie. He is of the energetic, scientific type, heartily, even violently interested in everything that can be studied as a scientific subject, and careless about himself and other people, including their feelings. He is, in fact, but for his years and size, rather like a very impetuous baby "taking notice" eagerly and loudly, and requiring almost as much watching to keep him out of unintended mischief. His manner varies from genial bullying when he is in a good humor to stormy petulance when anything goes wrong; but he is so entirely frank and void of malice that he remains likeable even in his least reasonable moments.)*

HIGGINS (*as he shuts the last drawer*):   Well, I think thats the whole show.

PICKERING: It's really amazing. I havnt taken half of it in, you know.

HIGGINS: Would you like to go over any of it again?

PICKERING (*rising and coming to the fireplace, where he plants himself with his back to the fire*):   No, thank you; not now. I'm quite done up for this morning.

HIGGINS (*following him, and standing beside him on his left*):   Tired of listening to sounds?

PICKERING: Yes. It's a fearful strain. I rather fancied myself because I can pronounce twenty-four distinct vowel sounds; but your hundred and thirty beat me. I cant hear a bit of difference between most of them.

HIGGINS (*chuckling, and going over to the piano to eat sweets*):   Oh, that comes with practice. You hear no difference at first; but you keep on listening, and presently you find theyre all as different as A from B. (MRS PEARCE *looks in: she is* HIGGINS'S *housekeeper*). Whats the matter?

MRS PEARCE (*hesitating, evidently perplexed*):   A young woman wants to see you, sir.

HIGGINS: A young woman! What does she want?

MRS PEARCE: Well, sir, she says youll be glad to see her when you know what shes come about. Shes quite a common girl, sir. Very common indeed. I should have sent her away, only I thought perhaps you wanted her to talk into your machines. I hope Ive not done wrong; but really you see such queer people sometimes—youll excuse me, I'm sure, sir—

HIGGINS: Oh, thats all right, Mrs Pearce. Has she an interesting accent?

MRS PEARCE: Oh, something dreadful, sir, really. I dont know how you can take an interest in it.

HIGGINS (*to* PICKERING):   Lets have her up. Shew her up, Mrs Pearce (*he rushes across to his working table and picks out a cylinder to use on the phonograph*).

MRS PEARCE (*only half resigned to it*):   Very well, sir. Its for you to say. (*She goes downstairs*).

HIGGINS: This is rather a bit of luck. I'll shew you how I make records. We'll set her talking; and I'll take it down first in Bell's visible Speech; then in broad Romic; and then we'll get her on the phonograph so that you can turn her on as often as you like with the written transcript before you.

MRS PEARCE (*returning*):   This is the young woman, sir.

(THE FLOWER GIRL *enters in state. She has a hat with three ostrich feathers, orange, sky-blue, and red. She has a nearly clean apron, and the shoddy coat has been tidied a little. The pathos of this deplorable figure, with its innocent vanity and consequential air, touches* PICKERING, *who has already straightened himself in the presence of* MRS PEARCE. *But as to* HIGGINS, *the only distinction he makes between men and women is that*

when he is neither bullying nor exclaiming to the heav-
ens against some featherweight cross, he coaxes women
as a child coaxes its nurse when it wants to get anything
out of her.)

HIGGINS (*brusquely, recognizing her with unconcealed dis-*
appointment, and at once, babylike, making an intolera-
ble grievance of it): Why, this is the girl I jotted down
last night. Shes no use: Ive got all the records I want
of the Lisson Grove lingo; and I'm not going to waste
another cylinder on it. (*To the girl*) Be off with you: I
dont want you.

THE FLOWER GIRL: Dont you be so saucy. You aint heard
what I come for yet. (*To* MRS PEARCE, *who is waiting*
at the door for further instructions) Did you tell him I
come in a taxi?

MRS PEARCE: Nonsense, girl! what do you think a gentleman like Mr Higgins cares what you came in?

THE FLOWER GIRL: Oh, we are proud! He aint above giving lessons, not him: I heard him say so. Well, I aint
come here to ask for any compliment; and if my money's not good enough I can go elsewhere.

HIGGINS: Good enough for what?

THE FLOWER GIRL: Good enough for ye-oo. Now you
know, dont you? I'm come to have lessons, I am. And
to pay for em too: make no mistake.

HIGGINS (*stupent*): Well!!! (*Recovering his breath with a*
gasp) What do you expect me to say to you?

THE FLOWER GIRL: Well, if you was a gentleman, you
might ask me to sit down, I think. Dont I tell you I'm
bringing you business?

HIGGINS: Pickering: shall we ask this baggage to sit
down, or shall we throw her out of the window?

THE FLOWER GIRL (*running away in terror to the piano,*
where she turns at bay): Ah-ah-oh-ow-ow-ow-oo!
(*Wounded and whimpering*) I wont be called a baggage
when Ive offered to pay like any lady.

(*Motionless, the two men stare at her from the other*
side of the room, amazed.)

PICKERING (*gently*):   What is it you want, my girl?

THE FLOWER GIRL: I want to be a lady in a flower shop stead of selling at the corner of Tottenham Court Road. But they wont take me unless I can talk more genteel. He said he could teach me. Well, here I am ready to pay him—not asking any favor—and he treats me as if I was dirt.

MRS PEARCE: How can you be such a foolish ignorant girl as to think you could afford to pay Mr Higgins?

THE FLOWER GIRL: Why shouldnt I? I know what lessons cost as well as you do; and I'm ready to pay.

HIGGINS: How much?

THE FLOWER GIRL (*coming back to him, triumphant*):   Now youre talking! I thought youd come off it when you saw a chance of getting back a bit of what you chucked at me last night. (*Confidentially*) Youd had a drop in, hadnt you?

HIGGINS (*peremptorily*):   Sit down.

THE FLOWER GIRL: Oh, if youre going to make a compliment of it—

HIGGINS (*thundering at her*):   Sit down.

MRS PEARCE (*severely*):   Sit down, girl. Do as youre told.

(*She places the stray chair near the hearthrug between* HIGGINS *and* PICKERING, *and stands behind it waiting for the girl to sit down*).

THE FLOWER GIRL: Ah-ah-ah-ow-ow-oo! (*She stands, half rebellious, half bewildered*).

PICKERING (*very courteous*):   Wont you sit down?

LIZA (*coyly*):   Dont mind if I do. (*She sits down.* PICKERING *returns to the hearthrug*).

HIGGINS: Whats your name?

THE FLOWER GIRL: Liza Doolittle.

HIGGINS (*declaiming gravely*):
> *Eliza, Elizabeth, Betsy and Bess,*
> *They went to the woods to get a bird's nes':*

PICKERING: *They found a nest with four eggs in it:*

HIGGINS: *They took one apiece, and left three in it.*

(*They laugh heartily at their own wit.*)

LIZA: Oh, dont be silly.

MRS PEARCE: You mustnt speak to the gentleman like that.

LIZA: Well, why wont he speak sensible to me?

HIGGINS: Come back to business. How much do you propose to pay me for the lessons?

LIZA: Oh, I know whats right. A lady friend of mine gets French lessons for eighteenpence an hour from a real French gentleman. Well, you wouldnt have the face to ask me the same for teaching me my own language as you would for French; so I wont give more than a shilling. Take it or leave it.

HIGGINS (*walking up and down the room, rattling his keys and his cash in his pockets*): You know, Pickering, if you consider a shilling, not as a simple shilling, but as a percentage of this girl's income, it works out as fully equivalent to sixty or seventy guineas from a millionaire.

PICKERING: How so?

HIGGINS: Figure it out. A millionaire has about £150 a day. She earns about half-a-crown.

LIZA (*haughtily*): Who told you I only—

HIGGINS (*continuing*): She offers me two-fifths of her day's income for a lesson. Two-fifths of a millionaire's income for a day would be somewhere about £60. It's handsome. By George, it's enormous! it's the biggest offer I ever had.

LIZA (*rising, terrified*): Sixty pounds! What are you talking about? I never offered you sixty pounds. Where would I get—

HIGGINS: Hold your tongue.

LIZA (*weeping*): But I aint got sixty pounds. Oh—

MRS PEARCE: Dont cry, you silly girl. Sit down. Nobody is going to touch your money.

HIGGINS: Somebody is going to touch you, with a broomstick, if you dont stop snivelling. Sit down.

LIZA (*obeying slowly*): Ah-ah-ah-ow-oo-o! One would think you was my father.

HIGGINS: If I decide to teach you, I'll be worse than two fathers to you. Here (*he offers her his silk handkerchief*)!

LIZA: Whats this for?

HIGGINS: To wipe your eyes. To wipe any part of your face that feels moist. Remember: thats your handkerchief; and thats your sleeve. Dont mistake the one for the other if you wish to become a lady in a shop.

(LIZA, *utterly bewildered, stares helplessly at him.*)

MRS PEARCE: It's no use talking to her like that, Mr Higgins: she doesnt understand you. Besides, youre quite wrong: she doesnt do it that way at all (*she takes the handkerchief*).

LIZA (*snatching it*): Here! You give me that handkerchief. He give it to me, not to you.

PICKERING (*laughing*): He did. I think it must be regarded as her property, Mrs Pearce.

MRS PEARCE (*resigning herself*): Serve you right, Mr Higgins.

PICKERING: Higgins: I'm interested. What about the ambassador's garden party? I'll say youre the greatest teacher alive if you make that good. I'll bet you all the expenses of the experiment you cant do it. And I'll pay for the lessons.

LIZA: Oh, you are real good. Thank you, Captain.

HIGGINS (*tempted, looking at her*): It's almost irresistible. Shes so deliciously low—so horribly dirty—

LIZA (*protesting extremely*): Ah-ah-ah-ah-ow-ow-oo-oo!!! I aint dirty: I washed my face and hands afore I come, I did.

PICKERING: Youre certainly not going to turn her head with flattery, Higgins.

MRS PEARCE (*uneasy*): Oh, don't say that, sir: theres more ways than one of turning a girl's head; and nobody can do it better than Mr Higgins, though he may not always mean it. I do hope, sir, you wont encourage him to do anything foolish.

HIGGINS (*becoming excited as the idea grows on him*): What is life but a series of inspired follies? The diffi-

culty is to find them to do. Never lose a chance: it
doesnt come everyday. I shall make a duchess of this
draggletailed guttersnipe.

LIZA (*strongly deprecating this view of her*): Ah-ah-ah-
ow-ow-oo!

HIGGINS (*carried away*): Yes: in six months—in three if
she has a good ear and a quick tongue—I'll take her
anywhere and pass her off as anything. We'll start to-
day: now! this moment! Take her away and clean her,
Mrs Pearce. Monkey Brand, if it wont come off any
other way. Is there a good fire in the kitchen?

MRS PEARCE (*protesting*): Yes; but—

HIGGINS (*storming on*): Take all her clothes off and burn
them. Ring up Whiteley or somebody for new ones.
Wrap her up in brown paper til they come.

LIZA: Youre no gentleman, youre not, to talk of such
things. I'm a good girl, I am; and I know what the like
of you are, I do.

HIGGINS: We want none of your Lisson Grove prudery
here, young woman. Youve got to learn to behave like
a duchess. Take her away, Mrs Pearce. If she gives you
any trouble, wallop her.

LIZA (*springing up and running between* PICKERING *and*
MRS PEARCE *for protection*): No! I'll call the police, I
will.

MRS PEARCE: But Ive no place to put her.

HIGGINS: Put her in the dustbin.

LIZA: Ah-ah-ah-ow-ow-oo!

PICKERING: Oh come, Higgins! be reasonable.

MRS PEARCE (*resolutely*): You must be reasonable, Mr
Higgins: really you must. You cant walk over everybody like this.

(HIGGINS, *thus scolded, subsides. The hurricane is succeeded by a zephyr of amiable surprise.*)

HIGGINS (*with professional exquisiteness of modula-
tion*): *I* walk over everybody! My dear Mrs Pearce,
my dear Pickering, I never had the slightest intention
of walking over anyone. All I propose is that we should

be kind to this poor girl. We must help her to prepare
and fit herself for her new station in life. If I did not
express myself clearly it was because I did not wish to
hurt her delicacy, or yours.

(LIZA, *reassured, steals back to her chair.*)

MRS PEARCE (*to* PICKERING):   Well, did you ever hear
anything like that, sir?

PICKERING (*laughing heartily*):   Never, Mrs Pearce: never.

HIGGINS (*patiently*):   Whats the matter?

MRS PEARCE: Well, the matter is, sir, that you cant take
a girl up like that as if you were picking up a pebble
on the beach.

HIGGINS: Why not?

MRS PEARCE: Why not! But you dont know anything
about her. What about her parents? She may be married.

LIZA: Garn!

HIGGINS: There! As the girl very properly says, Garn!
Married indeed! Dont you know that a woman of that
class looks a worn out drudge of fifty a year after shes
married?

LIZA: Whood marry me?

HIGGINS (*suddenly resorting to the most thrillingly beautiful low tones in his best elocutionary style*):   By
George, Eliza, the streets will be strewn with the bodies
of men shooting themselves for your sake before Ive
done with you.

MRS PEARCE: Nonsense, sir. You mustnt talk like that to
her.

LIZA (*rising and squaring herself determinedly*):   I'm
going away. He's off his chump, he is. I dont want no
balmies teaching me.

HIGGINS (*wounded in his tenderest point by her insensibil-
ity to his elocution*):   Oh, indeed! I'm mad, am I? Very
well, Mrs Pearce: you neednt order the new clothes for
her. Throw her out.

LIZA (*whimpering*):   Nah-ow. You got no right to touch
me.

MRS PEARCE: You see now what comes of being saucy.
(*Indicating the door*) This way, please.

LIZA (*almost in tears*):   I didn't want no clothes. I
wouldnt have taken them (*she throws away the handkerchief*). I can buy my own clothes.

HIGGINS (*deftly retrieving the handkerchief and inter-
cepting her on her reluctant way to the door*):   Youre
an ungrateful wicked girl. This is my return for offering
to take you out of the gutter and dress you beautifully
and make a lady of you.

MRS PEARCE: Stop, Mr Higgins. I wont allow it. It's you
that are wicked. Go home to your parents, girl; and tell
them to take better care of you.

LIZA: I aint got no parents. They told me I was big
enough to earn my own living and turned me out.

MRS PEARCE: Wheres your mother?

LIZA: I aint got no mother. Her that turned me out was
my sixth stepmother. But I done without them. And I'm
a good girl, I am.

HIGGINS: Very well, then, what on earth is all this fuss
about? The girl doesnt belong to anybody—is no use to
anybody but me. (*He goes to* MRS PEARCE *and begins
coaxing.*) You can adopt her, Mrs Pearce: I'm sure a
daughter would be a great amusement to you. Now dont
make any more fuss. Take her downstairs; and—

MRS PEARCE: But whats to become of her? Is she to be
paid anything? Do be sensible, sir.

HIGGINS: Oh, pay her whatever is necessary: put it down
in the housekeeping book. (*Impatiently*) What on earth
will she want with money? She'll have her food and
her clothes. She'll only drink if you give her money.

LIZA (*turning on him*):   Oh you are a brute. It's a lie:
nobody ever saw the sign of liquor on me. (*She goes
back to her chair and plants herself there defiantly*).

PICKERING (*in good-humored remonstrance*):   Does it
occur to you, Higgins, that the girl has some feelings?

HIGGINS (*looking critically at her*):   Oh no, I dont think
so. Not any feelings that we need bother about. (*Cheer-
ily*) Have you, Eliza?

LIZA: I got my feelings same as anyone else.

HIGGINS (*to* PICKERING, *reflectively*):   You see the difficulty?

PICKERING: Eh? What difficulty?

HIGGINS: To get her to talk grammar. The mere pronunciation is easy enough.

LIZA: I dont want to talk grammar. I want to talk like a lady.

MRS PEARCE: Will you please keep to the point, Mr Higgins. I want to know on what terms the girl is to be here. Is she to have any wages? And what is to become of her when youve finished your teaching? You must look ahead a little.

HIGGINS (*impatiently*):   Whats to become of her if I leave her in the gutter? Tell me that, Mrs Pearce.

MRS PEARCE: Thats her own business, not yours, Mr Higgins.

HIGGINS: Well, when Ive done with her, we can throw her back into the gutter; and then it will be her own business again; so thats all right.

LIZA: Oh, youve no feeling heart in you: you dont care for nothing but yourself (*she rises and takes the floor resolutely*). Here! Ive had enough of this. I'm going (*making for the door*). You ought to be ashamed of yourself, you ought.

HIGGINS (*snatching a chocolate cream from the piano, his eyes suddenly beginning to twinkle with mischief*): Have some chocolates, Eliza.

LIZA (*halting, tempted*):   How do I know what might be in them? Ive heard of girls being drugged by the like of you.

(HIGGINS *whips out his penknife; cuts a chocolate in two; puts one half into his mouth and bolts it; and offers her the other half.*)

HIGGINS: Pledge of good faith, Eliza. I eat one half: you eat the other. (LIZA *opens her mouth to retort: he pops the half chocolate into it*). You shall have boxes of

them, barrels of them, every day. You shall live on
them. Eh?

LIZA (*who has disposed of the chocolate after being nearly
choked by it*): I wouldn't have ate it, only I'm too
ladylike to take it out of my mouth.

HIGGINS: Listen, Eliza. I think you said you came in a
taxi.

LIZA: Well, what if I did? Ive as good a right to take a
taxi as anyone else.

HIGGINS: You have, Eliza; and in future you shall have
as many taxis as you want. You shall go up and down
and round the town in a taxi every day. Think of that,
Eliza.

MRS PEARCE: Mr Higgins: youre tempting the girl. It's
not right. She should think of the future.

HIGGINS: At her age! Nonsense! Time enough to think
of the future when you havnt any future to think of.
No, Eliza: do as this lady does: think of other people's
futures; but never think of your own. Think of chocolates, and taxis, and gold, and diamonds.

LIZA: No: I dont want no gold and no diamonds. I'm a
good girl, I am. (*She sits down again, with an attempt
at dignity*).

HIGGINS: You shall remain so, Eliza, under the care of
Mrs Pearce. And you shall marry an officer in the
Guards, with a beautiful moustache: the son of a
marquis, who will disinherit him for marrying you, but
will relent when he sees your beauty and goodness—

PICKERING: Excuse me, Higgins; but I really must interfere. Mrs Pearce is quite right. If this girl is to put
herself in your hands for six months for an experiment
in teaching, she must understand thoroughly what shes
doing.

HIGGINS: How can she? Shes incapable of understanding
anything. Besides, do any of us understand what we are
doing? If we did, would we ever do it?

PICKERING: Very clever, Higgins; but not sound sense.
(*To* ELIZA) Miss Doolittle—

LIZA (*overwhelmed*): Ah-ah-ow-oo!

HIGGINS: There! Thats all youll get out of Eliza. Ah-ah-
ow-oo! No use explaining. As a military man you ought
to know that. Give her her orders: thats what she wants.
Eliza: you are to live here for the next six months,
learning how to speak beautifully, like a lady in a florist's shop. If youre good and do whatever youre told,
you shall sleep in a proper bedroom, and have lots to
eat, and money to buy chocolates and take rides in taxis.
If youre naughty and idle you will sleep in the back
kitchen among the black beetles, and be walloped by
Mrs Pearce with a broomstick. At the end of six months
you shall go to Buckingham Palace in a carriage, beautifully dressed. If the King finds out youre not a lady,
you will be taken by the police to the Tower of London,
where your head will be cut off as a warning to other
presumptuous flower girls. If you are not found out,
you shall have a present of seven-and-sixpence to start
life with as a lady in a shop. If you refuse this offer
you will be a most ungrateful and wicked girl; and
the angels will weep for you. (*To* PICKERING) Now are
you satisfied, Pickering? (*To* MRS PEARCE) Can I put it
more plainly and fairly, Mrs Pearce?

MRS PEARCE (*patiently*):   I think youd better let me speak
to the girl properly in private. I dont know that I can
take charge of her or consent to the arrangement at all.
Of course I know you dont mean her any harm; but
when you get what you call interested in people's accents, you never think or care what may happen to them
or you. Come with me, Eliza.

HIGGINS: Thats all right. Thank you, Mrs Pearce. Bundle
her off to the bath-room.

LIZA (*rising reluctantly and suspiciously*):   Youre a great
bully, you are. I wont stay here if I dont like. I wont
let nobody wallop me. I never asked to go to Bucknam
Palace, I didn't. I was never in trouble with the police,
not me. I'm a good girl—

MRS PEARCE: Don't answer back, girl. You dont understand the gentleman. Come with me. (*She leads the way
to the door, and holds it open for* ELIZA).

LIZA (*as she goes out*):   Well, what I say is right. I wont
go near the king, not if I'm going to have my head cut
off. If I'd known what I was letting myself in for, I
wouldnt have come here. I always been a good girl;
and I never offered to say a word to him; and I dont
owe him nothing; and I dont care; and I wont be put
upon; and I have my feelings the same as anyone else—

(MRS PEARCE *shuts the door; and* ELIZA'*s plaints are no
longer audible.* PICKERING *comes from the hearth to the
chair and sits astride it with his arms on the back.*)

PICKERING: Excuse the straight question, Higgins. Are you
a man of good character where women are concerned?
HIGGINS   (*moodily*):   Have you ever met a man of good
character where women are concerned?
PICKERING: Yes: very frequently.
HIGGINS   (*dogmatically, lifting himself on his hands to
the level of the piano, and sitting on it with a
bounce*):   Well, I havnt. I find that the moment I let a
woman make friends with me, she becomes jealous,
exacting, suspicious, and a damned nuisance. I find that
the moment I let myself make friends with a woman, I
become selfish and tyrannical. Women upset everything.
When you let them into your life, you find that the
woman is driving at one thing and youre driving at
another.
PICKERING: At what, for example?
HIGGINS   (*coming off the piano restlessly*):   Oh, Lord
knows! I suppose the woman wants to live her own life;
and the man wants to live his; and each tries to drag
the other on to the wrong track. One wants to go north
and the other south; and the result is that both have to
go east, though they both hate the east wind. (*He sits
down on the bench at the keyboard*). So here I am, a
confirmed old bachelor, and likely to remain so.
PICKERING   (*rising and standing over him gravely*):
Come, Higgins! You know what I mean. If I'm to be
in this business I shall feel responsible for that girl. I

hope it's understood that no advantage is to be taken of her position.

HIGGINS: What! That thing! Sacred, I assure you. (*Rising to explain*) You see, she'll be a pupil; and teaching would be impossible unless pupils were sacred. Ive taught scores of American millionairesses how to speak English: the best looking women in the world. I'm seasoned. They might as well be blocks of wood. *I* might as well be a block of wood. It's—

(MRS PEARCE *opens the door. She has* ELIZA's *hat in her hand.* PICKERING *retires to the easy chair at the hearth and sits down.*)

HIGGINS (*eagerly*): Well, Mrs Pearce: is it all right?

MRS PEARCE (*at the door*): I just wish to trouble you with a word, if I may, Mr Higgins.

HIGGINS: Yes, certainly. Come in. (*She comes forward*). Dont burn that, Mrs Pearce. I'll keep it as a curiosity. (*He takes the hat*).

MRS PEARCE: Handle it carefully, sir, please. I had to promise her not to burn it; but I had better put it in the oven for a while.

HIGGINS (*putting it down hastily on the piano*): Oh! thank you. Well, what have you to say to me?

PICKERING: Am I in the way?

MRS PEARCE: Not at all, sir. Mr Higgins: will you please be very particular what you say before the girl?

HIGGINS (*sternly*): Of course. I'm always particular about what I say. Why do you say this to me?

MRS PEARCE (*unmoved*): No, sir: youre not at all particular when youve mislaid anything or when you get a little impatient. Now it doesnt matter before me: I'm used to it. But you really must not swear before the girl.

HIGGINS (*indignantly*): *I* swear! (*Most emphatically*) I never swear. I detest the habit. What the devil do you mean?

MRS PEARCE (*stolidly*): Thats what I mean, sir. You swear a great deal too much. I dont mind your damning and blasting, and what the devil and where the devil and who the devil—

HIGGINS: Mrs Pearce: this language from your lips! Really!

MRS PEARCE (*not to be put off*): —but there is a certain word I must ask you not to use. The girl has just used it herself because the bath was too hot. It begins with the same letter as bath. She knows no better: she learnt it at her mother's knee. But she must not hear it from your lips.

HIGGINS (*loftily*): I cannot charge myself with having ever uttered it, Mrs Pearce. (*She looks at him steadfastly. He adds, hiding an uneasy conscience with a judicial air*) Except perhaps in a moment of extreme and justifiable excitement.

MRS PEARCE: Only this morning, sir, you applied it to your boots, to the butter, and to the brown bread.

HIGGINS: Oh, that! Mere alliteration, Mrs Pearce, natural to a poet.

MRS PEARCE: Well, sir, whatever you choose to call it, I beg you not to let the girl hear you repeat it.

HIGGINS: Oh, very well, very well. Is that all?

MRS PEARCE: No, sir. We shall have to be very particular with this girl as to personal cleanliness.

HIGGINS: Certainly. Quite right. Most important.

MRS PEARCE: I mean not to be slovenly about her dress or untidy in leaving things about.

HIGGINS (*going to her solemnly*): Just so. I intended to call your attention to that. (*He passes on to* PICKERING, *who is enjoying the conversation immensely*). It is these little things that matter, Pickering. Take care of the pence and the pounds will take care of themselves is as true of personal habits as of money. (*He comes to anchor on the hearthrug, with the air of a man in an unassailable position*).

MRS PEARCE: Yes, sir. Then might I ask you not to come down to breakfast in your dressing-gown, or at any rate not to use it as a napkin to the extent you do, sir. And if you would be so good as not to eat everything off the same plate, and to remember not to put the porridge saucepan out of your hand on the clean tablecloth, it would be a better example to the girl. You know you nearly choked yourself with a fishbone in the jam only last week.

HIGGINS (*routed from the hearthrug and drifting back to the piano*): I may do these things sometimes in absence of mind; but surely I dont do them habitually. (*Angrily*) By the way: my dressing-gown smells most damnably of benzine.

MRS PEARCE: No doubt it does, Mr Higgins. But if you will wipe your fingers—

HIGGINS (*yelling*): Oh very well, very well: I'll wipe them in my hair in future.

MRS PEARCE: I hope youre not offended, Mr Higgins.

HIGGINS (*shocked at finding himself thought capable of an unamiable sentiment*): Not at all, not at all. Youre quite right, Mrs Pearce: I shall be particularly careful before the girl. Is that all?

MRS PEARCE: No, sir. Might she use some of those Japanese dresses you brought from abroad? I really cant put her back into her old things.

HIGGINS: Certainly. Anything you like. Is that all?

MRS PEARCE: Thank you, sir. Thats all. (*She goes out*).

HIGGINS: You know, Pickering, that woman has the most extraordinary ideas about me. Here I am, a shy, diffident sort of man. Ive never been able to feel really grown-up and tremendous, like other chaps. And yet shes firmly persuaded that I'm an arbitrary overbearing bossing kind of person. I cant account for it.

(MRS PEARCE *returns*.)

MRS PEARCE: If you please, sir, the trouble's beginning already. Theres a dustman downstairs, Alfred Doolittle, wants to see you. He says you have his daughter here.

PICKERING (*rising*): Phew! I say! (*He retreats to the hearthrug*).

HIGGINS (*promptly*): Send the blackguard up.

MRS PEARCE: Oh, very well, sir. (*She goes out*).

PICKERING: He may not be a blackguard, Higgins.

HIGGINS: Nonsense. Of course hes a blackguard.

PICKERING: Whether he is or not, I'm afraid we shall have some trouble with him.

HIGGINS (*confidently*):   Oh no: I think not. If theres any trouble he shall have it with me, not I with him. And we are sure to get something interesting out of him.

PICKERING: About the girl?

HIGGINS: No. I mean his dialect.

PICKERING: Oh!

MRS PEARCE (*at the door*):   Doolittle, sir. (*She admits* DOOLITTLE *and retires*).

(ALFRED DOOLITTLE *is an elderly but vigorous dustman, clad in the costume of his profession, including a hat with a back brim covering his neck and shoulders. He has well marked and rather interesting features, and seems equally free from fear and conscience. He has a remarkably expressive voice, the result of a habit of giving vent to his feelings without reserve. His present pose is that of wounded honor and stern resolution.*)

DOOLITTLE (*at the door, uncertain which of the two gentlemen is his man*):   Professor Higgins?

HIGGINS: Here. Good morning. Sit down.

DOOLITTLE: Morning, Governor. (*He sits down magisterially*) I come about a very serious matter, Governor.

HIGGINS (*to* PICKERING):   Brought up in Hounslow. Mother Welsh, I should think. (DOOLITTLE *opens his mouth, amazed. Higgins continues*) What do you want, Doolittle?

DOOLITTLE (*menacingly*):   I want my daughter: thats what I want. See?

HIGGINS: Of course you do. Youre her father, arnt you? You dont suppose anyone else wants her, do you? I'm glad to see you have some spark of family feeling left. Shes upstairs. Take her away at once.

DOOLITTLE (*rising, fearfully taken aback*):   What!

HIGGINS: Take her away. Do you suppose I'm going to keep your daughter for you?

DOOLITTLE (*remonstrating*): Now, now, look here, Governor. Is this reasonable? Is it fairity to take advantage of a man like this? The girl belongs to me. You got her. Where do I come in? (*He sits down again*).

HIGGINS: Your daughter had the audacity to come to my house and ask me to teach her how to speak properly so that she could get a place in a flower-shop. This gentleman and my housekeeper have been here all the time. (*Bullying him*) How dare you come here and attempt to blackmail me? You sent her here on purpose.

DOOLITTLE (*protesting*): No, Governor.

HIGGINS: You must have. How else could you possibly know that she is here?

DOOLITTLE: Dont take a man up like that, Governor.

HIGGINS: The police shall take you up. This is a plant— a plot to extort money by threats. I shall telephone for the police (*he goes resolutely to the telephone and opens the directory*).

DOOLITTLE: Have I asked you for a brass farthing? I leave it to the gentleman here: have I said a word about money?

HIGGINS (*throwing the book aside and marching down on* DOOLITTLE *with a poser*): What else did you come for?

DOOLITTLE (*sweetly*): Well, what would a man come for? Be human, Governor.

HIGGINS (*disarmed*): Alfred: did you put her up to it?

DOOLITTLE: So help me, Governor, I never did. I take my Bible oath I aint seen the girl these two months past.

HIGGINS: Then how did you know she was here?

DOOLITTLE (*"most musical, most melancholy"*): I'll tell you, Governor, if youll only let me get a word in. I'm willing to tell you. I'm wanting to tell you. I'm waiting to tell you.

HIGGINS: Pickering: this chap has a certain natural gift of rhetoric. Observe the rhythm of his native woodnotes wild. "I'm willing to tell you: I'm wanting to tell you: I'm waiting to tell you." Sentimental rhetoric! thats the

Welsh strain in him. It also accounts for his mendacity and dishonesty.

PICKERING: Oh, please, Higgins: I'm west country myself. (*To* DOOLITTLE) How did you know the girl was here if you didnt send her?

DOOLITTLE: It was like this, Governor. The girl took a boy in the taxi to give him a jaunt. Son of her landlady, he is. He hung about on the chance of her giving him another ride home. Well, she sent him back for her luggage when she heard you was willing for her to stop here. I met the boy at the corner of Long Acre and Endell Street.

HIGGINS: Public house. Yes?

DOOLITTLE: The poor man's club, Governor: why shouldnt I?

PICKERING: Do let him tell his story, Higgins.

DOOLITTLE: He told me what was up. And I ask you, what was my feelings and my duty as a father? I says to the boy, "You bring me the luggage," I says—

PICKERING: Why didnt you go for it yourself?

DOOLITTLE: Landlady wouldnt have trusted me with it, Governor. Shes that kind of woman: you know. I had to give the boy a penny afore he trusted me with it, the little swine. I brought it to her just to oblige you like, and make myself agreeable. Thats all.

HIGGINS: How much luggage?

DOOLITTLE: Musical instrument, Governor. A few pictures, a trifle of jewlery, and a bird-cage. She said she didnt want no clothes. What was I to think from that, Governor? I ask you as a parent what was I to think?

HIGGINS: So you came to rescue her from worse than death, eh?

DOOLITTLE (*appreciatively: relieved at being so well understood*): Just so, Governor. Thats right.

PICKERING: But why did you bring her luggage if you intended to take her away?

DOOLITTLE: Have I said a word about taking her away? Have I now?

HIGGINS (*determinedly*): Youre going to take her away,

double quick. (*He crosses to the hearth and rings the bell*).

DOOLITTLE (*rising*): No, Governor. Dont say that. I'm not the man to stand in my girl's light. Heres a career opening for her, as you might say; and—

(MRS PEARCE *opens the door and awaits orders.*)

HIGGINS: Mrs Pearce: this is Eliza's father. He has come to take her away. Give her to him. (*He goes back to the piano, with an air of washing his hands of the whole affair*).

DOOLITTLE: No. This is a misunderstanding. Listen here—

MRS PEARCE: He cant take her away, Mr Higgins: how can he? You told me to burn her clothes.

DOOLITTLE: Thats right. I cant carry the girl through the streets like a blooming monkey, can I? I put it to you.

HIGGINS: You have put it to me that you want your daughter. Take your daughter. If she has no clothes go out and buy her some.

DOOLITTLE (*desperate*): Wheres the clothes she come in? Did I burn them or did your missus here?

MRS PEARCE: I am the housekeeper, if you please. I have sent for some clothes for your girl. When they come you can take her away. You can wait in the kitchen. This way, please.

(DOOLITTLE, *much troubled, accompanies her to the door; then hesitates; finally turns confidentially to* HIGGINS.)

DOOLITTLE: Listen here, Governor. You and me is men of the world, aint we?

HIGGINS: Oh! Men of the world, are we? Youd better go, Mrs Pearce.

MRS PEARCE: I think so, indeed, sir. (*She goes, with dignity*).

PICKERING: The floor is yours, Mr Doolittle.

DOOLITTLE (*to* PICKERING): I thank you, Governor. (*To* HIGGINS, *who takes refuge on the piano bench, a little overwhelmed by the proximity of his visitor; for* DOOLIT-

TLE *has a professional flavor of dust about him*). Well,
the truth is, Ive taken a sort of fancy to you, Governor;
and if you want the girl, I'm not so set on having
her back home again but what I might be open to an
arrangement. Regarded in the light of a young woman,
shes a fine handsome girl. As a daughter shes not worth
her keep; and so I tell you straight. All I ask is my
rights as a father; and youre the last man alive to expect
me to let her go for nothing; for I can see youre one of
the straight sort, Governor. Well, whats a five pound
note to you? And whats Eliza to me? (*He returns to his
chair and sits down judicially*).

PICKERING: I think you ought to know, Doolittle, that
Mr Higgins's intentions are entirely honorable.

DOOLITTLE: Course they are, Governor. If I thought they
wasnt, Id ask fifty.

HIGGINS (*revolted*): Do you mean to say, you callous
rascal, that you would sell your daughter for £50?

DOOLITTLE: Not in a general way I wouldnt; but to oblige
a gentleman like you I'd do a good deal, I do assure
you.

PICKERING: Have you no morals, man?

DOOLITTLE (*unabashed*): Cant afford them, Governor.
Neither could you if you was as poor as me. Not that
I mean any harm, you know. But if Liza is going to
have a bit out of this, why not me too?

HIGGINS (*troubled*): I dont know what to do, Pickering.
There can be no question that as a matter of morals it's
a positive crime to give this chap a farthing. And yet I
feel a sort of rough justice in his claim.

DOOLITTLE: Thats it, Governor. Thats all I say. A father's heart, as it were.

PICKERING: Well, I know the feeling; but really it seems
hardly right—

DOOLITTLE: Dont say that, Governor. Dont look at it that
way. What am I, Governors both? I ask you, what am
I? I'm one of the undeserving poor: thats what I am.
Think of what that means to a man. It means that hes
up agen middle class morality all the time. If theres

anything going, and I put in for a bit of it, it's always
the same story: "Youre undeserving; so you cant have
it." But my needs is as great as the most deserving
widow's that ever got money out of six different charities in one week for the death of the same husband. I
dont need less than a deserving man: I need more. I
dont eat less hearty than him; and I drink a lot more.
I want a bit of amusement, cause I'm a thinking man.
I want cheerfulness and a song and a band when I feel
low. Well, they charge me just the same for everything
as they charge the deserving. What is middle class morality? Just an excuse for never giving me anything.
Therefore, I ask you, as two gentlemen, not to play
that game on me. I'm playing straight with you. I aint
pretending to be deserving. I'm undeserving; and I mean
to go on being undeserving. I like it; and thats the truth.
Will you take advantage of a man's nature to do him
out of the price of his own daughter what hes brought
up and fed and clothed by the sweat of his brow until
shes growed big enough to be interesting to you two
gentlemen? Is five pounds unreasonable? I put it to you;
and I leave it to you.

HIGGINS (*rising, and going over to Pickering*): Pickering: if we were to take this man in hand for three
months, he could choose between a seat in the Cabinet
and a popular pulpit in Wales.

PICKERING: What do you say to that, Doolittle?

DOOLITTLE: Not me, Governor, thank you kindly. Ive
heard all the preachers and all the prime ministers—for
I'm a thinking man and game for politics or religion or
social reform same as all the other amusements—and I
tell you it's a dog's life anyway you look at it. Undeserving poverty is my line. Taking one station in society
with another, it's—it's—well, it's the only one that has
any ginger in it, to my taste.

HIGGINS: I suppose we must give him a fiver.

PICKERING: He'll make a bad use of it, I'm afraid.

DOOLITTLE: Not me, Governor, so help me I wont. Dont
you be afraid that I'll save it and spare it and live idle

on it. There wont be a penny of it left by Monday: I'll
have to go to work same as if I'd never had it. It wont
pauperize me, you bet. Just one good spree for myself
and the missus, giving pleasure to ourselves and employment to others, and satisfaction to you to think it's
not been throwed away. You couldnt spend it better.

HIGGINS   (*taking out his pocket book and coming between*
DOOLITTLE *and the piano*):   This is irresistible. Lets
give him ten. (*He offers two notes to the dustman*).

DOOLITTLE: No, Governor. She wouldnt have the heart
to spend ten; and perhaps I shouldnt neither. Ten pounds
is a lot of money: it makes a man feel prudent like; and
then goodbye to happiness. You give me what I ask
you, Governor: not a penny more, and not a penny less.

PICKERING: Why dont you marry that missus of yours?
I rather draw the line at encouraging that sort of
immorality.

DOOLITTLE: Tell her so, Governor: tell her so. *I*'m willing. It's me that suffers by it. Ive no hold on her. I got
to be agreeable to her. I got to give her presents. I got
to buy her clothes something sinful. I'm a slave to that
woman, Governor, just because I'm not her lawful husband. And she knows it too. Catch her marrying me!
Take my advice, Governor: marry Eliza while shes
young and dont know no better. If you dont youl! be
sorry for it after. If you do, she'll be sorry for it after;
but better you than her, because youre a man, and shes
only a woman and dont know how to be happy anyhow.

HIGGINS: Pickering: if we listen to this man another minute, we shall have no convictions left. (*To* DOOLIT-
TLE)   Five pounds I think you said.

DOOLITTLE: Thank you kindly, Governor.

HIGGINS: Youre sure you wont take ten?

DOOLITTLE: Not now. Another time, Governor.

HIGGINS   (*handing him a five-pound note*):   Here you are.

DOOLITTLE: Thank you, Governor. Good morning. (*He
hurries to the door, anxious to get away with his booty.
When he opens it he is confronted with a dainty and
exquisitely clean young Japanese lady in a simple blue*

*cotton kimono printed cunningly with small white jas-
mine blossoms.* MRS PEARCE *is with her. He gets out
of her way deferentially and apologizes).* Beg pardon,
miss.

THE JAPANESE LADY: Garn! Dont you know your own
daughter?

DOOLITTLE:	*(exclaiming*	Bly me! it's Eliza!
HIGGINS:	*simul-*	Whats that! This!
PICKERING:	*taneously)*	By Jove!

LIZA: Dont I look silly?

HIGGINS: Silly?

MRS PEARCE (*at the door*): Now, Mr Higgins, please
dont say anything to make the girl conceited about
herself.

HIGGINS (*conscientiously*): Oh! Quite right, Mrs Pearce.
(*To* ELIZA) Yes: damned silly.

MRS PEARCE: Please, sir.

HIGGINS (*correcting himself*): I mean extremely silly.

LIZA: I should look all right with my hat on. (*She takes
up her hat; puts it on; and walks across the room to
the fireplace with a fashionable air*).

HIGGINS: A new fashion, by George! And it ought to
look horrible!

DOOLITTLE (*with fatherly pride*): Well, I never thought
she'd clean up as good looking as that, Governor. Shes
a credit to me, aint she?

LIZA: I tell you, it's easy to clean up here. Hot and cold
water on tap, just as much as you like, there is. Woolly
towels, there is; and a towel horse so hot, it burns your
fingers. Soft brushes to scrub yourself, and a wooden
bowl of soap smelling like primroses. Now I know why
ladies is so clean. Washing's a treat for them. Wish
they saw what it is for the like of me!

HIGGINS: I'm glad the bath-room met with your approval.

LIZA: It didnt: not all of it; and I dont care who hears
me say it. Mrs Pearce knows.

HIGGINS: What was wrong, Mrs Pearce?

MRS PEARCE (*blandly*): Oh, nothing, sir. It doesnt
matter.

LIZA: I had a good mind to break it. I didnt know which way to look. But I hung a towel over it, I did.

HIGGINS: Over what?

MRS PEARCE: Over the looking-glass, sir.

HIGGINS: Doolittle: you have brought your daughter up too strictly.

DOOLITTLE: Me! I never brought her up at all, except to give her a lick of a strap now and again. Dont put it on me, Governor. She aint accustomed to it, you see: thats all. But she'll soon pick up your free-and-easy ways.

LIZA: I'm a good girl, I am; and I wont pick up no free and easy ways.

HIGGINS: Eliza: if you say again that youre a good girl, your father shall take you home.

LIZA: Not him. You dont know my father. All he come here for was to touch you for some money to get drunk on.

DOOLITTLE: Well, what else would I want money for? To put into the plate in church, I suppose. (*She puts out her tongue at him. He is so incensed by this that* PICKERING *presently finds it necessary to step between them*). Dont you give me none of your lip; and dont let me hear you giving this gentleman any of it neither, or youll hear from me about it. See?

HIGGINS: Have you any further advice to give her before you go, Doolittle? Your blessing, for instance.

DOOLITTLE: No, Governor: I aint such a mug as to put up my children to all I know myself. Hard enough to hold them in without that. If you want Eliza's mind improved, Governor, you do it yourself with a strap. So long, gentlemen. (*He turns to go*).

HIGGINS (*impressively*): Stop. Youll come regularly to see your daughter. It's your duty, you know. My brother is a clergyman; and he could help you in your talks with her.

DOOLITTLE (*evasively*): Certainly. I'll come, Governor. Not just this week, because I have a job at a distance. But later on you may depend on me. Afternoon, gentle-

men. Afternoon, maam. (*He takes off his hat to* MRS
PEARCE, *who disdains the salutation and goes out. He
winks at* HIGGINS, *thinking him probably a fellow-
sufferer from* MRS PEARCE'S *difficult disposition, and
follows her*).

LIZA: Dont you believe the old liar. He'd as soon you
set a bull-dog on him as a clergyman. You wont see
him again in a hurry.

HIGGINS: I dont want to, Eliza. Do you?

LIZA: Not me. I dont want never to see him again, I
dont. Hes a disgrace to me, he is, collecting dust, instead of working at his trade.

PICKERING: What is his trade, Eliza?

LIZA: Talking money out of other people's pockets into
his own. His proper trade's a navvy; and he works at
it sometimes too—for exercise—and earns good money
at it. Aint you going to call me Miss Doolittle anymore?

PICKERING: I beg your pardon, Miss Doolittle. It was a
slip of the tongue.

LIZA: Oh, I dont mind; only it sounded so genteel. I
should just like to take a taxi to the corner of Tottenham
Court Road and get out there and tell it to wait for me,
just to put the girls in their place a bit. I wouldnt speak
to them, you know.

PICKERING: Better wait til we get you something really
fashionable.

HIGGINS: Besides, you shouldnt cut your old friends now
that you have risen in the world. Thats what we call
snobbery.

LIZA: You dont call the like of them my friends now, I
should hope. Theyve took it out of me often enough
with their ridicule when they had the chance; and now
I mean to get a bit of my own back. But if I'm to have
fashionable clothes, I'll wait. I should like to have
some. Mrs Pearce says youre going to give me some to
wear in bed at night different to what I wear in the
daytime; but it do seem a waste of money when you
could get something to shew. Besides, I never could
fancy changing into cold things on a winter night.

MRS PEARCE (*coming back*): Now, Eliza. The new things have come for you to try on.

LIZA: Ah-ow-oo-ooh! (*She rushes out*).

MRS PEARCE (*following her*): Oh, dont rush about like that, girl. (*She shuts the door behind her*).

HIGGINS: Pickering: we have taken on a stiff job.

PICKERING (*with conviction*): Higgins: we have.

Act III

(*It is* MRS HIGGINS'*s at-home day. Nobody has yet ar-rived. Her drawing-room, in a flat on Chelsea embank-ment, has three windows looking on the river; and the ceiling is not so lofty as it would be in an older house of the same pretension. The windows are open, giving access to a balcony with flowers in pots. If you stand with your face to the windows, you have the fireplace on your left and the door in the right-hand wall close to the corner nearest the windows.*

MRS HIGGINS *was brought up on Morris and Burne Jones; and her room, which is very unlike her son's room in Wimpole Street, is not crowded with furniture and little tables and nick-nacks. In the middle of the room there is a big ottoman; and this, with the carpet, the Morris wall-papers, and the Morris chintz window curtains and brocade covers of the ottoman and its cushions, supply all the ornament, and are much too handsome to be hidden by odds and ends of useless things. A few good oil-paintings from the exhibitions in the Gros-venor Gallery thirty years ago (the Burne Jones, not the Whistler side of them) are on the walls. The only landscape is a Cecil Lawson on the scale of a Rubens. There is a portrait of* MRS HIGGINS *as she was when she defied fashion in her youth in one of the beautiful Rossettian costumes which, when caricatured by people who did not understand, led to the absurdities of popu-lar estheticism in the eighteen-seventies.*

In the corner diagonally opposite the door MRS HIG-GINS, *now over sixty and long past taking the trouble to dress out of the fashion, sits writing at an elegantly simple writing-table with a bell button within reach of her hand. There is a Chippendale chair further back in the room between her and the window nearest her side. At the other side of the room, further forward, is an Elizabethan chair roughly carved in the taste of Inigo Jones. On the same side a piano in a decorated case. The corner between the fireplace and the window is occupied by a divan cushioned in Morris chintz.*

It is between four and five in the afternoon.

The door is opened violently; and HIGGINS *enters with his hat on.)*

MRS HIGGINS (*dismayed*): Henry (*scolding him*)! What are you doing here to-day? It is my at-home day: you promised not to come. (*As he bends to kiss her, she takes his hat off, and presents it to him*).

HIGGINS: Oh bother! (*He throws the hat down on the table*).

MRS HIGGINS: Go home at once.

HIGGINS (*kissing her*): I know, mother. I came on purpose.

MRS HIGGINS: But you mustnt. I'm serious, Henry. You offend all my friends: they stop coming whenever they meet you.

HIGGINS: Nonsense! I know I have no small talk; but people dont mind. (*He sits on the settee*).

MRS HIGGINS: Oh! dont they? Small talk indeed! What about your large talk? Really, dear, you mustnt stay.

HIGGINS: I must. Ive a job for you. A phonetic job.

MRS HIGGINS: No use, dear. I'm sorry; but I cant get round your vowels; and though I like to get pretty post-cards in your patent shorthand, I always have to read the copies in ordinary writing you so thoughtfully send me.

HIGGINS: Well, this isnt a phonetic job.

MRS HIGGINS: You said it was.

HIGGINS: Not your part of it. Ive picked up a girl.

MRS HIGGINS: Does that mean that some girl has picked you up?

HIGGINS: Not at all. I dont mean a love affair.

MRS HIGGINS: What a pity!

HIGGINS: Why?

MRS HIGGINS: Well, you never fall in love with anyone under forty-five. When will you discover that there are some rather nice-looking young women about?

HIGGINS: Oh, I cant be bothered with young women. My idea of a lovable woman is something as like you as possible. I shall never get into the way of seriously liking young women: some habits lie too deep to be changed. (*Rising abruptly and walking about, jingling his money and his keys in his trouser pockets*) Besides, theyre all idiots.

MRS HIGGINS: Do you know what you would do if you really loved me, Henry?

HIGGINS: Oh bother! What? Marry, I suppose?

MRS HIGGINS: No. Stop fidgeting and take your hands out of your pockets. (*With a gesture of despair, he obeys and sits down again*). Thats a good boy. Now tell me about the girl.

HIGGINS: Shes coming to see you.

MRS HIGGINS: I dont remember asking her.

HIGGINS: You didnt. *I* asked her. If youd known her you wouldnt have asked her.

MRS HIGGINS: Indeed! Why?

HIGGINS: Well, it's like this. Shes a common flower girl. I picked her off the kerbstone.

MRS HIGGINS: And invited her to my at-home!

HIGGINS (*rising and coming to her to coax her*): Oh, thatll be all right. Ive taught her to speak properly; and she has strict orders as to her behavior. Shes to keep to two subjects: the weather and everybody's health—Fine day and How do you do, you know—and not to let herself go on things in general. That will be safe.

MRS HIGGINS: Safe! To talk about our health! about our insides! perhaps about our outsides! How could you be so silly, Henry?

HIGGINS (*impatiently*): Well, she must talk about something. (*He controls himself and sits down again*). Oh, she'll be all right: dont you fuss. Pickering is in it with me. Ive a sort of bet on that I'll pass her off as a duchess in six months. I started on her some months ago; and shes getting on like a house on fire. I shall win my bet. She has a quick ear; and shes been easier to teach than my middle-class pupils because shes had to learn a complete new language. She talks English almost as you talk French.

MRS HIGGINS: Thats satisfactory, at all events.

HIGGINS: Well, it is and it isnt.

MRS HIGGINS: What does that mean?

HIGGINS: You see, Ive got her pronunciation all right; but you have to consider not only how a girl pronounces, but what she pronounces; and thats where—

(*They are interrupted by* THE PARLOR-MAID, *announcing guests.*)

THE PARLOR-MAID: Mrs and Miss Eynsford Hill. (*She withdraws*).

HIGGINS: Oh Lord! (*He rises; snatches his hat from the table; and makes for the door; but before he reaches it his mother introduces him*).

(MRS *and* MISS EYNSFORD HILL *are the mother and daughter who sheltered from the rain in Covent Garden. The mother is well bred, quiet, and has the habitual anxiety of straitened means. The daughter has acquired a gay air of being very much at home in society: the bravado of genteel poverty.*)

MRS EYNSFORD HILL (*to* MRS HIGGINS): How do you do? (*They shake hands*).

MISS EYNSFORD HILL: How d'you do? (*She shakes*).

MRS HIGGINS (*introducing*): My son Henry.

MRS EYNSFORD HILL: Your celebrated son! I have so longed to meet you, Professor Higgins.

HIGGINS (*glumly, making no movement in her direction*): Delighted. (*He backs against the piano and bows brusquely*).

MISS EYNSFORD HILL (*going to him with confident familiarity*):   How do you do?

HIGGINS (*staring at her*):   Ive seen you before somewhere. I havnt the ghost of a notion where; but Ive heard your voice. (*Drearily*) It doesnt matter. Youd better sit down.

MRS HIGGINS: I'm sorry to say that my celebrated son has no manners. You mustnt mind him.

MISS EYNSFORD HILL (*gaily*):   I dont. (*She sits in the Elizabethan chair*).

MRS EYNSFORD HILL (*a little bewildered*):   Not at all. (*She sits on the ottoman between her daughter and* MRS HIGGINS, *who has turned her chair away from the writing-table*).

HIGGINS: Oh, have I been rude? I didnt mean to be.

(*He goes to the central window, through which, with his back to the company, he contemplates the river and the flowers in Battersea Park on the opposite bank as if they were a frozen desert.*)

THE PARLOR-MAID *returns, ushering in* PICKERING.

THE PARLOR-MAID: Colonel Pickering. (*She withdraws*).

PICKERING: How do you do, Mrs Higgins?

MRS HIGGINS: So glad youve come. Do you know Mrs Eynsford Hill—Miss Eynsford Hill? (*Exchange of bows. The Colonel brings the Chippendale chair a little forward between* MRS HILL *and* MRS HIGGINS, *and sits down*).

PICKERING: Has Henry told you what weve come for?

HIGGINS (*over his shoulder*):   We were interrupted: damn it!

MRS HIGGINS: Oh Henry, Henry, really!

MRS EYNSFORD HILL (*half rising*):   Are we in the way?

MRS HIGGINS (*rising and making her sit down again*):   No, no. You couldnt have come more fortunately: we want you to meet a friend of ours.

HIGGINS (*turning hopefully*):   Yes, by George! We want two or three people. Youll do as well as anybody else.

(THE PARLOR-MAID *returns, ushering* FREDDY.)

THE PARLOR-MAID: Mr Eynsford Hill.

HIGGINS (*almost audibly, past endurance*): God of Heaven! another of them.

FREDDY (*shaking hands with* MRS HIGGINS): Ahdedo?

MRS HIGGINS: Very good of you to come. (*Introducing*) Colonel Pickering.

FREDDY (*bowing*): Ahdedo?

MRS HIGGINS: I dont think you know my son, Professor Higgins.

FREDDY (*going to* HIGGINS): Ahdedo?

HIGGINS (*looking at him much as if he were a pickpocket*): I'll take my oath Ive met you before somewhere. Where was it?

FREDDY: I dont think so.

HIGGINS (*resignedly*): It dont matter, anyhow. Sit down.

(*He shakes* FREDDY'S *hand, and almost slings him on to the ottoman with his face to the windows; then comes round to the other side of it.*)

HIGGINS: Well, here we are, anyhow! (*He sits down on the ottoman next* MRS EYNSFORD HILL, *on her left*). And now, what the devil are we going to talk about until Eliza comes?

MRS HIGGINS: Henry: you are the life and soul of the Royal Society's soirées; but really youre rather trying on more commonplace occasions.

HIGGINS: Am I? Very sorry. (*Beaming suddenly*) I suppose I am, you know. (*Uproariously*) Ha, ha!

MISS EYNSFORD HILL (*who considers* HIGGINS *quite eligible matrimonially*): I sympathize. *I* havnt any small talk. If people would only be frank and say what they really think!

HIGGINS (*relapsing into gloom*): Lord forbid!

MRS EYNSFORD HILL (*taking up her daughter's cue*): But why?

HIGGINS: What they think they ought to think is bad enough, Lord knows; but what they really think would break up the whole show. Do you suppose it would be really agreeable if I were to come out now with what *I* really think?

MISS EYNSFORD HILL (*gaily*):   Is it so very cynical?

HIGGINS: Cynical! Who the dickens said it was cynical? I mean it wouldnt be decent.

MRS EYNSFORD HILL (*seriously*):   Oh! I'm sure you dont mean that, Mr Higgins.

HIGGINS: You see, we're all savages, more or less. We're supposed to be civilized and cultured—to know all about poetry and philosophy and art and science, and so on; but how many of us know even the meanings of these names? (*To* MISS HILL)   What do you know of poetry? (*To* MRS HILL)   What do you know of science? (*Indicating* FREDDY)   What does he know of art or science or anything else? What the devil do you imagine I know of philosophy?

MRS HIGGINS (*warningly*):   Or of manners, Henry?

THE PARLOR-MAID (*opening the door*):   Miss Doolittle. (*She withdraws*).

HIGGINS (*rising hastily and running to* MRS HIGGINS):   Here she is, mother. (*He stands on tiptoe and makes signs over his mother's head to* ELIZA *to indicate to her which lady is her hostess*).

(ELIZA, *who is exquisitely dressed, produces an impression of such remarkable distinction and beauty as she enters that they all rise, quite fluttered. Guided by* HIGGINS'S *signals, she comes to* MRS HIGGINS *with studied grace*.)

LIZA (*speaking with pedantic correctness of pronunciation and great beauty of tone*):   How do you do, Mrs Higgins? (*She gasps slightly in making sure of the H in Higgins, but is quite successful*).   Mr Higgins told me I might come.

MRS HIGGINS (*cordially*):   Quite right: I'm very glad indeed to see you.

PICKERING: How do you do, Miss Doolittle?

LIZA (*shaking hands with him*): Colonel Pickering, is it not?

MRS EYNSFORD HILL: I feel sure we have met before, Miss Doolittle. I remember your eyes.

LIZA: How do you do? (*She sits down on the ottoman gracefully in the place just left vacant by* HIGGINS).

MRS EYNSFORD HILL (*introducing*): My daughter Clara.

LIZA: How do you do?

CLARA (*impulsively*): How do you do? (*She sits down on the ottoman beside* ELIZA, *devouring her with her eyes*).

FREDDY (*coming to their side of the ottoman*): Ive certainly had the pleasure.

MRS EYNSFORD HILL (*introducing*): My son Freddy.

LIZA: How do you do?

(FREDDY *bows and sits down in the Elizabethan chair, infatuated.*)

HIGGINS (*suddenly*): By George, yes: it all comes back to me! (*They stare at him*). Covent Garden! (*Lamentably*) What a damned thing!

MRS HIGGINS: Henry, please! (*He is about to sit on the edge of the table*). Dont sit on my writing-table: youll break it.

HIGGINS (*sulkily*): Sorry.

(*He goes to the divan, stumbling into the fender and over the fire-irons on his way; extricating himself with muttered imprecations; and finishing his disastrous journey by throwing himself so impatiently on the divan that he almost breaks it.* MRS HIGGINS *looks at him, but controls herself and says nothing.*

A long and painful pause ensues.)

MRS HIGGINS (*at last, conversationally*): Will it rain, do you think?

LIZA: The shallow depression in the west of these islands is likely to move slowly in an easterly direction. There are no indications of any great change in the barometrical situation.

FREDDY: Ha! ha! how awfully funny!

LIZA: What is wrong with that, young man? I bet I got it right.

FREDDY: Killing!

MRS EYNSFORD HILL: I'm sure I hope it wont turn cold. Theres so much influenza about. It runs right through our whole family regularly every spring.

LIZA (*darkly*): My aunt died of influenza: so they said.

MRS EYNSFORD HILL (*clicks her tongue sympathetically*): ! ! !

LIZA (*in the same tragic tone*): But it's my belief they done the old woman in.

MRS HIGGINS (*puzzled*): Done her in?

LIZA: Y-e-e-e-es, Lord love you! Why should she die of influenza? She come through diphtheria right enough the year before. I saw her with my own eyes. Fairly blue with it, she was. They all thought she was dead; but my father he kept ladling gin down her throat til she came to so sudden that she bit the bowl off the spoon.

MRS EYNSFORD HILL (*startled*): Dear me!

LIZA (*piling up the indictment*): What call would a woman with that strength in her have to die of influenza? What become of her new straw hat that should have come to me? Somebody pinched it; and what I say is, them as pinched it done her in.

MRS EYNSFORD HILL: What does doing her in mean?

HIGGINS (*hastily*): Oh, thats the new small talk. To do a person in means to kill them.

MRS EYNSFORD HILL (*to* ELIZA, *horrified*): You surely dont believe that your aunt was killed?

LIZA: Do I not! Them she lived with would have killed her for a hat-pin, let alone a hat.

MRS EYNSFORD HILL: But it cant have been right for your father to pour spirits down her throat like that. It might have killed her.

LIZA: Not her. Gin was mother's milk to her. Besides, he'd poured so much down his own throat that he knew the good of it.

MRS EYNSFORD HILL: Do you mean that he drank?

LIZA: Drank! My word! Something chronic.

MRS EYNSFORD HILL: How dreadful for you!

LIZA: Not a bit. It never did him no harm what I could see. But then he did not keep it up regular. (*Cheerfully*) On the burst, as you might say, from time to time. And always more agreeable when he had a drop in. When he was out of work, my mother used to give him fourpence and tell him to go out and not come back until he'd drunk himself cheerful and loving-like. Theres lots of women has to make their husbands drunk to make them fit to live with. (*Now quite at her ease*) You see, it's like this. If a man has a bit of a conscience, it always takes him when he's sober; and then it makes him low-spirited. A drop of booze just takes that off and makes him happy. (*To* FREDDY, *who is in convulsions of suppressed laughter*) Here! what are you sniggering at?

FREDDY: The new small talk. You do it so awfully well.

LIZA: If I was doing it proper, what was you laughing at? (*To* HIGGINS) Have I said anything I oughtnt?

MRS HIGGINS (*interposing*): Not at all, Miss Doolittle.

LIZA: Well, thats a mercy, anyhow. (*Expansively*) What I always say is—

HIGGINS (*rising and looking at his watch*): Ahem!

LIZA (*looking round at him; taking the hint; and rising*): Well: I must go. (*They all rise.* FREDDY *goes to the door*). So pleased to have met you. Good-bye. (*She shakes hands with* MRS HIGGINS).

MRS HIGGINS: Good-bye.

LIZA: Good-bye, Colonel Pickering.

PICKERING: Good-bye, Miss Doolittle. (*They shake hands*).

LIZA (*nodding to the others*): Good-bye, all.

FREDDY (*opening the door for her*): Are you walking across the Park, Miss Doolittle? If so—

LIZA: Walk! Not bloody likely. (*Sensation*). I am going in a taxi. (*She goes out*).

(PICKERING *gasps and sits down.* FREDDY *goes out on the balcony to catch another glimpse of* ELIZA.)

MRS EYNSFORD HILL (*suffering from shock*): Well, I really cant get used to the new ways.

CLARA (*throwing herself discontentedly into the Elizabethan chair*): Oh, it's all right, mamma, quite right. People will think we never go anywhere or see anybody if you are so old-fashioned.

MRS EYNSFORD HILL: I daresay I am very old-fashioned; but I do hope you wont begin using that expression, Clara. I have got accustomed to hear you talking about men as rotters, and calling everything filthy and beastly; though I do think it horrible and unladylike. But this last is really too much. Dont you think so, Colonel Pickering?

PICKERING: Dont ask me. Ive been away in India for several years; and manners have changed so much that I sometimes dont know whether I'm at a respectable dinner-table or in a ship's forecastle.

CLARA: It's all a matter of habit. Theres no right or wrong in it. Nobody means anything by it. And it's so quaint, and gives such a smart emphasis to things that are not in themselves very witty. I find the new small talk delightful and quite innocent.

MRS EYNSFORD HILL (*rising*): Well, after that, I think it's time for us to go.

(PICKERING *and* HIGGINS *rise.*)

CLARA (*rising*): Oh yes: we have three at-homes to go to still. Good-bye, Mrs Higgins. Good-bye, Colonel Pickering. Good-bye, Professor Higgins.

HIGGINS (*coming grimly at her from the divan, and accompanying her to the door*): Good-bye. Be sure you try on that small talk at the three at-homes. Dont be nervous about it. Pitch it in strong.

CLARA (*all smiles*): I will. Good-bye. Such nonsense, all this early Victorian prudery!

HIGGINS (*tempting her*): Such damned nonsense!

CLARA: Such bloody nonsense!

MRS EYNSFORD HILL (*convulsively*): Clara!

CLARA: IIa! ha! (*She goes out radiant, conscious of being thoroughly up to date, and is heard descending the stairs in a stream of silvery laughter*).

FREDDY (*to the heavens at large*): Well, I ask you—
(*He gives it up, and comes to* MRS HIGGINS). Good-bye.

MRS HIGGINS (*shaking hands*): Good-bye. Would you
like to meet Miss Doolittle again?

FREDDY (*eagerly*): Yes, I should, most awfully.

MRS HIGGINS: Well, you know my days.

FREDDY: Yes. Thanks awfully. Good-bye. (*He goes out*).

MRS EYNSFORD HILL: Good-bye, Mr Higgins.

HIGGINS: Good-bye. Good-bye.

MRS EYNSFORD HILL (*to* PICKERING): It's no use. I shall
never be able to bring myself to use that word.

PICKERING: Dont. It's not compulsory, you know. Youll
get on quite well without it.

MRS EYNSFORD HILL: Only, Clara is so down on me if I
am not positively reeking with the latest slang. Good-
bye.

PICKERING: Good-bye (*They shake hands*).

MRS EYNSFORD HILL (*to* MRS HIGGINS): You mustnt mind
Clara. (PICKERING, *catching from her lowered tone that
this is not meant for him to hear, discreetly joins* HIG-
GINS *at the window*). We're so poor! and she gets so
few parties, poor child! She doesnt quite know. (MRS
HIGGINS, *seeing that her eyes are moist, takes her hand
sympathetically and goes with her to the door*). But the
boy is nice. Dont you think so?

MRS HIGGINS: Oh, quite nice. I shall always be delighted
to see him.

MRS EYNSFORD HILL: Thank you, dear. Good-bye. (*She
goes out*).

HIGGINS (*eagerly*): Well? Is Eliza presentable (*he swoops
on his mother and drags her to the ottoman, where she
sits down in* ELIZA'S *place with her son on her left*)?

(PICKERING *returns to his chair on her right.*)

MRS HIGGINS: You silly boy, of course shes not presentable. Shes a triumph of your art and of her dressmak-
er's; but if you suppose for a moment that she doesnt
give herself away in every sentence she utters, you must
be perfectly cracked about her.

PICKERING: But dont you think something might be done? I mean something to eliminate the sanguinary element from her conversation.

MRS HIGGINS: Not as long as she is in Henry's hands.

HIGGINS (*aggrieved*): Do you mean that my language is improper?

MRS HIGGINS: No, dearest: it would be quite proper—say on a canal barge; but it would not be proper for her at a garden party.

HIGGINS (*deeply injured*): Well I must say—

PICKERING (*interrupting him*): Come, Higgins: you must learn to know yourself. I havnt heard such language as yours since we used to review the volunteers in Hyde Park twenty years ago.

HIGGINS (*sulkily*): Oh, well, if you say so, I suppose I dont always talk like a bishop.

MRS HIGGINS (*quieting* HENRY *with a touch*): Colonel Pickering: will you tell me what is the exact state of things in Wimpole Street?

PICKERING (*cheerfully: as if this completely changed the subject*): Well, I have come to live there with Henry. We work together at my Indian Dialects; and we think it more convenient—

MRS HIGGINS: Quite so. I know all about that: it's an excellent arrangement. But where does this girl live?

HIGGINS: With us, of course. Where would she live?

MRS HIGGINS: But on what terms? Is she a servant? If not, what is she?

PICKERING (*slowly*): I think I know what you mean, Mrs Higgins.

HIGGINS: Well, dash me if *I* do! Ive had to work at the girl every day for months to get her to her present pitch. Besides, shes useful. She knows where my things are, and remembers my appointments and so forth.

MRS HIGGINS: How does your housekeeper get on with her?

HIGGINS: Mrs Pearce? Oh, shes jolly glad to get so much taken off her hands; for before Eliza came, she used to have to find things and remind me of my appointments.

But shes got some silly bee in her bonnet about Eliza. She keeps saying "You dont think, sir": doesnt she, Pick?

PICKERING: Yes: thats the formula. "You dont think, sir." Thats the end of every conversation about Eliza.

HIGGINS: As if I ever stop thinking about the girl and her confounded vowels and consonants. I'm worn out, thinking about her, and watching her lips and her teeth and her tongue, not to mention her soul, which is the quaintest of the lot.

MRS HIGGINS: You certainly are a pretty pair of babies, playing with your live doll.

HIGGINS: Playing! The hardest job I ever tackled: make no mistake about that, mother. But you have no idea how frightfully interesting it is to take a human being and change her into a quite different human being by creating a new speech for her. It's filling up the deepest gulf that separates class from class and soul from soul.

PICKERING (*drawing his chair closer to* MRS HIGGINS *and bending over to her eagerly*): Yes: it's enormously interesting. I assure you, Mrs Higgins, we take Eliza very seriously. Every week—every day almost—there is some new change. (*Closer again*) We keep records of every stage—dozens of gramophone disks and photographs—

HIGGINS (*assailing her at the other ear*): Yes, by George: it's the most absorbing experiment I ever tackled. She regularly fills our lives up: doesnt she, Pick?

PICKERING: We're always talking Eliza.

HIGGINS: Teaching Eliza.

PICKERING: Dressing Eliza.

MRS HIGGINS: What!

HIGGINS: Inventing new Elizas.

HIGGINS: } (*speaking together*) { You know, she has the most extraordinary quickness of ear:

PICKERING: } { I assure you, my dear Mrs Higgins, that girl

HIGGINS:	just like a parrot. Ive tried her with every
PICKERING:	is a genius. She can play the piano quite beautifully.
HIGGINS:	possible sort of sound that a human being can make—
PICKERING:	We have taken her to classical concerts and to music
HIGGINS:	Continental dialects, African dialects, Hottentot
PICKERING: *(speaking together)*	halls; and it's all the same to her: she plays everything
HIGGINS:	clicks, things it took me years to get hold of; and
PICKERING:	she hears right off when she comes home, whether it's
HIGGINS:	she picks them up like a shot, right away, as if she had
PICKERING:	Beethoven and Brahms or Lehar and Lionel Monckton;
HIGGINS:	been at it all her life.
PICKERING:	though six months ago, she'd never as much as touched a piano—

MRS HIGGINS (*putting her fingers in her ears, as they are by this time shouting one another down with an intolerable noise*): Sh-sh-sh—sh! (*They stop*).

PICKERING: I beg your pardon. (*He draws his chair back apologetically*).

HIGGINS: Sorry. When Pickering starts shouting nobody can get a word in edgeways.

MRS HIGGINS: Be quiet, Henry. Colonel Pickering: dont you realize that when Eliza walked into Wimpole Street, something walked in with her?

PICKERING: Her father did. But Henry soon got rid of him.

MRS HIGGINS: It would have been more to the point if

her mother had. But as her mother didnt something else did.

PICKERING: But what?

MRS HIGGINS (*unconsciously dating herself by the word*): A problem.

PICKERING: Oh, I see. The problem of how to pass her off as a lady.

HIGGINS: I'll solve that problem. Ive half solved it already.

MRS HIGGINS: No, you two infinitely stupid male creatures: the problem of what is to be done with her afterwards.

HIGGINS: I dont see anything in that. She can go her own way, with all the advantages I have given her.

MRS HIGGINS: The advantages of that poor woman who was here just now! The manners and habits that disqualify a fine lady from earning her own living without giving her a fine lady's income! Is that what you mean?

PICKERING (*indulgently, being rather bored*): Oh, that will be all right, Mrs Higgins. (*He rises to go*).

HIGGINS (*rising also*): We'll find her some light employment.

PICKERING: Shes happy enough. Dont you worry about her. Good-bye. (*He shakes hands as if he were consoling a frightened child, and makes for the door*).

HIGGINS: Anyhow, theres no good bothering now. The thing's done. Good-bye, mother. (*He kisses her, and follows* PICKERING).

PICKERING (*turning for a final consolation*): There are plenty of openings. We'll do whats right. Good-bye.

HIGGINS (*to* PICKERING *as they go out together*): Let's take her to the Shakespear exhibition at Earls Court.

PICKERING: Yes: lets. Her remarks will be delicious.

HIGGINS: She'll mimic all the people for us when we get home.

PICKERING: Ripping. (*Both are heard laughing as they go downstairs*).

MRS HIGGINS (*rises with an impatient bounce, and returns to her work at the writing-table. She sweeps a litter of*

*disarranged papers out of her way; snatches a sheet of
paper from her stationery case; and tries resolutely
to write. At the third line she gives it up; flings down
her pen; grips the table angrily and exclaims*):   Oh,
men! men!! men!!!

Act IV

(The Wimpole Street laboratory. Midnight. Nobody in the room. The clock on the mantelpiece strikes twelve. The fire is not alight: it is a summer night.

Presently HIGGINS *and* PICKERING *are heard on the stairs.)*

HIGGINS *(calling down to* PICKERING): I say, Pick: lock up, will you. I shant be going out again.

PICKERING: Right. Can Mrs Pearce go to bed? We dont want anything more, do we?

HIGGINS: Lord, no!

*(*ELIZA *opens the door and is seen on the lighted landing in opera cloak, brilliant evening dress, and diamonds, with fan, flowers, and all accessories. She comes to the hearth, and switches on the electric lights there. She is tired: her pallor contrasts strongly with her dark eyes and hair; and her expression is almost tragic. She takes off her cloak; puts her fan and flowers on the piano; and sits down on the bench, brooding and silent.* HIGGINS, *in evening dress, with overcoat and hat, comes in, carrying a smoking jacket which he has picked up downstairs. He takes off the hat and overcoat; throws them carelessly on the newspaper stand; disposes of his coat in the same way; puts on the smoking jacket; and throws himself wearily into the easy-chair at the hearth.* PICKERING, *similarly attired, comes in. He also takes off his hat and overcoat, and is about to throw them on* HIGGINS's *when he hesitates.)*

PICKERING: I say: Mrs Pearce will row if we leave these things lying about in the drawing-room.

HIGGINS: Oh, chuck them over the bannisters into the hall. She'll find them there in the morning and put them away all right. She'll think we were drunk.

PICKERING: We are, slightly. Are there any letters?

HIGGINS: I didnt look. (PICKERING *takes the overcoats and hats and goes downstairs.* HIGGINS *begins half singing half yawning an air from La Fanciulla del Golden West. Suddenly he stops and exclaims*) I wonder where the devil my slippers are!

(ELIZA *looks at him darkly; then rises suddenly and leaves the room.*

HIGGINS *yawns again, and resumes his song.*

PICKERING *returns, with the contents of the letter-box in his hand.*)

PICKERING: Only circulars, and this coroneted billet-doux for you. (*He throws the circulars into the fender, and posts himself on the hearthrug, with his back to the grate*).

HIGGINS (*glancing at the billet-doux*): Money-lender. (*He throws the letter after the circulars*).

(ELIZA *returns with a pair of large down-at-heel slippers. She places them on the carpet before* HIGGINS, *and sits as before without a word.*)

HIGGINS (*yawning again*): Oh Lord! What an evening! What a crew! What a silly tomfoolery! (*He raises his shoe to unlace it, and catches sight of the slippers. He stops unlacing and looks at them as if they had appeared there of their own accord*). Oh! theyre there, are they?

PICKERING (*stretching himself*): Well, I feel a bit tired. It's been a long day. The garden party, a dinner party, and the opera! Rather too much of a good thing. But youve won your bet, Higgins. Eliza did the trick, and something to spare, eh?

HIGGINS (*fervently*): Thank God it's over!

(ELIZA *flinches violently; but they take no notice of her;
and she recovers herself and sits stonily as before.*)

PICKERING: Were you nervous at the garden party? *I* was.
Eliza didnt seem a bit nervous.

HIGGINS: Oh, she wasnt nervous. I knew she'd be all
right. No: it's the strain of putting the job through all
these months that has told on me. It was interesting
enough at first, while we were at the phonetics; but after
that I got deadly sick of it. If I hadnt backed myself to
do it I should have chucked the whole thing up two
months ago. It was a silly notion: the whole thing has
been a bore.

PICKERING: Oh come! the garden party was frightfully
exciting. My heart began beating like anything.

HIGGINS: Yes, for the first three minutes. But when I
saw we were going to win hands down, I felt like a
bear in a cage, hanging about doing nothing. The dinner
was worse: sitting gorging there for over an hour, with
nobody but a damned fool of a fashionable woman to
talk to! I tell you, Pickering, never again for me. No
more artificial duchesses. The whole thing has been simple purgatory.

PICKERING: Youve never been broken in properly to the
social routine. (*Strolling over to the piano*) I rather
enjoy dipping into it occasionally myself: it makes me
feel young again. Anyhow, it was a great success: an
immense success. I was quite frightened once or twice
because Eliza was doing it so well. You see, lots of the
real people cant do it at all: theyre such fools that they
think style comes by nature to people in their position;
and so they never learn. Theres always something professional about doing a thing superlatively well.

HIGGINS: Yes: thats what drives me mad: the silly people
dont know their own silly business. (*Rising*) However,
it's over and done with; and now I can go to bed at last
without dreading tomorrow.

(ELIZA'S *beauty becomes murderous.*)

PICKERING: I think I shall turn in too. Still, it's been a great occasion: a triumph for you. Good-night. (*He goes*).

HIGGINS (*following him*): Good-night. (*Over his shoulder, at the door*) Put out the lights, Eliza; and tell Mrs Pearce not to make coffee for me in the morning: I'll take tea. (*He goes out*).

(ELIZA *tries to control herself and feel indifferent as she rises and walks across to the hearth to switch off the lights. By the time she gets there she is on the point of screaming. She sits down in* HIGGINS'*s chair and holds on hard to the arms. Finally she gives way and flings herself furiously on the floor, raging.*)

HIGGINS (*in despairing wrath outside*): What the devil have I done with my slippers? (*He appears at the door*).

LIZA (*snatching up the slippers, and hurling them at him one after the other with all her force*): There are your slippers. And there. Take your slippers; and may you never have a day's luck with them!

HIGGINS (*astounded*): What on earth—! (*He comes to her*). Whats the matter? Get up. (*He pulls her up*). Anything wrong?

LIZA (*breathless*): Nothing wrong—with you. Ive won your bet for you, havnt I? Thats enough for you. *I* dont matter, I suppose.

HIGGINS: You won my bet! You! Presumptuous insect! *I* won it. What did you throw those slippers at me for?

LIZA: Because I wanted to smash your face. I'd like to kill you, you selfish brute. Why didnt you leave me where you picked me out of—in the gutter? You thank God it's all over, and that now you can throw me back again there, do you? (*She crisps her fingers frantically*).

HIGGINS (*looking at her in cool wonder*): The creature is nervous, after all.

LIZA (*gives a suffocated scream of fury, and instinctively darts her nails at his face*): !!

HIGGINS (*catching her wrists*): Ah! would you? Claws in, you cat. How dare you shew your temper to me?

Sit down and be quiet. (*He throws her roughly into the easy chair*).

LIZA (*crushed by superior strength and weight*): Whats to become of me? Whats to become of me?

HIGGINS: How the devil do I know whats to become of you? What does it matter what becomes of you?

LIZA: You dont care. I know you dont care. You wouldnt care if I was dead. I'm nothing to you—not so much as them slippers.

HIGGINS (*thundering*): Those slippers.

LIZA (*with bitter submission*): Those slippers. I didnt think it made any difference now.

(*A pause.* ELIZA *hopeless and crushed.* HIGGINS *a little uneasy.*)

HIGGINS (*in his loftiest manner*): Why have you begun going on like this? May I ask whether you complain of your treatment here?

LIZA: No.

HIGGINS: Has anybody behaved badly to you? Colonel Pickering? Mrs Pearce? Any of the servants?

LIZA: No.

HIGGINS: I presume you dont pretend that *I* have treated you badly?

LIZA: No.

HIGGINS: I am glad to hear it. (*He moderates his tone*). Perhaps youre tired after the strain of the day. Will you have a glass of champagne? (*He moves towards the door*).

LIZA: No. (*Recollecting her manners*) Thank you.

HIGGINS (*good-humored again*): This has been coming on you for some days. I suppose it was natural for you to be anxious about the garden party. But thats all over now. (*He pats her kindly on the shoulder. She writhes*). Theres nothing more to worry about.

LIZA: No. Nothing more for you to worry about. (*She suddenly rises and gets away from him by going to the piano bench, where she sits and hides her face*). Oh God! I wish I was dead.

HIGGINS (*staring after her in sincere surprise*): Why? In heaven's name, why? (*Reasonably, going to her*) Listen to me, Eliza. All this irritation is purely subjective.

LIZA: I dont understand. I'm too ignorant.

HIGGINS: It's only imagination. Low spirits and nothing else. Nobody's hurting you. Nothing's wrong. You go to bed like a good girl and sleep it off. Have a little cry and say your prayers: that will make you comfortable.

LIZA: I heard your prayers. "Thank God it's all over!"

HIGGINS (*impatiently*): Well, dont you thank God it's all over? Now you are free and can do what you like.

LIZA (*pulling herself together in desperation*): What am I fit for? What have you left me fit for? Where am I to go? What am I to do? Whats to become of me?

HIGGINS (*enlightened, but not at all impressed*): Oh, thats whats worrying you, is it? (*He thrusts his hands into his pockets, and walks about in his usual manner, rattling the contents of his pockets, as if condescending to a trivial subject out of pure kindness*). I shouldnt bother about it if I were you. I should imagine you wont have much difficulty in settling yourself somewhere or other, though I hadnt quite realized that you were going away. (*She looks quickly at him: he does not look at her, but examines the dessert stand on the piano and decides that he will eat an apple*). You might marry, you know. (*He bites a large piece out of the apple and munches it noisily*). You see, Eliza, all men are not confirmed old bachelors like me and the Colonel. Most men are the marrying sort (poor devils!); and youre not bad-looking: it's quite a pleasure to look at you sometimes—not now, of course, because youre crying and looking as ugly as the very devil; but when youre all right and quite yourself, youre what I should call attractive. That is, to the people in the marrying line, you understand. You go to bed and have a good nice rest; and then get up and look at yourself in the glass; and you wont feel so cheap.

(ELIZA *again looks at him, speechless, and does not stir.*

The look is quite lost on him: he eats his apple with a dreamy expression of happiness, as it is quite a good one.)

HIGGINS (*a genial afterthought occurring to him*):   I daresay my mother could find some chap or other who would do very well.

LIZA: We were above that at the corner of Tottenham Court Road.

HIGGINS (*waking up*):   What do you mean?

LIZA: I sold flowers. I didnt sell myself. Now youve made a lady of me I'm not fit to sell anything else. I wish youd left me where you found me.

HIGGINS (*slinging the core of the apple decisively into the grate*):   Tosh, Eliza. Dont you insult human relations by dragging all this cant about buying and selling into it. You neednt marry the fellow if you dont like him.

LIZA: What else am I to do?

HIGGINS: Oh, lots of things. What about your old idea of a florist's shop? Pickering could set you up in one: hes lots of money. (*Chuckling*) He'll have to pay for all those togs you have been wearing to-day; and that, with the hire of the jewellery, will make a big hole in two hundred pounds. Why, six months ago you would have thought it the millennium to have a flower shop of your own. Come! youll be all right. I must clear off to bed: I'm devilish sleepy. By the way, I came down for something: I forget what it was.

LIZA: Your slippers.

HIGGINS: Oh yes, of course. You shied them at me. (*He picks them up, and is going out when she rises and speaks to him*).

LIZA: Before you go, sir—

HIGGINS (*dropping the slippers in his surprise at her calling him Sir*):   Eh?

LIZA: Do my clothes belong to me or to Colonel Pickering?

HIGGINS (*coming back into the room as if her question were the very climax of unreason*):   What the devil use would they be to Pickering?

LIZA: He might want them for the next girl you pick up to experiment on.

HIGGINS (*shocked and hurt*): Is that the way you feel towards us?

LIZA: I dont want to hear anything more about that. All I want to know is whether anything belongs to me. My own clothes were burnt.

HIGGINS: But what does it matter? Why need you start bothering about that in the middle of the night?

LIZA: I want to know what I may take away with me. I dont want to be accused of stealing.

HIGGINS (*now deeply wounded*): Stealing! You shouldnt have said that, Eliza. That shews a want of feeling.

LIZA: I'm sorry. I'm only a common ignorant girl; and in my station I have to be careful. There cant be any feelings between the like of you and the like of me. Please will you tell me what belongs to me and what doesnt?

HIGGINS (*very sulky*): You may take the whole damned houseful if you like. Except the jewels. Theyre hired. Will that satisfy you? (*He turns on his heel and is about to go in extreme dudgeon*).

LIZA (*drinking in his emotion like nectar, and nagging him to provoke a further supply*): Stop, please. (*She takes off her jewels*). Will you take these to your room and keep them safe? I dont want to run the risk of their being missing.

HIGGINS (*furious*): Hand them over. (*She puts them into his hands*). If these belonged to me instead of to the jeweller, I'd ram them down your ungrateful throat. (*He perfunctorily thrusts them into his pockets, unconsciously decorating himself with the protruding ends of the chains*).

LIZA (*taking a ring off*): This ring isnt the jeweller's: it's the one you bought me in Brighton. I dont want it now. (HIGGINS *dashes the ring violently into the fireplace, and turns on her so threateningly that she crouches over the piano with her hands over her face, and exclaims*). Dont you hit me.

HIGGINS: Hit you! You infamous creature, how dare you accuse me of such a thing? It is you who have hit me. You have wounded me to the heart.

LIZA (*thrilling with hidden joy*): I'm glad. Ive got a little of my own back, anyhow.

HIGGINS (*with dignity, in his finest professional style*): You have caused me to lose my temper: a thing that has hardly ever happened to me before. I prefer to say nothing more tonight. I am going to bed.

LIZA (*pertly*): Youd better leave a note for Mrs Pearce about the coffee; for she wont be told by me.

HIGGINS (*formally*): Damn Mrs Pearce; and damn the coffee; and damn you; and damn my own folly in having lavished hard-earned knowledge and the treasure of my regard and intimacy on a heartless guttersnipe. (*He goes out with impressive decorum, and spoils it by slamming the door savagely*).

(ELIZA *smiles for the first time; expresses her feelings by a wild pantomime in which an imitation of* HIGGINS'*s exit is confused with her own triumph; and finally goes down on her knees on the hearthrug to look for the ring.*)

Act V

(MRS HIGGINS'*s drawing-room. She is at her writing-table as before.* THE PARLOR-MAID *comes in.*)

THE PARLOR-MAID (*at the door*): Mr Henry, mam, is downstairs with Colonel Pickering.

MRS HIGGINS: Well, shew them up.

THE PARLOR-MAID: Theyre using the telephone, mam. Telephoning to the police, I think.

MRS HIGGINS: What!

THE PARLOR-MAID (*coming further in and lowering her voice*): Mr Henry is in a state, mam. I thought I'd better tell you.

MRS HIGGINS: If you had told me that Mr Henry was not in a state it would have been more surprising. Tell them to come up when theyve finished with the police. I suppose hes lost something.

THE PARLOR-MAID: Yes, mam (*going*).

MRS HIGGINS: Go upstairs and tell Miss Doolittle that Mr Henry and the Colonel are here. Ask her not to come down til I send for her.

THE PARLOR-MAID: Ycs, mam.

(HIGGINS *bursts in. He is, as* THE PARLOR-MAID *has said, in a state.*)

HIGGINS: Look here, mother: heres a confounded thing!

MRS HIGGINS: Yes, dear. Good-morning. (*He checks his impatience and kisses her, whilst* THE PARLOR-MAID *goes out*). What is it?

HIGGINS: Eliza's bolted.

MRS HIGGINS (*calmly continuing her writing*):   You must have frightened her.

HIGGINS: Frightened her! nonsense! She was left last night, as usual, to turn out the lights and all that; and instead of going to bed she changed her clothes and went right off: her bed wasnt slept in. She came in a cab for her things before seven this morning; and that fool Mrs Pearce let her have them without telling me a word about it. What am I to do?

MRS HIGGINS: Do without, I'm afraid, Henry. The girl has a perfect right to leave if she chooses.

HIGGINS (*wandering distractedly across the room*):   But I cant find anything. I dont know what appointments Ive got. I'm— (PICKERING *comes in.* MRS HIGGINS *puts down her pen and turns away from the writing-table*).

PICKERING (*shaking hands*):   Good-morning, Mrs Higgins. Has Henry told you? (*He sits down on the ottoman*).

HIGGINS: What does that ass of an inspector say? Have you offered a reward?

MRS HIGGINS (*rising in indignant amazement*):   You dont mean to say you have set the police after Eliza.

HIGGINS: Of course. What are the police for? What else could we do? (*He sits in the Elizabethan chair*).

PICKERING: The inspector made a lot of difficulties. I really think he suspected us of some improper purpose.

MRS HIGGINS: Well, of course he did. What right have you to go to the police and give the girl's name as if she were a thief, or a lost umbrella, or something? Really! (*She sits down again, deeply vexed*).

HIGGINS: But we want to find her.

PICKERING: We cant let her go like this, you know, Mrs Higgins. What were we to do?

MRS HIGGINS: You have no more sense, either of you, than two children. Why—

(THE PARLOR-MAID *comes in and breaks off the conversation*.)

THE PARLOR-MAID: Mr Henry: a gentleman wants to see

you very particular. Hes been sent on from Wimpole
Street.

HIGGINS: Oh, bother! I cant see anyone now. Who is it?

THE PARLOR-MAID: A Mr Doolittle, sir.

PICKERING: Doolittle! Do you mean the dustman?

THE PARLOR-MAID: Dustman! Oh no, sir: a gentleman.

HIGGINS (*springing up excitedly*):   By George, Pick, it's
some relative of hers that shes gone to. Somebody we
know nothing about. (*To* THE PARLOR-MAID)   Send him
up, quick.

THE PARLOR-MAID: Yes, sir. (*She goes*).

HIGGINS (*eagerly, going to his mother*):   Genteel rela-
tives! now we shall hear something. (*He sits down in
the Chippendale chair*).

MRS HIGGINS: Do you know any of her people?

PICKERING: Only her father: the fellow we told you
about.

THE PARLOR-MAID (*announcing*):   Mr Doolittle. (*She
withdraws*).

(DOOLITTLE *enters. He is brilliantly dressed in a new
fashionable frock-coat, with white waistcoat and grey
trousers. A flower in his buttonhole, a dazzling silk hat,
and patent leather shoes complete the effect. He is too
concerned with the business he has come on to notice*
MRS HIGGINS. *He walks straight to* HIGGINS, *and accosts
him with vehement reproach.*)

DOOLITTLE (*indicating his own person*):   See here! Do
you see this? You done this.

HIGGINS: Done what, man?

DOOLITTLE: This, I tell you. Look at it. Look at this hat.
Look at this coat.

PICKERING: Has Eliza been buying you clothes?

DOOLITTLE: Eliza! not she. Not half. Why would she buy
me clothes?

MRS HIGGINS: Good-morning, Mr Doolittle. Wont you sit
down?

DOOLITTLE (*taken aback as he becomes conscious that he
has forgotten his hostess*):   Asking your pardon, maam.

(*He approaches her and shakes her proffered hand*).
Thank you. (*He sits down on the ottoman, on* PICKER-
ING's *right*). I am that full of what has happened to me
that I cant think of anything else.

HIGGINS: What the dickens has happened to you?

DOOLITTLE: I shouldnt mind if it had only happened to
me: anything might happen to anybody and nobody to
blame but Providence, as you might say. But this is
something that you done to me: yes, you, Henry
Higgins.

HIGGINS: Have you found Eliza? Thats the point.

DOOLITTLE: Have you lost her?

HIGGINS: Yes.

DOOLITTLE: You have all the luck, you have. I aint found
her; but she'll find me quick enough now after what
you done to me.

MRS HIGGINS: But what has my son done to you, Mr
Doolittle?

DOOLITTLE: Done to me! Ruined me. Destroyed my happiness. Tied me up and delivered me into the hands of
middle class morality.

HIGGINS (*rising intolerantly and standing over* DOOLIT-
TLE):   Youre raving. Youre drunk. Youre mad. I gave
you five pounds. After that I had two conversations with
you, at half-a-crown an hour. Ive never seen you since.

DOOLITTLE: Oh! Drunk! am I? Mad! am I? Tell me this.
Did you or did you not write a letter to an old blighter
in America that was giving five millions to found Moral
Reform Societies all over the world, and that wanted
you to invent a universal language for him?

HIGGINS: What! Ezra D. Wannafeller! Hes dead. (*He sits
down again carelessly*).

DOOLITTLE: Yes: hes dead; and I'm done for. Now did
you or did you not write a letter to him to say that the
most original moralist at present in England, to the best
of your knowledge, was Alfred Doolittle, a common
dustman.

HIGGINS: Oh, after your last visit I remember making
some silly joke of the kind.

DOOLITTLE: Ah! you may well call it a silly joke. It put
the lid on me right enough. Just give him the chance
he wanted to shew that Americans is not like us: that
they recognize and respect merit in every class of life,
however humble. Them words is in his blooming will,
in which, Henry Higgins, thanks to your silly joking,
he leaves me a share in his Pre-digested Cheese Trust
worth three thousand a year on condition that I lecture
for his Wannafeller Moral Reform World League as
often as they ask me up to six times a year.

HIGGINS: The devil he does! Whew! (*Brightening suddenly*)   What a lark!

PICKERING: A safe thing for you, Doolittle. They wont
ask you twice.

DOOLITTLE: It aint the lecturing I mind. I'll lecture them
blue in the face, I will, and not turn a hair. It's making
a gentleman of me that I object to. Who asked him to
make a gentleman of me? I was happy. I was free. I
touched pretty nigh everybody for money when I wanted
it, same as I touched you, Henry Higgins. Now I am
worrited; tied neck and heels; and everybody touches me
for money. It's a fine thing for you, says my solicitor. Is
it? says I. You mean it's a good thing for you, I says.
When I was a poor man and had a solicitor once when
they found a pram in the dust cart, he got me off, and
got shut of me and got me shut of him as quick as he
could. Same with the doctors: used to shove me out of
the hospital before I could hardly stand on my legs, and
nothing to pay. Now they finds out that I'm not a
healthy man and cant live unless they looks after me
twice a day. In the house I'm not let do a hand's turn
for myself: somebody else must do it and touch me for
it. A year ago I hadnt a relative in the world except
two or three that wouldnt speak to me. Now Ive fifty,
and not a decent week's wages among the lot of them.
I have to live for others and not for myself: thats middle
class morality. You talk of losing Eliza. Dont you be
anxious: I bet shes on my doorstep by this: she that
could support herself easy by selling flowers if I wasnt

respectable. And the next one to touch me will be you,
Henry Higgins. I'll have to learn to speak middle class
language from you, instead of speaking proper English.
Thats where youll come in; and I daresay thats what
you done it for.

MRS HIGGINS: But, my dear Mr Doolittle, you need not
suffer all this if you are really in earnest. Nobody can
force you to accept this bequest. You can repudiate it.
Isnt that so, Colonel Pickering?

PICKERING: I believe so.

DOOLITTLE (*softening his manner in deference to her sex*):
Thats the tragedy of it, maam. It's easy to say chuck
it; but I havnt the nerve. Which of us has? We're all
intimidated. Intimidated, maam: thats what we are.
What is there for me if I chuck it but the workhouse in
my old age? I have to dye my hair already to keep my
job as a dustman. If I was one of the deserving poor,
and had put by a bit, I could chuck it; but then why
should I, acause the deserving poor might as well be
millionaires for all the happiness they ever has. They
dont know what happiness is. But I, as one of the undeserving poor, have nothing between me and the pauper's
uniform but this here blasted three thousand a year that
shoves me into the middle class. (Excuse the expression, maam: youd use it yourself if you had my provocation.) Theyve got you every way you turn: it's a
choice between the Skilly of the workhouse and the
Char Bydis of the middle class; and I havnt the nerve
for the workhouse. Intimidated: thats what I am. Broke.
Bought up. Happier men than me will call for my dust,
and touch me for their tip; and I'll look on helpless,
and envy them. And thats what your son has brought
me to. (*He is overcome by emotion*).

MRS HIGGINS: Well, I'm very glad youre not going to do
anything foolish, Mr Doolittle. For this solves the problem of Eliza's future. You can provide for her now.

DOOLITTLE (*with melancholy resignation*): Yes, maam:
I'm expected to provide for everyone now, out of three
thousand a year.

HIGGINS (*jumping up*): Nonsense! he cant provide for

her. He shant provide for her. She doesnt belong to him. I paid him five pounds for her. Doolittle: either youre an honest man or a rogue.

DOOLITTLE (*tolerantly*): A little of both, Henry, like the rest of us: a little of both.

HIGGINS: Well, you took that money for the girl; and you have no right to take her as well.

MRS HIGGINS: Henry: dont be absurd. If you want to know where Eliza is, she is upstairs.

HIGGINS (*amazed*): Upstairs!!! Then I shall jolly soon fetch her downstairs. (*He makes resolutely for the door*).

MRS HIGGINS (*rising and following him*): Be quiet, Henry. Sit down.

HIGGINS: I—

MRS HIGGINS: Sit down, dear; and listen to me.

HIGGINS: Oh very well, very well, very well. (*He throws himself ungraciously on the ottoman, with his face towards the windows*). But I think you might have told us this half an hour ago.

MRS HIGGINS: Eliza came to me this morning. She passed the night partly walking about in a rage, partly trying to throw herself into the river and being afraid to, and partly in the Carlton Hotel. She told me of the brutal way you two treated her.

HIGGINS (*bounding up again*): What!

PICKERING (*rising also*): My dear Mrs Higgins, shes been telling you stories. We didnt treat her brutally. We hardly said a word to her; and we parted on particularly good terms. (*Turning on* HIGGINS). Higgins: did you bully her after I went to bed?

HIGGINS: Just the other way about. She threw my slippers in my face. She behaved in the most outrageous way. I never gave her the slightest provocation. The slippers came bang into my face the moment I entered the room—before I had uttered a word. And used perfectly awful language.

PICKERING (*astonished*): But why? What did we do to her?

MRS HIGGINS: I think I know pretty well what you did.

The girl is naturally rather affectionate, I think. Isnt she, Mr Doolittle?

DOOLITTLE: Very tender-hearted, maam. Takes after me.

MRS HIGGINS: Just so. She had become attached to you both. She worked very hard for you, Henry! I dont think you quite realize what anything in the nature of brain work means to a girl like that. Well, it seems that when the great day of trial came, and she did this wonderful thing for you without making a single mistake, you two sat there and never said a word to her, but talked together of how glad you were that it was all over and how you had been bored with the whole thing. And then you were surprised because she threw your slippers at you! *I* should have thrown the fire-irons at you.

HIGGINS: We said nothing except that we were tired and wanted to go to bed. Did we, Pick?

PICKERING (*shrugging his shoulders*): That was all.

MRS HIGGINS (*ironically*): Quite sure?

PICKERING: Absolutely. Really, that was all.

MRS HIGGINS: You didnt thank her, or pet her, or admire her, or tell her how splendid she'd been.

HIGGINS (*impatiently*): But she knew all about that. We didnt make speeches to her, if thats what you mean.

PICKERING (*conscience stricken*): Perhaps we were a little inconsiderate. Is she very angry?

MRS HIGGINS (*returning to her place at the writing-table*): Well, I'm afraid she wont go back to Wimpole Street, especially now that Mr Doolittle is able to keep up the position you have thrust on her; but she says she is quite willing to meet you on friendly terms and to let bygones be bygones.

HIGGINS (*furious*): Is she, by George? Ho!

MRS HIGGINS: If you promise to behave yourself, Henry, I'll ask her to come down. If not, go home; for you have taken up quite enough of my time.

HIGGINS: Oh, all right. Very well. Pick: you behave yourself. Let us put on our best Sunday manners for this creature that we picked out of the mud. (*He flings himself sulkily into the Elizabethan chair*).

DOOLITTLE (*remonstrating*): Now, now, Henry Higgins! have some consideration for my feelings as a middle class man.

MRS HIGGINS: Remember your promise, Henry. (*She presses the bell-button on the writing-table*). Mr Doolittle: will you be so good as to step out on the balcony for a moment. I dont want Eliza to have the shock of your news until she has made it up with these two gentlemen. Would you mind?

DOOLITTLE: As you wish, lady. Anything to help Henry to keep her off my hands. (*He disappears through the window*).

(THE PARLOR-MAID *answers the bell.* PICKERING *sits down in* DOOLITTLE'*s place.*)

MRS HIGGINS: Ask Miss Doolittle to come down, please.

THE PARLOR-MAID: Yes, mam. (*She goes out*).

MRS HIGGINS: Now, Henry: be good.

HIGGINS: I am behaving myself perfectly.

PICKERING: He is doing his best, Mrs Higgins.

(*A pause.* HIGGINS *throws back his head; stretches out his legs; and begins to whistle.*)

MRS HIGGINS: Henry, dearest, you dont look at all nice in that attitude.

HIGGINS (*pulling himself together*): I was not trying to look nice, mother.

MRS HIGGINS: It doesnt matter, dear. I only wanted to make you speak.

HIGGINS: Why?

MRS HIGGINS: Because you cant speak and whistle at the same time.

(HIGGINS *groans. Another very trying pause.*)

HIGGINS (*springing up, out of patience*): Where the devil is that girl? Are we to wait here all day?

(ELIZA *enters, sunny, self-possessed, and giving a staggeringly convincing exhibition of ease of manner. She*

carries a little work-basket, and is very much at home.
PICKERING *is too much taken aback to rise.*)

LIZA: How do you do, Professor Higgins? Are you quite
well?

HIGGINS (*choking*):   Am I— (*He can no more*).

LIZA: But of course you are: you are never ill. So glad
to see you again, Colonel Pickering. (*He rises hastily;
and they shake hands*). Quite chilly this morning, isnt
it? (*She sits down on his left. He sits beside her*).

HIGGINS: Dont you dare try this game on me. I taught it
to you; and it doesnt take me in. Get up and come
home; and dont be a fool.

(ELIZA *takes a piece of needlework from her basket, and
begins to stitch at it, without taking the least notice of
this outburst.*)

MRS HIGGINS: Very nicely put, indeed, Henry. No
woman could resist such an invitation.

HIGGINS: You let her alone, mother. Let her speak for
herself. You will jolly soon see whether she has an idea
that I havnt put into her head or a word that I havnt
put into her mouth. I tell you I have created this thing
out of the squashed cabbage leaves of Covent Garden;
and now she pretends to play the fine lady with me.

MRS HIGGINS (*placidly*):   Yes, dear; but youll sit down,
wont you?

(HIGGINS *sits down again, savagely.*)

LIZA (*to* PICKERING, *taking no apparent notice of* HIGGINS,
and working away deftly):   Will you drop me altogether
now that the experiment is over, Colonel Pickering?

PICKERING: Oh dont. You mustnt think of it as an experiment. It shocks me, somehow.

LIZA: Oh, I'm only a squashed cabbage leaf—

PICKERING (*impulsively*):   No.

LIZA (*continuing quietly*):   —but I owe so much to you
that I should be very unhappy if you forgot me.

PICKERING: It's very kind of you to say so, Miss
Doolittle.

LIZA: It's not because you paid for my dresses. I know you are generous to everybody with money. But it was from you that I learnt really nice manners; and that is what makes one a lady, isnt it? You see it was so very difficult for me with the example of Professor Higgins always before me. I was brought up to be just like him, unable to control myself, and using bad language on the slightest provocation. And I should never have known that ladies and gentlemen didnt behave like that if you hadnt been there.

HIGGINS: Well!!

PICKERING: Oh, thats only his way, you know. He doesnt mean it.

LIZA: Oh, *I* didnt mean it either, when I was a flower girl. It was only my way. But you sec I did it; and thats what makes the difference after all.

PICKERING: No doubt. Still, he taught you to speak; and I couldnt have done that, you know.

LIZA (*trivially*): Of course: that is his profession.

HIGGINS: Damnation!

LIZA (*continuing*): It was just like learning to dance in the fashionable way: there was nothing more than that in it. But do you know what began my real education?

PICKERING: What?

LIZA (*stopping her work for a moment*): Your calling me Miss Doolittle that day when I first came to Wimpole Street. That was the beginning of self-respect for me. (*She resumes her stitching*). And there were a hundred little things you never noticed, because they came naturally to you. Things about standing up and taking off your hat and opening doors—

PICKERING: Oh, that was nothing.

LIZA: Yes: things that shewed you thought and felt about me as if I were something better than a scullery-maid; though of course I know you would have been just the same to a scullery-maid if she had been let into the drawing-room. You never took off your boots in the dining-room when I was there.

PICKERING: You mustnt mind that. Higgins takes off his boots all over the place.

LIZA: I know. I am not blaming him. It is his way, isnt it? But it made such a difference to me that you didnt do it. You see, really and truly, apart from the things anyone can pick up (the dressing and the proper way of speaking, and so on), the difference between a lady and a flower girl is not how she behaves, but how shes treated. I shall always be a flower girl to Professor Higgins, because he always treats me as a flower girl, and always will; but I know I can be a lady to you, because you always treat me as a lady, and always will.

MRS HIGGINS: Please dont grind your teeth, Henry.

PICKERING: Well, this is really very nice of you, Miss Doolittle.

LIZA: I should like you to call me Eliza, now, if you would.

PICKERING: Thank you. Eliza, of course.

LIZA: And I should like Professor Higgins to call me Miss Doolittle.

HIGGINS: I'll see you damned first.

MRS HIGGINS: Henry! Henry!

PICKERING (*laughing*): Why dont you slang back at him? Dont stand it. It would do him a lot of good.

LIZA: I cant. I could have done it once; but now I cant go back to it. Last night, when I was wandering about, a girl spoke to me; and I tried to get back into the old way with her; but it was no use. You told me, you know, that when a child is brought to a foreign country, it picks up the language in a few weeks, and forgets its own. Well, I am a child in your country. I have forgotten my own language, and can speak nothing but yours. Thats the real break-off with the corner of Tottenham Court Road. Leaving Wimpole Street finishes it.

PICKERING (*much alarmed*): Oh! but youre coming back to Wimpole Street, arnt you? Youll forgive Higgins?

HIGGINS (*rising*): Forgive! Will she, by George! Let her go. Let her find out how she can get on without us. She will relapse into the gutter in three weeks without me at her elbow.

(DOOLITTLE *appears at the centre window. With a look of dignified reproach at* HIGGINS, *he comes slowly and silently to his daughter, who, with her back to the window, is unconscious of his approach.*)

PICKERING: Hes incorrigible, Eliza. You wont relapse, will you?

LIZA: No: not now. Never again. I have learnt my lesson. I dont believe I could utter one of the old sounds if I tried. (DOOLITTLE *touches her on her left shoulder. She drops her work, losing her self-possession utterly at the spectacle of her father's splendor*) A-a-a-a-a-ah-ow-ooh!

HIGGINS (*with a crow of triumph*): Aha! Just so. A-a-a-a-ahowooh! A-a-a-a-ahowooh! A-a-a-a-ahowooh! Victory! Victory! (*He throws himself on the divan, folding his arms, and spraddling arrogantly*).

DOOLITTLE: Can you blame the girl? Dont look at me like that, Eliza. It aint my fault. Ive come into some money.

LIZA: You must have touched a millionaire this time, dad.

DOOLITTLE: I have. But I'm dressed something special today. I'm going to St. George's, Hanover Square. Your stepmother is going to marry me.

LIZA (*angrily*): Youre going to let yourself down to marry that low common woman!

PICKERING (*quietly*): He ought to, Eliza. (*To* DOOLITTLE) Why has she changed her mind?

DOOLITTLE (*sadly*): Intimidated, Governor. Intimidated. Middle class morality claims its victim. Wont you put on your hat, Liza, and come and see me turned off?

LIZA: If the Colonel says I must, I—I'll (*almost sobbing*) I'll demean myself. And get insulted for my pains, like enough.

DOOLITTLE: Dont be afraid: she never comes to words with anyone now, poor woman! respectability has broke all the spirit out of her.

PICKERING (*squeezing* ELIZA's *elbow gently*): Be kind to them, Eliza. Make the best of it.

LIZA (*forcing a little smile for him through her vexation*):   Oh well, just to shew theres no ill feeling. I'll be back in a moment. (*She goes out*).

DOOLITTLE (*sitting down beside* PICKERING):   I feel uncommon nervous about the ceremony, Colonel. I wish youd come and see me through it.

PICKERING: But youve been through it before, man. You were married to Eliza's mother.

DOOLITTLE: Who told you that, Colonel?

PICKERING: Well, nobody told me. But I concluded—naturally—

DOOLITTLE: No: that aint the natural way, Colonel: it's only the middle class way. My way was always the undeserving way. But dont say nothing to Eliza. She dont know: I always had a delicacy about telling her.

PICKERING: Quite right. We'll leave it so, if you dont mind.

DOOLITTLE: And youll come to the church, Colonel, and put me through straight?

PICKERING: With pleasure. As far as a bachelor can.

MRS HIGGINS: May I come, Mr Doolittle? I should be very sorry to miss your wedding.

DOOLITTLE: I should indeed be honored by your condescension, maam; and my poor old woman would take it as a tremendous compliment. Shes been very low, thinking of the happy days that are no more.

MRS HIGGINS (*rising*):   I'll order the carriage and get ready. (*The men rise, except* HIGGINS). I shant be more than fifteen minutes. (*As she goes to the door* ELIZA *comes in, hatted and buttoning her gloves*). I'm going to the church to see your father married, Eliza. You had better come in the brougham with me. Colonel Pickering can go on with the bridegroom.

(MRS HIGGINS *goes out.* ELIZA *comes to the middle of the room between the centre window and the ottoman.* PICKERING *joins her.*)

DOOLITTLE: Bridegroom! What a word! It makes a man realize his position, somehow. (*He takes up his hat and goes towards the door*).

PICKERING: Before I go, Eliza, do forgive him and come back to us.

LIZA: I dont think papa would allow me. Would you, dad?

DOOLITTLE (*sad but magnanimous*):   They played you off very cunning, Eliza, them two sportsmen. If it had been only one of them, you could have nailed him. But you see, there was two; and one of them chaperoned the other, as you might say. (*To* PICKERING)   It was artful of you, Colonel; but I bear no malice: I should have done the same myself. I been the victim of one woman after another all my life; and I dont grudge you two getting the better of Eliza. I shant interfere. It's time for us to go, Colonel. So long, Henry. See you in St. George's, Eliza. (*He goes out*).

PICKERING (*coaxing*):   Do stay with us, Eliza. (*He follows* DOOLITTLE).

(ELIZA *goes out on the balcony to avoid being alone with* HIGGINS. *He rises and joins her there. She immediately comes back into the room and makes for the door; but he goes along the balcony quickly and gets his back to the door before she reaches it.*)

HIGGINS: Well, Eliza, youve had a bit of your own back, as you call it. Have you had enough? and are you going to be reasonable? Or do you want any more?

LIZA: You want me back only to pick up your slippers and put up with your tempers and fetch and carry for you.

HIGGINS: I havnt said I wanted you back at all.

LIZA: Oh, indeed. Then what are we talking about?

HIGGINS: About you, not about me. If you come back I shall treat you just as I have always treated you. I cant change my nature; and I dont intend to change my manners. My manners are exactly the same as Colonel Pickering's.

LIZA: Thats not true. He treats a flower girl as if she was a duchess.

HIGGINS: And I treat a duchess as if she was a flower girl.

LIZA: I see. (*She turns away composedly, and sits on the ottoman, facing the window*). The same to everybody.

HIGGINS: Just so.

LIZA: Like father.

HIGGINS (*grinning, a little taken down*): Without accepting the comparison at all points, Eliza, it's quite true that your father is not a snob, and that he will be quite at home in any station of life to which his eccentric destiny may call him. (*Seriously*) The great secret, Eliza, is not having bad manners or good manners or any other particular sort of manners, but having the same manner for all human souls: in short, behaving as if you were in Heaven, where there are no third-class carriages, and one soul is as good as another.

LIZA: Amen. You are a born preacher.

HIGGINS (*irritated*): The question is not whether I treat you rudely, but whether you ever heard me treat anyone else better.

LIZA (*with sudden sincerity*): I dont care how you treat me. I dont mind your swearing at me. I dont mind a black eye: Ive had one before this. But (*standing up and facing him*) I wont be passed over.

HIGGINS: Then get out of my way; for I wont stop for you. You talk about me as if I were a motor bus.

LIZA: So you are a motor bus: all bounce and go, and no consideration for anyone. But I can do without you: dont think I cant.

HIGGINS: I know you can. I told you you could.

LIZA (*wounded, getting away from him to the other side of the ottoman with her face to the hearth*): I know you did, you brute. You wanted to get rid of me.

HIGGINS: Liar.

LIZA: Thank you. (*She sits down with dignity*).

HIGGINS: You never asked yourself, I suppose, whether *I* could do without you.

LIZA (*earnestly*): Dont you try to get round me. Youll have to do without me.

HIGGINS (*arrogant*): I can do without anybody. I have my own soul: my own spark of divine fire. But (*with sudden humility*) I shall miss you, Eliza. (*He sits down near her on the ottoman*). I have learnt something from your idiotic notions: I confess that humbly and gratefully. And I have grown accustomed to your voice and appearance. I like them, rather.

LIZA: Well, you have both of them on your gramophone and in your book of photographs. When you feel lonely without me, you can turn the machine on. It's got no feelings to hurt.

HIGGINS: I cant turn your soul on. Leave me those feelings; and you can take away the voice and the face. They are not you.

LIZA: Oh, you are a devil. You can twist the heart in a girl as easy as some could twist her arms to hurt her. Mrs Pearce warned me. Time and again she has wanted to leave you; and you always got round her at the last minute. And you dont care a bit for her. And you dont care a bit for me.

HIGGINS: I care for life, for humanity; and you are a part of it that has come my way and been built into my house. What more can you or anyone ask?

LIZA: I wont care for anybody that doesnt care for me.

HIGGINS: Commercial principles, Eliza. Like (*reproducing her Covent Garden pronunciation with professional exactness*) s'yollin voylets (selling violets), isnt it?

LIZA: Dont sneer at me. It's mean to sneer at me.

HIGGINS: I have never sneered in my life. Sneering doesnt become either the human face or the human soul. I am expressing my righteous contempt for Commercialism. I dont and wont trade in affection. You call me a brute because you couldnt buy a claim on me by fetching my slippers and finding my spectacles. You were a fool: I think a woman fetching a man's slippers is a disgusting sight: did I ever fetch your slippers? I think a good deal more of you for throwing them in my face.

No use slaving for me and then saying you want to be cared for: who cares for a slave? If you come back, come back for the sake of good fellowship; for youll get nothing else. Youve had a thousand times as much out of me as I have out of you; and if you dare to set up your little dog's tricks of fetching and carrying slippers against my creation of a Duchess Eliza, I'll slam the door in your silly face.

LIZA: What did you do it for if you didnt care for me?

HIGGINS (*heartily*): Why, because it was my job.

LIZA: You never thought of the trouble it would make for me.

HIGGINS: Would the world ever have been made if its maker had been afraid of making trouble? Making life means making trouble. Theres only one way of escaping trouble; and thats killing things. Cowards, you notice, are always shrieking to have troublesome people killed.

LIZA: I'm no preacher: I dont notice things like that. I notice that you dont notice me.

HIGGINS (*jumping up and walking about intolerantly*): Eliza: youre an idiot. I waste the treasures of my Miltonic mind by spreading them before you. Once for all, understand that I go my way and do my work without caring twopence what happens to either of us. I am not intimidated, like your father and your stepmother. So you can come back or go to the devil: which you please.

LIZA: What am I to come back for?

HIGGINS (*bouncing up on his knees on the ottoman and leaning over it to her*): For the fun of it. Thats why I took you on.

LIZA (*with averted face*): And you may throw me out tomorrow if I dont do everything you want me to?

HIGGINS: Yes; and you may walk out tomorrow if I dont do everything you want me to.

LIZA: And live with my stepmother?

HIGGINS: Yes, or sell flowers.

LIZA: Oh! if I only could go back to my flower basket! I should be independent of both you and father and all the world! Why did you take my independence from me? Why did I give it up? I'm a slave now, for all my fine clothes.

HIGGINS: Not a bit. I'll adopt you as my daughter and settle money on you if you like. Or would you rather marry Pickering?

LIZA (*looking fiercely round at him*): I wouldnt marry you if you asked me; and youre nearer my age than what he is.

HIGGINS (*gently*): Than he is: not "than what he is."

LIZA (*losing her temper and rising*): I'll talk as I like. Youre not my teacher now.

HIGGINS (*reflectively*): I dont suppose Pickering would, though. Hes as confirmed an old bachelor as I am.

LIZA: Thats not what I want; and dont you think it. Ive always had chaps enough wanting me that way. Freddy Hill writes to me twice and three times a day, sheets and sheets.

HIGGINS (*disagreeably surprised*): Damn his impudence! (*He recoils and finds himself sitting on his heels*).

LIZA: He has a right to if he likes, poor lad. And he does love me.

HIGGINS (*getting off the ottoman*): You have no right to encourage him.

LIZA: Every girl has a right to be loved.

HIGGINS: What! By fools like that?

LIZA: Freddy's not a fool. And if hes weak and poor and wants me, may be hed make me happier than my betters that bully me and dont want me.

HIGGINS: Can he make anything of you? Thats the point.

LIZA: Perhaps I could make something of him. But I never thought of us making anything of one another; and you never think of anything else. I only want to be natural.

HIGGINS: In short, you want me to be as infatuated about you as Freddy? Is that it?

LIZA: No I dont. Thats not the sort of feeling I want from you. And dont you be too sure of yourself or of me. I could have been a bad girl if I'd liked. Ive seen more of some things than you, for all your learning.

Girls like me can drag gentlemen down to make love to them easy enough. And they wish each other dead the next minute.

HIGGINS: Of course they do. Then what in thunder are we quarrelling about?

LIZA (*much troubled*): I want a little kindness. I know I'm a common ignorant girl, and you a book-learned gentleman; but I'm not dirt under your feet. What I done (*correcting herself*) what I did was not for the dresses and the taxis: I did it because we were pleasant together and I come—came—to care for you; not to want you to make love to me, and not forgetting the difference between us, but more friendly like.

HIGGINS: Well, of course. Thats just how I feel. And how Pickering feels. Eliza: youre a fool.

LIZA: Thats not a proper answer to give me (*she sinks on the chair at the writing-table in tears*).

HIGGINS: It's all youll get until you stop being a common idiot. If youre going to be a lady, youll have to give up feeling neglected if the men you know dont spend half their time snivelling over you and the other half giving you black eyes. If you cant stand the coldness of my sort of life, and the strain of it, go back to the gutter. Work til you are more a brute than a human being; and then cuddle and squabble and drink til you fall asleep. Oh, it's a fine life, the life of the gutter. It's real: it's warm: it's violent: you can feel it through the thickest skin: you can taste it and smell it without any training or any work. Not like Science and Literature and Classical Music and Philosophy and Art. You find me cold, unfeeling, selfish, dont you? Very well: be off with you to the sort of people you like. Marry some sentimental hog or other with lots of money, and a thick pair of lips to kiss you with and a thick pair of boots to kick you with. If you cant appreciate what youve got, youd better get what you can appreciate.

LIZA (*desperate*): Oh, you are a cruel tyrant. I cant talk to you: you turn everything against me: I'm always in the wrong. But you know very well all the time that

youre nothing but a bully. You know I cant go back to
the gutter, as you call it, and that I have no real friends
in the world but you and the Colonel. You know well
I couldnt bear to live with a low common man after
you two; and it's wicked and cruel of you to insult me
by pretending I could. You think I must go back to
Wimpole Street because I have nowhere else to go but
father's. But dont you be too sure that you have me
under your feet to be trampled on and talked down. I'll
marry Freddy, I will, as soon as hes able to support
me.

HIGGINS (*sitting down beside her*): Rubbish! you shall
marry an ambassador. You shall marry the Governor-
General of India or the Lord-Lieutenant of Ireland, or
somebody who wants a deputy-queen. I'm not going to
have my masterpiece thrown away on Freddy.

LIZA: You think I like you to say that. But I havnt forgot
what you said a minute ago; and I wont be coaxed round
as if I was a baby or a puppy. If I cant have kindness,
I'll have independence.

HIGGINS: Independence? Thats middle class blasphemy.
We are all dependent on one another, every soul of us
on earth.

LIZA (*rising determinedly*): I'll let you see whether I'm
dependent on you. If you can preach, I can teach. I'll
go and be a teacher.

HIGGINS: Whatll you teach, in heaven's name?

LIZA: What you taught me. I'll teach phonetics.

HIGGINS: Ha! ha! ha!

LIZA: I'll offer myself as an assistant to Professor
Nepean.

HIGGINS (*rising in a fury*): What! That impostor! that
humbug! that toadying ignoramus! Teach him my methods! my discoveries! You take one step in his direction
and I'll wring your neck. (*He lays hands on her*). Do
you hear?

LIZA (*defiantly non-resistant*): Wring away. What do I
care? I knew youd strike me some day. (*He lets her go,
stamping with rage at having forgotten himself, and*

recoils so hastily that he stumbles back into his seat on
the ottoman). Aha! Now I know how to deal with you.
What a fool I was not to think of it before! You cant
take away the knowledge you gave me. You said I had
a finer ear than you. And I can be civil and kind to
people, which is more than you can. Aha! Thats done
you, Henry Higgins, it has. Now I dont care that (*snap-*
ping her fingers) for your bullying and your big talk.
I'll advertize it in the papers that your duchess is only
a flower girl that you taught, and that she'll teach anybody to be a duchess just the same in six months for a
thousand guineas. Oh, when I think of myself crawling
under your feet and being trampled on and called
names, when all the time I had only to lift up my finger
to be as good as you, I could just kick myself.

HIGGINS (*wondering at her*):   You damned impudent slut,
you! But it's better than snivelling; better than fetching
slippers and finding spectacles, isnt it? (*Rising*) By
George, Eliza, I said I'd make a woman of you; and I
have. I like you like this.

LIZA: Yes: you turn round and make up to me now that
I'm not afraid of you, and can do without you.

HIGGINS: Of course I do, you little fool. Five minutes
ago you were like a millstone round my neck. Now
youre a tower of strength: a consort battleship. You and
I and Pickering will be three old bachelors together instead of only two men and a silly girl.

(MRS HIGGINS *returns, dressed for the wedding.* ELIZA
instantly becomes cool and elegant.)

MRS HIGGINS: The carriage is waiting, Eliza. Are you
ready?

LIZA: Quite. Is the Professor coming?

MRS HIGGINS: Certainly not. He cant behave himself in
church. He makes remarks out loud all the time on the
clergyman's pronunciation.

LIZA: Then I shall not see you again, Professor. Good-
bye. (*She goes to the door*).

MRS HIGGINS (*coming to* HIGGINS):   Good-bye, dear.

HIGGINS: Good-bye, mother. (*He is about to kiss her, when he recollects something*). Oh, by the way, Eliza, order a ham and a Stilton cheese, will you? And buy me a pair of reindeer gloves, number eights, and a tie to match that new suit of mine, at Eale & Binman's. You can choose the color. (*His cheerful, careless, vigorous voice shows that he is incorrigible*).

LIZA (*disdainfully*): Buy them yourself. (*She sweeps out*).

MRS HIGGINS: I'm afraid youve spoiled that girl, Henry. But never mind, dear: I'll buy you the tie and gloves.

HIGGINS (*sunnily*): Oh, dont bother. She'll buy em all right enough. Good-bye.

(*They kiss.* MRS HIGGINS *runs out.* HIGGINS, *left alone, rattles his cash in his pocket; chuckles; and disports himself in a highly self-satisfied manner.*)

The rest of the story need not be shewn in action, and indeed, would hardly need telling if our imaginations were not so enfeebled by their lazy dependence on the ready-mades and reach-me-downs of the ragshop in which Romance keeps its stock of "happy endings" to misfit all stories. Now, the history of Eliza Doolittle, though called a romance because the transfiguration it records seems exceedingly improbable, is common enough. Such transfigurations have been achieved by hundreds of resolutely ambitious young women since Nell Gwynne set them the example by playing queens and fascinating kings in the theatre in which she began by selling oranges. Nevertheless, people in all directions have assumed, for no other reason than that she became the heroine of a romance, that she must have married the hero of it. This is unbearable, not only because her little drama, if acted on such a thoughtless assumption, must be spoiled, but because the true sequel is patent to anyone with a sense of human nature in general, and of feminine instinct in particular.

Eliza, in telling Higgins she would not marry him if he asked her, was not coquetting: she was announcing a well-considered decision. When a bachelor interests, and dominates, and teaches, and becomes important to a spinster, as Higgins with Eliza, she always, if she has character enough to be capable of it, considers very seriously indeed whether she will play for becoming that bachelor's wife, especially if he is so little interested in marriage that a determined and devoted woman might capture him if she set herself resolutely to do it. Her decision will depend a good deal on whether she is really free to choose; and that, again, will depend on her age and income. If she is at the end of her youth, and has no security for her livelihood, she will marry him because she must marry anybody who will provide for her. But at Eliza's age a good-looking girl does not feel that pressure: she feels free to pick and choose. She is therefore guided by her instinct in the matter. Eliza's instinct tells her not to marry Higgins. It does not tell her to give him up. It is not in the slightest doubt as to his remaining one of the strongest personal interests in her life. It would be very sorely strained if there was another woman likely to supplant her with him. But as she feels sure of him on that last point, she has no doubt at all as to her course, and would not have any, even if the difference of twenty years in age, which seems so great to youth, did not exist between them.

As our own instincts are not appealed to by her conclusion, let us see whether we cannot discover some reason in it. When Higgins excused his indifference to young women on the ground that they had an irresistible rival in his mother, he gave the clue to his inveterate old-bachelordom. The case is uncommon only to the extent that remarkable mothers are uncommon. If an imaginative boy has a sufficiently rich mother who has intelligence, personal grace, dignity of character without harshness, and a cultivated sense of the best art of her time to enable her to make her house beautiful, she sets a standard for him against which very few women can struggle, besides effecting for him a disengagement of his affections, his sense of beauty, and his idealism from his specifically sexual impulses. This makes him a standing puzzle to the huge number of uncultivated people who have been brought up in tasteless homes by commonplace or disagreeable parents, and to whom, consequently, literature, painting, sculpture, music, and affectionate personal relations come as modes of sex if they come at all. The word passion means nothing else to them; and that Higgins could have a passion for phonetics and idealize his mother instead of Eliza, would seem to them absurd and unnatural. Nevertheless, when we look round and see that hardly anyone is too ugly or disagreeable to find a wife or a husband if he or she wants one, whilst many old maids and bachelors are above the average in quality and culture, we cannot help suspecting that the disentanglement of sex from the associations with which it is so commonly confused, a disentanglement which persons of genius achieve by sheer intellectual analysis, is sometimes produced or aided by parental fascination.

Now, though Eliza was incapable of thus explaining to herself Higgins's formidable powers of resistance to the charm that prostrated Freddy at the first glance, she was instinctively aware that she could never obtain a complete grip of him, or come between him and his mother (the first necessity of the married woman). To put it shortly, she knew that for some mysterious reason he had not the makings of a married man in him, according to her conception of a husband as one to whom she would be his nearest and fondest and warmest interest. Even had there been no mother-rival, she would still have refused to accept an interest in herself that was secondary to philosophic interests. Had Mrs Higgins died, there would still have been Milton and the Universal Alphabet. Landor's remark that to those who have the greatest power of loving, love is a secondary affair, would not have recommended Landor to Eliza. Put that along with her resentment of Higgins's domineering superiority, and her mistrust of his coaxing cleverness in getting round her and evading her wrath when he had gone too far with his impetuous bullying, and you will see that Eliza's instinct had good grounds for warning her not to marry her Pygmalion.

And now, whom did Eliza marry? For if Higgins was a predestinate old bachelor, she was most certainly not a predestinate old maid. Well, that can be told very shortly to those who have not guessed it from the indications she has herself given them.

Almost immediately after Eliza is stung into proclaiming her considered determination not to marry Higgins, she mentions the fact that young Mr Frederick Eynsford Hill is pouring out his love for her daily through the post. Now Freddy is young, practically twenty years younger than Higgins: he is a gentleman (or, as Eliza would qualify him, a toff), and speaks like one; he is nicely dressed, is treated by the Colonel as an equal, loves her unaffectedly, and is not her master, nor ever likely to dominate her in spite of his advantage of social standing. Eliza has no use for the foolish romantic tradition that all women love to be mastered, if not actually bullied and beaten. "When you go to women," says Nietzsche, "take your whip with you." Sensible despots have never confined that precaution to women: they have taken their whips with them when they have dealt with men, and been slavishly idealized by the men over whom they have flourished the whip much more than by women. No doubt there are slavish women as well as slavish men; and women, like men, admire those that are stronger than themselves. But to admire a strong person and to live under that strong person's thumb are two different things. The weak may not be admired and hero-worshipped; but they are by no means disliked or shunned; and they never seem to have the least difficulty in marrying people who are too good for them. They may fail in emergencies; but life is not one long emergency: it is mostly a string of situations for which no exceptional strength is needed, and with which even rather weak people can cope if they have a stronger partner to help them out. Accordingly, it is a truth everywhere in evidence that strong people, masculine or feminine, not only do not marry stronger people, but do not shew any preference for them in selecting their friends. When a lion meets another with a louder roar "the first lion thinks the last a bore." The man or woman who feels strong enough for two, seeks for every other quality in a partner than strength.

The converse is also true. Weak people want to marry strong people who do not frighten them too much; and this often leads them to make the mistake we describe metaphorically as "biting off more than they can chew." They want too much for too little; and when the bargain is unreasonable beyond all bearing, the union becomes impossible: it ends in the weaker party being either discarded or borne as a cross, which is worse. People who are not only weak, but silly or obtuse as well, are often in these difficulties.

This being the state of human affairs, what is Eliza fairly sure to do when she is placed between Freddy and Higgins? Will she look forward to a lifetime of fetching Higgins's slippers or to a lifetime of Freddy fetching hers? There can be no doubt about the answer. Unless Freddy is biologically repulsive to her, and Higgins biologically attractive to a degree that overwhelms all her other instincts, she will, if she marries either of them, marry Freddy.

And that is just what Eliza did.

Complications ensued; but they were economic, not romantic. Freddy had no money and no occupation. His mother's jointure, a last relic of the opulence of Largelady Park, had enabled her to struggle along in Earlscourt with an air of gentility, but not to procure any serious secondary education for her children, much less give the boy a profession. A clerkship at thirty shillings a week was beneath Freddy's dignity, and extremely distasteful to him besides. His prospects consisted of a hope that if he kept up appearances somebody would do something for him. The something appeared vaguely to his imagination as a private secretaryship or a sinecure of some sort. To his mother it perhaps appeared as a marriage to some lady of means who could not resist her boy's niceness. Fancy her feelings when he married a flower girl who had become déclassée under extraordinary circumstances which were now notorious!

It is true that Eliza's situation did not seem wholly ineligible. Her father, though formerly a dustman, and now fantastically disclassed, had become extremely popular in the smartest society by a social talent which triumphed over every prejudice and every disadvantage. Rejected by the middle class, which he loathed, he had shot up at once into the highest circles by his wit, his dustmanship (which he carried like a banner), and his Nietzschean transcendence of good and evil. At intimate ducal dinners he sat on the right hand of the Duchess; and in country houses he smoked in the pantry and was made much of by the butler when he was not feeding in the dining-room and being consulted by cabinet ministers. But he found it almost as hard to do all this on four thousand a year as Mrs Eynsford Hill to live in Earlscourt on an income so pitiably smaller that I have not the heart to disclose its exact figure. He absolutely refused to add the last straw to his burden by contributing to Eliza's support.

Thus Freddy and Eliza, now Mr and Mrs Eynsford Hill, would have spent a penniless honeymoon but for a wedding present of £500 from the Colonel to Eliza. It lasted a long time because Freddy did not know how to spend money, never having had any to spend, and Eliza, socially trained by a pair of old bachelors, wore her clothes as long as they held together and looked pretty, without the least regard to their being many months out of fashion. Still, £500 will not last two young people for ever; and they both knew, and Eliza felt as well, that they must shift for themselves in the end. She could quarter herself on Wimpole Street because it had come to be her home; but she was quite aware that she ought not to quarter Freddy there, and that it would not be good for his character if she did.

Not that the Wimpole Street bachelors objected. When

she consulted them, Higgins declined to be bothered about her housing problem when that solution was so simple. Eliza's desire to have Freddy in the house with her seemed of no more importance than if she had wanted an extra piece of bedroom furniture. Pleas as to Freddy's character, and the moral obligation on him to earn his own living, were lost on Higgins. He denied that Freddy had any character, and declared that if he tried to do any useful work some competent person would have the trouble of undoing it: a procedure involving a net loss to the community, and great unhappiness to Freddy himself, who was obviously intended by Nature for such light work as amusing Eliza, which, Higgins declared, was a much more useful and honorable occupation than working in the city. When Eliza referred again to her project of teaching phonetics, Higgins abated not a jot of his violent opposition to it. He said she was not within ten years of being qualified to meddle with his pet subject; and as it was evident that the Colonel agreed with him, she felt she could not go against them in this grave matter, and that she had no right, without Higgins's consent, to exploit the knowledge he had given her; for his knowledge seemed to her as much his private property as his watch: Eliza was no communist. Besides, she was superstitiously devoted to them both, more entirely and frankly after her marriage than before it.

It was the Colonel who finally solved the problem, which had cost him much perplexed cogitation. He one day asked Eliza, rather shyly, whether she had quite given up her notion of keeping a flower shop. She replied that she had thought of it, but had put it out of her head, because the Colonel had said, that day at Mrs Higgins's, that it would never do. The Colonel confessed that when he said that, he had not quite recovered from the dazzling impression of the day before. They broke the matter to Higgins that evening. The sole comment vouchsafed by him very nearly led to a serious quarrel with Eliza. It was to the effect that she would have in Freddy an ideal errand boy.

Freddy himself was next sounded on the subject. He

said he had been thinking of a shop himself; though it had presented itself to his pennilessness as a small place in which Eliza should sell tobacco at one counter whilst he sold newspapers at the opposite one. But he agreed that it would be extraordinarily jolly to go early every morning with Eliza to Covent Garden and buy flowers on the scene of their first meeting: a sentiment which earned him many kisses from his wife. He added that he had always been afraid to propose anything of the sort, because Clara would make an awful row about a step that must damage her matrimonial chances, and his mother could not be expected to like it after clinging for so many years to that step of the social ladder on which retail trade is impossible.

This difficulty was removed by an event highly unexpected by Freddy's mother. Clara, in the course of her incursions into those artistic circles which were the highest within her reach, discovered that her conversational qualifications were expected to include a grounding in the novels of Mr H. G. Wells. She borrowed them in various directions so energetically that she swallowed them all within two months. The result was a conversion of a kind quite common to-day. A modern Acts of the Apostles would fill fifty whole Bibles if anyone were capable of writing it.

Poor Clara, who appeared to Higgins and his mother as a disagreeable and ridiculous person, and to her own mother as in some inexplicable way a social failure, had never seen herself in either light; for, though to some extent ridiculed and mimicked in West Kensington like everybody else there, she was accepted as a rational and normal—or shall we say inevitable?—sort of human being. At worst they called her The Pusher; but to them no more than to herself had it ever occurred that she was pushing the air, and pushing it in a wrong direction. Still, she was not happy. She was growing desperate. Her one asset, the fact that her mother was what the Epsom greengrocer called a carriage lady, had no exchange value, apparently. It had prevented her from getting educated, because the only education she could have afforded was education with the Earlscourt greengrocer's daughter. It had led her to seek the society of her mother's class; and that class simply would not have her, because she was much poorer than the greengrocer, and, far from being able to afford a maid, could not afford even a housemaid, and had to scrape along at home with an illiberally treated general servant. Under such circumstances nothing could give her an air of being a genuine product of Largelady Park. And yet its tradition made her regard a marriage with anyone within her reach as an unbearable humiliation. Commercial people and professional people in a small way were odious to her. She ran after painters and novelists; but she did not charm them; and her bold attempts to pick up and practise artistic and literary talk irritated them. She was, in short, an utter failure, an ignorant, incompetent, pretentious, unwelcome, penniless, useless little snob; and though she did not admit these disqualifications (for nobody ever faces unpleasant truths of this kind until the possibility of a way out dawns on them) she felt their effects too keenly to be satisfied with her position.

Clara had a startling eyeopener when, on being suddenly wakened to enthusiasm by a girl of her own age who dazzled her and produced in her a gushing desire to take her for a model, and gain her friendship, she discovered that this exquisite apparition had graduated from the gutter in a few months time. It shook her so violently, that when Mr H. G. Wells lifted her on the point of his puissant pen, and placed her at the angle of view from which the life she was leading and the society to which she clung appeared in its true relation to real human needs and worthy social structure, he effected a conversion and a conviction of sin comparable to the most sensational feats of General Booth or Gypsy Smith. Clara's snobbery went bang. Life suddenly began to move with her. Without knowing how or why, she began to make friends and enemies. Some of the acquaintances to whom she had been a tedious or indifferent or ridiculous affliction, dropped her: others became cordial. To her amazement

she found that some "quite nice" people were saturated
with Wells, and that this accessibility to ideas was the
secret of their niceness. People she had thought deeply
religious, and had tried to conciliate on that tack with
disastrous results, suddenly took an interest in her, and
revealed a hostility to conventional religion which she had
never conceived possible except among the most desperate
characters. They made her read Galsworthy; and Galsworthy exposed the vanity of Largelady Park and finished her.
It exasperated her to think that the dungeon in which she
had languished for so many unhappy years had been un-
locked all the time, and that the impulses she had so carefully struggled with and stifled for the sake of keeping
well with society, were precisely those by which alone she
could have come into any sort of sincere human contact.
In the radiance of these discoveries, and the tumult of
their reaction, she made a fool of herself as freely and
conspicuously as when she so rashly adopted Eliza's ex-
pletive in Mrs Higgins's drawing-room; for the new-born
Wellsian had to find her bearings almost as ridiculously
as a baby; but nobody hates a baby for its ineptitudes, or
thinks the worse of it for trying to eat the matches; and
Clara lost no friends by her follies. They laughed at her
to her face this time; and she had to defend herself and
fight it out as best she could.

When Freddy paid a visit to Earlscourt (which he never
did when he could possibly help it) to make the desolating
announcement that he and his Eliza were thinking of
blackening the Largelady scutcheon by opening a shop, he
found the little household already convulsed by a prior
announcement from Clara that she also was going to work
in an old furniture shop in Dover Street, which had been
started by a fellow Wellsian. This appointment Clara
owed, after all, to her old social accomplishment of Push.
She had made up her mind that, cost what it might, she
would see Mr. Wells in the flesh; and she had achieved
her end at a garden party. She had better luck than so
rash an enterprise deserved. Mr. Wells came up to her
expectations. Age had not withered him, nor could custom

stale his infinite variety in half an hour. His pleasant neatness and compactness, his small hands and feet, his teeming ready brain, his unaffected accessibility, and a certain fine apprehensiveness which stamped him as susceptible from his topmost hair to his tipmost toe, proved irresistible. Clara talked of nothing else for weeks and weeks afterwards. And as she happened to talk to the lady of the furniture shop, and that lady also desired above all things to know Mr. Wells and sell pretty things to him, she offered Clara a job on the chance of achieving that end through her.

And so it came about that Eliza's luck held, and the expected opposition to the flower shop melted away. The shop is in the arcade of a railway station not very far from the Victoria and Albert Museum; and if you live in that neighborhood you may go there any day and buy a buttonhole from Eliza.

Now here is a last opportunity for romance. Would you not like to be assured that the shop was an immense success, thanks to Eliza's charms and her early business experience in Covent Garden? Alas! the truth is the truth: the shop did not pay for a long time, simply because Eliza and her Freddy did not know how to keep it. True, Eliza had not to begin at the very beginning: she knew the names and prices of the cheaper flowers; and her elation was unbounded when she found that Freddy, like all youths educated at cheap, pretentious, and thoroughly inefficient schools, knew a little Latin. It was very little, but enough to make him appear to her a Porson or Bentley, and to put him at his ease with botanical nomenclature. Unfortunately he knew nothing else; and Eliza, though she could count money up to eighteen shillings or so, and had acquired a certain familiarity with the language of Milton from her struggles to qualify herself for winning Higgins's bet, could not write out a bill without utterly disgracing the establishment. Freddy's power of stating in Latin that Balbus built a wall and that Gaul was divided into three parts did not carry with it the slightest knowledge of accounts or business: Colonel Pickering had to explain to him what a cheque book and a bank account meant. And the pair were by no means easily teachable. Freddy backed up Eliza in her obstinate refusal to believe that they could save money by engaging a bookkeeper with some knowledge of the business. How, they argued, could you possibly save money by going to extra expense when you already could not make both ends meet? But the Colonel, after making the ends meet over and over again, at last gently insisted; and Eliza, humbled to the dust by having to beg from him so often, and stung by the uproarious derision of Higgins, to whom the notion of Freddy succeeding at anything was a joke that never palled, grasped the fact that business, like phonetics, has to be learned.

On the piteous spectacle of the pair spending their evenings in shorthand schools and polytechnic classes, learning bookkeeping and typewriting with incipient junior clerks, male and female, from the elementary schools, let me not dwell. There were even classes at the London School of Economics, and a humble personal appeal to the director of that institution to recommend a course bearing on the flower business. He, being a humorist, explained to them the method of the celebrated Dickensian essay on Chinese Metaphysics by the gentleman who read an article on China and an article on Metaphysics and combined the information. He suggested that they should combine the London School with Kew Gardens. Eliza, to whom the procedure of the Dickensian gentleman seemed perfectly correct (as in fact it was) and not in the least funny (which was only her ignorance) took his advice with entire gravity. But the effort that cost her the deepest humiliation was a request to Higgins, whose pet artistic fancy, next to Milton's verse, was caligraphy, and who himself wrote a most beautiful Italian hand, that he would teach her to write. He declared that she was congenitally incapable of forming a single letter worthy of the least of Milton's words; but she persisted; and again he suddenly threw himself into the task of teaching her with a combination of stormy intensity, concentrated patience, and occasional bursts of interesting disquisition on the beauty and nobility, the august mission and destiny, of human hand-writing. Eliza ended by acquiring an extremely uncommercial script which was a positive extension of her personal beauty, and spending three times as much on stationery as anyone else because certain qualities and shapes of paper became indispensable to her. She could not even address an envelope in the usual way because it made the margins all wrong.

Their commercial schooldays were a period of disgrace and despair for the young couple. They seemed to be learning nothing about flower shops. At last they gave it up as hopeless, and shook the dust of the shorthand schools, and the polytechnics, and the London School of Economics from their feet for ever. Besides, the business was in some mysterious way beginning to take care of itself. They had somehow forgotten their objections to employing other people. They came to the conclusion that their own way was the best, and that they had really a remarkable talent for business. The Colonel, who had been compelled for some years to keep a sufficient sum on current account at his bankers to make up their deficits, found that the provision was unnecessary: the young people were prospering. It is true that there was not quite fair play between them and their competitors in trade. Their week-ends in the country cost them nothing, and saved them the price of their Sunday dinners; for the motor car was the Colonel's; and he and Higgins paid the hotel bills. Mr. F. Hill, florist and greengrocer (they soon discovered that there was money in asparagus; and asparagus led to other vegetables), had an air which stamped the business as classy; and in private life he was still Frederick Eynsford Hill, Esquire. Not that there was any swank about him: nobody but Eliza knew that he had been christened Frederick Challoner. Eliza herself swanked like anything.

That is all. That is how it has turned out. It is astonishing how much Eliza still manages to meddle in the housekeeping at Wimpole Street in spite of the shop and her own family. And it is notable that though she never nags her husband, and frankly loves the Colonel as if she were his favorite daughter, she has never got out of the habit of nagging Higgins that was established on the fatal night when she won his bet for him. She snaps his head off on the faintest provocation, or on none. He no longer dares to tease her by assuming an abysmal inferiority of Freddy's mind to his own. He storms and bullies and derides; but she stands up to him so ruthlessly that the Colonel has to ask her from time to time to be kinder to Higgins; and it is the only request of his that brings a mulish expression into her face. Nothing but some emergency or calamity great enough to break down all likes and dislikes, and throw them both back on their common humanity—and may they be spared any such trial!—will ever alter this. She knows that Higgins does not need her, just as her father did not need her. The very scrupulousness with which he told her that day that he had become used to having her there, and dependent on her for all sorts of little services, and that he should miss her if she went away (it would never have occurred to Freddy or the Colonel to say anything of the sort) deepens her inner certainty that she is "no more to him than them slippers"; yet she has a sense, too, that his indifference is deeper than the infatuation of commoner souls. She is immensely interested in him. She has even secret mischievous moments in which she wishes she could get him alone, on a desert island, away from all ties and with nobody else in the world to consider, and just drag him off his pedestal and see him making love like any common man. We all have private imaginations of that sort. But when it comes to business, to the life that she really leads as distinguished from the life of dreams and fancies, she likes Freddy and she likes the Colonel; and she does not like Higgins and Mr. Doolittle. Galatea never does quite like Pygmalion: his relation to her is too godlike to be altogether agreeable.

THE END

Discover the world of

LOUISA MAY ALCOTT

Little Women
_____ 21275-3 $3.95/$4.95

Little Women is one of the best-loved books of all time. Lovely Meg, talented Jo, frail Beth, spoiled Amy: these are the four March sisters, who learn the hard lessons of poverty and of growing up in New England during the Civil War.

Jo's Boys
_____ 21449-7 $3.50/$4.50

Louisa May Alcott continues the story of her feisty protagonist Jo in this final novel chronicling the adventures and the misadventures of the March family.

*Bantam Classics bring you the world's greatest literature—
books that have stood the test of time. These beautifully designed
books will be proud additions to your bookshelf. You'll want
all these time-tested classics for your own reading pleasure.*

The survival adventures of Jack London

_____21233-8 THE CALL OF THE WILD and
        WHITE FANG $3.95/$4.95 Canada
_____21225-7 THE SEA WOLF $3.95/$4.95
_____21335-0 TO BUILD A FIRE
        AND OTHER STORIES $5.50/$7.50

The swashbuckling world of Alexandre Dumas

_____21350-4 THE COUNT OF MONTE CRISTO $4.95/$5.95
_____21337-7 THE THREE MUSKETEERS $5.95/$6.95

The frontier historicals of James Fenimore Cooper

_____21329-6 THE LAST OF THE MOHICANS $4.50/$5.95
_____21085-8 THE DEERSLAYER $4.95/$6.95

The haunting realism of Daniel Defoe

_____21373-3 ROBINSON CRUSOE $3.95/$4.95
_____21328-8 MOLL FLANDERS $3.50/$4.50
